Managing
Conflict
in
Organizations

Managing
Conflict
in
Organizations

Fourth Edition

M. Afzalur Rahim

Transaction Publishers
New Brunswick (U.S.A.) and London (U.K.)

Copyright (c) 2011 by Transaction Publishers, New Brunswick, New Jersey.

All rights reserved under International and Pan-American Copyright Conventions. No part of this book may be reproduced or transmitted in any form or by any means, electronic or mechanical, including photocopy, recording, or any information storage and retrieval system, without prior permission in writing from the publisher. All inquiries should be addressed to Transaction Publishers, Rutgers-The State University of New Jersey, 35 Berrue Circle, Piscataway, New Jersey 08854-8042. www.transactionpub.com

This book is printed on acid-free paper that meets the American National Standard for Permanence of Paper for Printed Library Materials.

Library of Congress Catalog Number: 2010017602
ISBN: 978-1-4128-1456-0
Printed in the United States of America

Library of Congress Cataloging-in-Publication Data

Rahim, M. Afzalur.
    Managing conflict in organizations / M. Afzalur Rahim. -- 4th ed.
        p. cm.
    Includes bibliographical references and index.
    ISBN 978-1-4128-1456-0
        1. Conflict management. I. Title.

HD42.R34 2010
658.4'053--dc22

2010017602

Contents

List of Tables and Figures

Tables

Figures

Preface

Now more than ever organizations need to learn and continuously change to improve their competitive positions. Change is associated with conflict, and dealing with conflict effectively is essential for realizing the benefits of change. Learning organizations like Honda, Motorola, Dow Corning, and General Electric have developed the kind of leadership, culture, and organizational design needed to manage conflict effectively, but many organizations still handle conflict ineffectively. The previous three editions of this book stated that managers and administrators attempt not so much to understand and deal with conflict functionally as to find ways of reducing, avoiding, or terminating it. It appears that this state of affairs has remained unchanged, wasting valuable resources as employees engage in dysfunctional conflict and miss the opportunity of utilizing conflict to improve organizational effectiveness.

This edition's major objective (i.e., to develop a design for the effective management of conflict at various levels in an organization) has remained unchanged. The thesis of this book continues to be that the management of organizational conflict involves the diagnosis of, and intervention in, conflict. A diagnosis is needed to determine whether and to what extent an intervention is needed to:

1. Minimize affective and process conflicts;
2. Minimize substantive conflict in routine tasks;
3. Attain and maintain a moderate amount of substantive conflict for non-routine tasks; and
4. Enable the organizational members to learn and use the various styles of behavior, such as integrating, obliging, dominating, avoiding, and compromising for handling different conflict situations effectively.

One of the goals is to present the reader with up-to-date scientific studies on conflict and conflict management that appeared in scholarly journals and books after the third edition of this work was published in 2001. Each chapter was revised and literature review updated to strengthen the conflict management model.

This edition can be used to supplement courses on Organizational Behavior, Organizational and Industrial Psychology, Organizational Communication, and

Organization Development. It will also be useful to the management practitioners and consultants on conflict management. While I expect that this edition's use will result in improved decisions and job performance, its enduring success as a text point to its continued relevance in guiding leadership thought.

I wish to express my special gratitude to Karen Jehn, Melbourne Business School, Clement Psenicka, Youngstown State University, Robert Golembiewski, University of Georgia, and James Carter, Harvard Medical School for helping me to improve several parts of the book. I want to express my thanks to my management students of Youngstown State and Western Kentucky Universities, who provided the data for preparing the collegiate norms of conflict and conflict styles. I want to express my appreciation to several anonymous reviewers for making comments on several parts of the book. Their opinions were useful in refining some of my thoughts on conflict and conflict management, but I am fully responsible for the final product.

The price that an author's family pays for a book is enormous. I would like to express my gratitude and indebtedness to my wife and son for their patience and supportiveness. My wife was very supportive during various stages of the revision. Without her help it would have been very difficult to accomplish this task.

—M. A. Rahim

1

Introduction

Conflict is inevitable among humans. It is a natural outcome of human interaction that begins when two or more social entities (i.e., individuals, groups, organizations, and nations) come in contact with one another in attaining their objectives. Relationships among such entities may become incompatible or inconsistent when two or more of them desire a similar resource that is in short supply; when they have partially exclusive behavioral preferences regarding their joint action; or when they have different attitudes, values, beliefs, and skills. Another definition of conflict would be "*perceived divergence of interest*, a belief that the parties' current aspirations are incompatible. In other words, conflict is a belief that if one party gets what it wants, the other (or others) will not be able to do so" (Pruitt & Kim, 2004, pp. 7–8).

The theme of conflict has been with us and has influenced our thinking from time immemorial. It received different degrees of emphasis from social and biological scientists during various periods of history. Over the years the phenomena relating to conflict have been investigated by the economists, historians, novelists, philosophers, political scientists, sociologists, psychologists, and theologians; and biologists have investigated the "struggle for existence" by species of differing genetic inheritance. Scholars in organization theory became interested in scientific investigation of conflict phenomena during the later part of the last century. There have been renewed interest and significant changes in the study of conflict in social and organizational contexts. The formation of the International Association for Conflict Management and Conflict Management Division of the Academy of Management to encourage research, teaching, and training and development on managing social and organizational conflicts and the publication of the *International Journal of Conflict Management* in 1990 attest to this renewed interest. In recent years, a number of universities in the United States have shown great interest in teaching and research on social and organizational conflicts.

Contributions from Various Disciplines

Most of the contributions to the theory of social conflict came from philosophy and sociology. A few contributions also came from other disciplines, such as biological science. A brief review of the major classical positions in these disciplines on the concept of conflict would be helpful at this point.

Philosophy

Plato and Aristotle. Although among the classical philosophers neither Plato (427–347 B.C.) nor Aristotle (384–322 B.C.) wrote a separate treatise on social conflict, both of them discussed in detail the need for order in a society. A brief review of the positions held by these philosophers on social conflict is as follows.

Plato was of the opinion that tension within society is natural and therefore some conflict is inevitable. However, he felt that social conflict could be kept at a minimum if an appropriate balance of the segments of a society could be obtained. This could be attained if each segment of a society knew the part it had to play and carried out its functions accordingly. Plato suggested that such a balance of the parts could be obtained only with appropriate leadership.

In *The Republic*, Plato suggested that the needs of the society could be satisfied if private property was eliminated. To satisfy the needs of society, he particularly felt the necessity for eliminating private property for those who would provide political leadership. Plato believed that the leaders could not do their job properly if they were motivated by private interests.

Aristotle, however, believed that Plato's philosophy called for "extreme unification," or communism, and that this was neither practical nor possible. This is not to say that Aristotle saw much usefulness of social conflict. On the contrary, although he disagreed with Plato on the form of the government, he shared Plato's sympathy for the need of order in the state. Plato and Aristotle stressed that an absence of conflict is a sine qua non for the attainment of the just form of life in the city-state. To them, "strife is a sign of imperfection and unhappiness. Order marks the good life and disorders the opposite. Conflict is a threat to the success of the state and should be kept at an absolute minimum and removed altogether if possible" (Sipka, 1969, p. 7). The conclusion is that both classical philosophers assigned social conflict a pathological status.

Hobbes and Locke. The seventeenth century social contact theory of the Englishmen Thomas Hobbes (1588–1679) and John Locke (1632–1704) suggested that the purpose of the government is to establish order in social relations, without which there would be constant violence between human beings. Hobbes considered "human beings as egotistical, the dupes of error, the slaves of sin, of passion, and of fear. Persons are their own enemies, or the enemies of others, or both" (Lourenco & Glidewell, 1975, p. 489). He took the position that the Sovereign (i.e., a monarch who is granted absolute and permanent power to control social conflict) should control human beings. Whatever the Sovereign decides becomes the law, and all the citizens must abide by it. Since they have given him the right and power to make them, they cannot object to his laws. This is the only way to control social conflict effectively.

Locke was critical of Hobbes's disposition for the political order, the Leviathan, which is empowered with absolute control. According to Locke, government is to be organized by the people through their common consent, and its duty was the preservation of lives, liberties, and estates. Although Locke disagreed with Hobbes on the type of government he considered appropriate, he concluded that government should control conflict.

While there are some differences in their approaches to social theory, those differences are at times not so great. Both "Hobbes and Locke had an extraordinary sensitivity to the dangers of social conflict and sought, through government, to control it as much as possible....not only did these men not see a growth or re-constructive potential in social conflict, but they considered it a flaw in the body politic....Though neither man insists that all conflict is to be removed, it is clear that this is their intention" (Sipka, 1969, pp. 15–16).

Hegel and Marx. A distinct shift of views on conflict in philosophy occurred during the nineteenth century. It is not possible to review all of the major philosophical contributions that held to a functional view of conflict, but it would be useful to review the works of two German intellectual giants like G. W. F. Hegel (1770–1831) and Karl Marx (1818–1883).

Hegel's philosophy is dominated by the notion of the dialectic, which has, over the years, developed four different meanings: (1) arriving at the truth, (2) dialogue or debate, (3) process of ascertaining the unrestricted truth, and (4) process of change through the conflict of opposing forces. Hegel's dialectic asserts that every finite concept (*thesis,* or the first doctrine) bears within itself its own opposite (*antithesis,* or the second doctrine). To overcome the opposition, one must reconcile the opposing concepts by coming to a third position (*synthesis,* or the third doctrine). The dialectical method thus affects a synthesis of opposites. The synthesis, in turn, becomes a new thesis, and the dialectical process continues until a fully developed synthesis (the Absolute Idea) is reached. Each stage in this process relates back to the previous idea but results in broadened knowledge.

The dialectics of Marx and Hegel are different. Marx saw human history as full of conflict between classes—bourgeoisie (business class) and proletariat (working class)—which is the mechanism of change and development. Marx was a revolutionary who wanted the capitalists to relinquish their power. He and his associate Engel were quite candid about their opinion on revolution.

They closed the *Communist Manifesto* with the following words: "The Communists...openly declare that their ends can be attained only by the forcible overthrow of all existing social conditions. Let the ruling classes tremble at a Communist revolution. The proletariats have nothing to lose but their chains. Workingmen of all countries, unite!"

The key to Marx's dialectic, therefore, is associated with class conflict rooted in economic disparities. Marx believed that this class struggle (between haves and have-nots) would ultimately lead to a classless society devoid of repression where human beings are, for the first time, truly free. This new society would be free from conflict and the individuals would be perfectly reconciled to themselves and their fellows.

Dewey. John Dewey (1859–1952) was an American philosopher, psychologist, and educational reformer who made significant contributions to the study of social conflict during the twentieth century. He was profoundly influenced by Darwin's theory of evolution and Hegel's dialectic process. For Dewey (1922/1957), "Conflict is the gadfly to thought. It stirs us to observation and memory. It instigates us to invention. It shocks us out to sheep-like passivity, and sets us at noting and contriving" (p. 300). He observed that when the relationship between human beings and environment is interrupted by obstacles or conflict, individuals must use their intelligence to readapt through a change in their accustomed modes of conduct and belief. In other words, an individual should examine a conflict situation to discover the various actions possible and choose the one that is most effective.

Biological Science

Darwin. Charles Darwin (1809–1882), was an English naturalist, formulated the "theory of natural selection," which indicated that biological species survive and grow by confronting the environmental challenges (Darwin, 1871). He concluded that organisms are in conflict one with another and/or with external nature. This called for a reexamination of the classical views of the role of social conflict in human development. Darwin and his followers (the social Darwinists) recognized the role that environmental conflict plays in human growth, which led to the development of the doctrine of "the survival of the fittest." Darwin concluded that humans have progressed to the present state through a struggle for existence; and if they want to advance still higher, they must remain subject to a severe struggle. Without struggle or conflict, the more gifted individuals would not be more successful in their life than the less gifted.

Darwin believed that the growth of human beings is a function of their response to conflict with the environment. If conflict were altogether absent—as appears to be the ideal in much of classical philosophy—the progress of human beings would be retarded. The evolutionary emphasis on the essential role of conflict in human development is a pennant of the nineteenth century. Through Darwin, it found its way into virtually all facets of science.

Sociology

Simmel. Georg Simmel (1858–1918) was a German philosopher-sociologist who made a significant contribution to the study of the various forms of conflict. Simmel acknowledged the dual nature of conflict—it has both functional and dysfunctional outcomes—and concluded that conflict may be as important for an effective social entity (individuals, group, nations) as cooperation. He firmly believed that conflict was a unifying force that may be instrumental in strengthening the solidarity and identity of a group.

He believed that in small groups such as the marital couple, "a certain amount of discord, inner divergence and outer controversy, is organically tied up with very elements that ultimately hold the group together; it cannot be separated from the unity of the sociological structure" (Simmel, 1908/1955, pp. 17–18). His general hypothesis was that a certain amount of conflict is as essential to the proper functioning of the groups as are stability and order.

Mayo. George Elton Mayo (1880–1949) was an Australian industrial psychologist who was introduced to sociology in 1926. He contributed to management theory through his research at Western Electric's Hawthorn Works at Chicago, which took place during 1927–1932. Mayo's (1933) studies, which led to the human relations movement, emphasized the need for cooperation for enhancing organizational effectiveness and over time the human relations theory found other supporters such as Lewin (1948), Likert (1967), and Whyte (1951).

To Mayo, conflict was dysfunctional and should be minimized or, if possible, eliminated from organizations altogether. Child (1995) concluded that Mayo had a "deep abhorrence of conflict in any form.... Mayo and his colleagues... assumed that ordinary employees were largely governed by a 'logic of sentiment,' which was of a different order from managers' rational appraisal of the situation in terms of costs and efficiency. Conflict with management was thus an aberration that threatened the effectiveness of organizations" (pp. 88–89; see also Baritz, 1960, p. 203).

Parsons. Talcott Parsons (1902–1979) was an American sociologist who formulated the structural functionalism theory, which considerably influenced social science thought following World War II. His theory is based on the assumption that society is innately stable, integrated, and functional, and as a result, change and conflict are viewed to be abnormal and dysfunctional. He emphasized that social structures are complimentary and they perform positive functions for each other and maintain social order and stability (Parsons, 1949).

One of the major criticisms of structural functionalism is its conservatism to maintain status quo and, therefore, its inability to deal with the process of change and conflict. Sipka's (1969) review suggests that Parsons's theory "is through and through an equilibrium model and the dynamics of conflict are relegated to the level of 'deviation.' All this stems, perhaps, from Parsons's extraordinary, Hobbesian preoccupation with the natural tendency of men to hostility, and the difficulty of controlling them adequately" (p. 70). Parsons's theory was a dominant perspective for analyzing society until 1960s, but today it is only of historical interest.

Coser. During the 1950s a number of theorists (Mills, 1959; Dahrendorf, 1959; Bernard, 1957) presented viewpoints opposing Parsons's analysis. Consequently, the interest in the study of the social phenomena of conflict began to grow. A publication by Lewis Coser (1913–2003)—*The Functions of Social Conflict* (Coser, 1956)—which focused on the productive potential of conflict, had much to do with this renewal of interest. Coser interpreted and expanded Simmel's essay in considerable detail. He reminded his fellow social scientists of the significant role that conflict plays for a society. His book was highly influential in setting the stage for a significant increase in the attention to conflict by sociologists during and after this period.

It should be pointed out here that at the beginning of the last century, there was considerable interest among some American sociologists in the study of social conflict. They were inspired by the works of Simmel (1908/1955) who associated conflict with positive functions against the tradition that considered conflict as a form of social deviation. They generally agreed with Park and Burgess (1921/1929): "Only where there is conflict is behavior conscious and self-conscious; only here are the conditions for rational conduct" (p. 578).

Two opposing viewpoints on the outcome of conflict were presented. A synthesis of these viewpoints regarding the usefulness of conflict is necessary. A realistic view of conflict is that it has productive as well as destructive potentials (Assael, 1969; Deutsch, 1969; Jehn, 1997a; de Dreu & Van de Vliert, 1997; Kelly & Kelly, 1998; Pelled, Eisenhardt, & Xin, 1999). The functional and dysfunctional outcomes of conflict in organizations are as follows:

Functional Outcomes

- Conflict may stimulate innovation, creativity, and change.
- Organizational decision making processes may be improved.
- Alternative solutions to a problem may be found.
- Conflict may lead to synergistic solutions to common problems.
- Individual and group performance may be enhanced.
- Individuals and groups may be forced to search for new approaches.
- Individuals and groups may be required to articulate and clarify their positions.

Dysfunctional Outcomes

- Conflict may cause job stress, burnout, and dissatisfaction.
- Communication between individuals and groups may be reduced.
- A climate of distrust and suspicion can be developed.
- Relationships may be damaged.
- Job performance may be reduced.
- Resistance to change can increase.
- Organizational commitment and loyalty may be affected.

The preceding discussion suggests that social conflict has both positive and negative consequences. If a social system is to benefit from conflict, the negative effects of conflict must be reduced, and positive effects must be enhanced.

Organizational Conflict

Having recognized that conflict is an important social concept, we can then look into the special case of organizational conflict. Conflict is certainly one of the major organizational phenomena. Pondy (1967) observed that organization theories "that do not admit conflict provide poor guidance in dealing with problems of organizational efficiency, stability, governance, and change, for conflict within and between organizations is intimately related as either symptom, cause, or effect, to each of these problems" (p. 504). It has been observed by Baron (1990) that, "organizational conflict is an important topic for both managers and for scientists interested in understanding the nature of organizational behavior and organizational processes" (p. 198). Content analysis of syllabi on organizational behavior courses for master of business administration (MBA) students by Rahim (1981) indicated that conflict was the fifth most frequently mentioned among sixty-five topics.

The Classical View of Organizational Conflict

The classical organization theorists (Fayol, 1916/1949; Gulick & Urwick, 1937; Taylor, 1911; Weber, 1929/1947) did not seem to appreciate different impacts that conflict can have on organizations. They implicitly assumed that conflict was detrimental to organizational efficiency and therefore should be minimized in organizations. They prescribed organization structures—rules and procedures, hierarchy, channel of command, and so on—so that organization members would be unlikely to engage in conflict. This approach to managing organizations was based on the assumption that harmony, cooperation, and the absence of conflict were appropriate for achieving organizational effectiveness.

Taylor. Frederick W. Taylor (1856–1915) was an American mechanical engineer who believed that the functioning of an organization would improve if the principles of scientific management were implemented. Some of these principles involved the following (Taylor, 1911):

1. The development of a true science of work that involves determining a fair day's work.
2. Scientific selection and progressive development of workers.
3. Fitting of workers to their respective tasks.
4. Constant and intimate cooperation of managers and workers.
5. Provision of means to encourage each person to the utmost utilization of his or her capacity.
6. Development of organization structures to control the various phases of production.

Taylor particularly insisted that the conflicts between labor and management would disappear if these principles were applied. Although scientific management led to significant advancement in industrial efficiency, it was not without opposition. During the later part of his life, Taylor was subjected to much criticism by labor. The opposition from organized labor was due to their belief that scientific management resulted in speedup of the workers. The unions also objected to the scientific determination of wages without resorting to collective bargaining. Scientific management also did not make any provision for the effective management of conflict between individuals and groups in an organization.

Fayol. Another classical organization theorist was Henry Fayol (1841–1925), a French executive. Today's organization theory is greatly indebted to Fayol (1916/1949). In some respects his work was superior to that of Taylor. Fayol advocated that the managerial functions, such as planning, organizing, command, coordination, and control, are applicable to all sorts of organized human endeavor. In addition to this, some of his organization principles, such as unity of command, span of control, division of work, and so on, are widely used today.

Although Fayol's approaches to management were broader and more systematic and broader than those of Taylor, both of them, as well as other classicists such as Gulick and Urwick (1937) and Mooney and Reiley (1939), saw organizations from a closed-system perspective. They implicitly assumed that conflict was detrimental to organizational effectiveness. They prescribed mechanistic organizational structures with clear lines of authority, hierarchical structures, division of labor, and so on, which would encourage harmony and cooperation and suppress or eliminate conflict among members.

Weber. Max Weber (1868–1933) was a distinguished German sociologist who is commonly described as a founding father (with Durkheim) of sociology. He proposed a structure of organization that he called bureaucracy and believed it to be the most efficient form of organization. Bureaucratic organizations must follow several fundamental principles (Weber, 1929/1947):

1. A well-defined hierarchy of authority.
2. Division of work based on functional specialization.
3. A system of rules covering the rights and duties of employees.
4. A system of procedures for dealing with work situations.
5. Impersonality in interpersonal relationships.
6. Selection of employees and their promotion based on technical competence.

Weber left no room for conflict or deviance in his model of bureaucracy. Although he was aware of some of the dysfunctions of bureaucracy, he maintained that bureaucratic structures were appropriate for organizational effectiveness.

Follett. Among the classical organization theorists, Mary Parker Follett (1868–1933) was a significant exception. Her strong behavioral orientation to management and organization in the 1920s placed her several decades ahead of her time. She noted the value of constructive conflict in an organization: "We can often measure our progress by watching the nature of our conflicts. Social progress is in this respect like individual progress; we become spiritually more and more developed as our conflicts rise to higher levels" (Follett, 1926/1940, p. 35; see also Child, 1995). She strongly advocated the need for an integrative (problem-solving) method for managing organizational conflict. She believed that other methods of handling conflict, such as suppression, avoidance, dominance, and compromise, were ineffective in dealing with conflict.

Concluding Comments on the Classical View of Organizational Conflict

Taylor, Fayol, Weber, and Mayo intended to reduce conflict for enhancing the organizational efficiency, but they followed different routes. Whereas Taylor, Fayol, and Weber attempted to reduce conflict by altering the technical–structural system of the organization, Mayo attempted to accomplish this by altering its social system.

Thus, it can be observed that the classical organization theorists, with the exception of Follett, did not incorporate a conflict variable into their models. These theorists "viewed conflict as undesirable, detrimental to the organization. Ideally it should not exist. The prescription was simple. Eliminate it" (Litterer, 1966, p. 178). The classicists did not, however, explicitly state that conflict should be eliminated from organizations. They, of course, implicitly assumed that conflict was not desirable for an organization and should be minimized. This approach to organization and management dominated the literature during the first half of the last century.

The Modern View of Organizational Conflict

Litterer (1966) argued that the preceding view of classical organization theorists is similar to the "view of others on the handling of tension within people. A fundamental position of many who analyzed individual behavior was that individuals were motivated by a desire for tension reduction. The prescription in both therapy and organization design therefore was to take steps or make arrangements which would reduce tension within individuals. More recently it has become accepted that tension is normal, even desirable, with the thought growing that 'healthy' personalities actually seek to increase tension" (pp. 178–179). Whyte (1967) stated clearly that goal of an organization is not harmony, but to design a system capable of recognizing and solving the problems it faces. Because conflict is inevitable in organizations, it is important that procedures for conflict management are included into the design of organizations.

The preceding line of reasoning is important in understanding the shift in conceptualization of conflict in organizations. Taking the lead from Litterer and Whyte, it can be observed that "healthy" organizations seek to increase intraorganizational conflict. It does not necessarily signify any organizational weakness as implied by the classical organization theorists or human relationists. Robbins (1974) presented three philosophies of organizational conflict.

1. The philosophy of conflict of the classicists or traditionalists, discussed earlier in this chapter, was based on the assumption that conflict was detrimental to an organization and, as such, must be reduced or eliminated.
2. The classical stage was followed by the behavioralists' philosophy, which can best be described as the recognition that conflict is inevitable in organizations. Behavioralists accept the presence of conflict and even occasionally advocate the enhancement of conflict for increasing organizational effectiveness. But they have not actively created conditions that generate conflict in organizations.
3. The philosophy of conflict of the interactionists is the third philosophy, which differs significantly from the previous two. It is characterized by the following:
    a. Recognition of the absolute necessity of conflict;
    b. Explicit encouragement of opposition;
    c. Defining conflict management to include stimulation as well as resolution methods; and
    d. Considering the management of conflict as a major responsibility of all administrators (Robbins, 1974, pp. 13–14).

The interactionist approach is similar to the pluralist theory, which "looks upon conflict as a means of generating agreements and of creating agreed upon terms of collaboration. . . . Conflict becomes an instrument of social change and influence rather than a symptom of a breakdown in social relationships. In fact, conflict behaviors must occur from time to time in order to demonstrate the will and capacity of action" (Nightingale, 1974, p. 150). Kerr (1964) was one of the leading figures in the application of this theory to the study of conflict in organizations.

Organizational conflict as it stands now is considered legitimate and inevitable and a positive indicator of effective organizational management. It is now recognized that conflict within certain limits is essential to productivity. Conflict can be functional to the extent to which it results in the formulation and creative solution to the right problems or the effective attainment of subsystem or organizational objectives that otherwise would not have been possible. Little or no conflict in organizations may lead to stagnation, poor decisions, and ineffectiveness. On the other hand, organizational conflict left uncontrolled may have dysfunctional outcomes. Therefore, the central theme is that *too little conflict may encourage stagnancy, mediocrity, and groupthink, but too much conflict may lead to organizational disintegration.* The preceding discussion leads to the conclusion, therefore, that too little or too much of conflict are both dysfunctional for an organization's effectiveness. A *moderate amount of conflict, handled in a constructive manner, is essential for attaining and maintaining an optimum level of organizational effectiveness* (Rahim & Bonoma, 1979). As discussed in Chapter 4, a moderate amount of substantive or task-related conflict, but not affective and process conflicts, is appropriate for attaining and maintaining an optimum level of organizational effectiveness.

Although the present attitude toward conflict is that it is essential for attaining and maintaining an optimum level of organizational effectiveness, some writers have overemphasized the dysfunctional consequences of conflict or failed to comprehend fully the functional aspects of conflict (e.g., McDonald, 1972). Not only did McDonald overemphasize the dysfunctional aspects of conflict at top management, but his prescription included comprehensive criteria for executive selection to reduce the likelihood of such conflict. This strategy may be able to reduce conflict, but it may also reduce the effectiveness or creativity of the top management group. Neuhauser (1988) is another writer who believes that organization conflict is destructive: "Conflict is a major source of increased stress and *decreased productivity for all managers and employees* in any department of any organization. It *almost always ends up affecting the quality of services* received by customers" (p. 3, emphasis added). One of the major problems with these writers is that they emphasized the dysfunctions of conflict in organizations but neglected to consider the consequences of creating conflict-free organizations. First, it is impossible to eliminate conflict from organizations. Second, an attempt on the part of managers to eliminate all conflict, in the long run, will affect individual, group, and organizational productivity.

De Bono (1986) is one of the writers on social conflict who equates conflict resolution with total elimination of conflict. He uses a new word, "confliction," to mean generating or creating conflict. He invented another word, "de-confliction," which is the opposite of confliction. "De-confliction does not refer to negotiation or bargaining or even to the resolution of conflicts. De-confliction is the effort required to evaporate a conflict. Just as confliction is the setting up of a conflict so de-confliction is the opposite process: the demolition of the conflict" (De Bono, 1986, p. 5). De Bono's approach to total elimination of conflict is no different from the approaches of the classicists. This approach to dealing with conflict is completely out of tune with modern thinking and, therefore, unsatisfactory.

A study sponsored by the American Management Association (AMA) shows that middle and top managers "have a lively and growing interest in learning more about both the prevention and management of conflict" (Thomas & Schmidt, 1976, p. 318). Some of the findings of this study are:

1. The chief executive officers, vice presidents, and middle managers spend about 18 percent, 21 percent, and 26 percent of their time, respectively, in dealing with conflict.
2. The respondents felt that their ability to manage conflict has become more important over the past ten years.
3. They rated conflict management as equal to, or slightly higher in importance than, the topics taught in AMA programs (which include planning, communication, motivation, and decision making).

This is a wonderful time for studying conflict. Professionals from various disciplines, such as anthropology, communication, law, philosophy, political science, sociology, and psychology, are contributing to our understanding of conflict. Recently a number of significant books on conflict were added to the growing list of publications on conflict.

It appears that there is a great need for enhancing the skill for managing conflict in organizations. The effectiveness of groups, organizations, and nations depends on their ability to handle conflict constructively. This is particularly important because the frequency of conflict is rising rapidly and accepted means of managing it is not often understood and used properly.

A word of caution. Although the preceding discussion shows that a moderate amount of conflict may be associated with the effective functioning of organizations, "dissent in organizations is not always tolerated and is rarely encouraged" (Stanley, 1981, p. 13). A study by Schwenk (1990) shows that managers of for-profit organizations consider conflict in decision making to be unpleasant, and high-conflict decisions are associated with low quality (see also Schweiger, Sandberg, & Ragan, 1986). However, the study also shows that although the managers of not-for-profit organizations consider conflict to be unpleasant, they believe that high-conflict decisions are positively associated with high quality. One possible explanation of the perception of this relationship between conflict and quality is that the managers of not-for-profit organizations are required to deal with decisions in which the needs of various groups and individuals are to be satisfied. The presence of conflict in the decision-making process possibly enables the administrators to do just that.

The implication of this study is that the managers of for-profit and not-for-profit organizations may respond to conflict situations differently. It appears that managers of for-profit organizations may deny the existence of conflict and deal with it through avoidance, suppression, or compromise. This will probably lead to groupthink, a concept discussed in Chapter 9. If this is true, managers of for-profit organizations are in particular need of training in conflict management.

Summary

The study of social conflict has received different emphases at different periods of history from scholars in philosophy, sociology, economics, political science, anthropology, and psychology. Most of the early contributions to the study of social conflict came from philosophers and sociologists. Management scholars became interested in it in recent years. It is generally agreed that social conflict has both functional and dysfunctional consequences.

Positions of classical philosophers on conflict, such as Plato and Aristotle, Hobbes, and Locke, and modern philosophers, such as Hegel and Marx, and Dewy, were briefly reviewed. This section also reviewed the viewpoints of the biological scientists on conflict, such as Darwin and the contributions of sociologists, such as Simmel, Mayo, Parsons, and Coser. A synthesis of the viewpoints presented by these scholars indicates that conflict in organizations has both functional and dysfunctional outcomes.

The study of organization theory is not complete without an understanding of the phenomena of conflict. The classical organization theorists implicitly assumed that conflict was detrimental to organizations, and, as a result, they attempted to eliminate it by designing mechanistic or bureaucratic organization structures. The neo-classical or human relation theorists also considered conflict to be dysfunctional, but they tried to eliminate it by improving the social system of the organization. The modern view of conflict, however, is that it is not necessarily dysfunctional for organizations. A moderate amount of conflict, handled in a constructive fashion, is necessary for attaining an optimum level of organizational effectiveness. Unfortunately, there are still writers who view conflict as dysfunctional and recommend its elimination.

Recent studies show that conflict management skills are important for managers and that managers are interested in learning more about organizational conflict and its management. Recent events show that there is a growing interest on teaching and research on conflict among scholars from various disciplines. Unfortunately, conflict in organizations is not always tolerated and rarely encouraged. It appears that managers from for-profit and not-for-profit organizations view the effects of decision conflict differently. Perception of high conflict is associated with high quality for managers of not-for-profit organizations but with low quality for managers of for-profit organizations.

Chapter 2 discusses the nature of conflict, with particular emphasis on organizational conflict. Chapter 3 discusses the relationships of conflict to organizational learning and effectiveness. Chapter 4 discusses the overall design or strategy for the management of organizational conflict. Chapters 5 through 8 provide the details for the management of intrapersonal, interpersonal, intragroup, and intergroup conflicts, respectively. These chapters present percentile and reference group norms of conflict from managerial and collegiate samples. Chapter 9 discusses ethics and morality. Chapter 10 discusses the measurement of conflict. Chapter 11 is the final chapter that summarizes the discussions of the previous 10 chapters and presents some concluding remarks. Appendixes A and B present cases and exercises, respectively.

2

Nature of Conflict

The concept of conflict was introduced in the previous chapter. The present chapter further explores the literature on conflict, especially organizational conflict, for a more theoretical understanding of its nature and implications.

Defining Conflict

The term "conflict" has no single clear meaning. Much of the confusion has been created by scholars in different disciplines who are interested in studying conflict. Reviews of the conflict literature show a conceptual sympathy for, but little consensual endorsement of, any generally accepted definition of conflict. There is tremendous variance in conflict definitions that include a range of definitions for specific interests and a variety of general definitions that attempt to be all-inclusive.

In the organizational area, March and Simon (1958, p. 112) consider conflict as a breakdown in the standard mechanisms of decision making, so that an individual or group experiences difficulty in selecting an alternative. This is a narrow conceptualization of conflict and is not very useful for research purposes. On the broad side, Pondy (1967) has argued that organizational conflict can best be understood as a dynamic process underlying organizational behavior. This is a very broad definition that excludes very little of anything transpiring in a group or individual. Tedeschi, Schlenker, and Bonoma (1973) take a middle position, defining conflict as "an interactive state in which the behaviors or goals of one actor are to some degree incompatible with the behaviors or goals of some other actor or actors" (p. 232). It is understood from their exposition that "actor" refers to any social entity, from the individual, to the corporate body itself. Smith (1966) also takes a similar position and defines conflict as "a situation in which the conditions, practices, or goals for the different participants are inherently incompatible" (p. 511). Another definition of conflict is "a type of behavior which occurs when two or more parties are in opposition or in battle as a result of a perceived relative deprivation from the activities of or interacting with another person or group" (Litterer, 1966, p. 180).

The difference between the last two authors in defining conflict is that whereas Smith considers conflict as a situation, Litterer considers it as a type of behavior. However, both of these authors and Tedeschi et al. consider conflict to result from incompatibility or opposition in goals, activities, or interaction among the social entities. Baron (1990; see also Mack & Snyder, 1957), after reviewing a number of recent definitions of conflict, concluded that although definitions are not identical, they overlap with respect to the following elements:

1. Conflict includes *opposing interests* between individuals or groups in a zero-sum situation;
2. Such opposed interests must be *recognized* for conflict to exist;
3. Conflict involves *beliefs*, by each side, that the other will thwart (or has already thwarted) its interests;
4. Conflict is a *process*; it develops out of existing relationships between individuals or groups and reflects their past interactions and the contexts in which these took place; and
5. Imply *actions* by one or both sides that do, in fact, produce thwarting of others' goals (p. 199).

These five elements are particularly useful in conceptualizing a zero-sum conflict situation. In nonzero-sum (i.e., positive-sum and mixed-motive) conflict situations some of the preceding elements may not be present. For example, say that two managers who respect each other's judgment disagree on their plans to enhance market share for a product. Although each manager believes that his or her plan is better than the other, each is of the opinion that the plan prepared by the other manager has some potentials for enhancing the product's market share. This conflict does not necessarily involve beliefs by each manager that the other will thwart (or has already thwarted) his or her interests.

Conflict is defined as an *interactive process manifested in incompatibility, disagreement, or dissonance within or between social entities (i.e., individual, group, organization, etc.).* Calling conflict an interactive state does not preclude the possibilities of intraindividual conflict, for it is known that a person often interacts with himself or herself. Obviously, one also interacts with others. Conflict occurs when one (two) social entity(ies):

1. Is required to engage in an activity that is incongruent with his or her needs or interests;
2. Holds behavioral preferences the satisfaction of which is incompatible with another person's implementation of his or her preferences;
3. Wants some mutually desirable resource that is in short supply, such that the wants of everyone may not be satisfied fully; and

4. Possesses attitudes, values, skills, and goals that are salient in directing one's behavior but that are perceived to be exclusive of the attitudes, values, skills, and goals held by the other(s).
5. Has partially exclusive behavioral preferences regarding joint actions; and
6. Is interdependent in the performance of functions or activities.

According to Roloff (1987), "organizational conflict occurs when members engage in activities that are incompatible with those of colleagues within their network, members of other collectivities, or unaffiliated individuals who utilize the services or products of the organization" (p. 496). This definition is consistent with the one just presented. Some of the manifestations of conflict behavior are expressing disagreement with the opponent, yelling, verbal abuse, interference, and so on.

Threshold of Conflict

This principle is consistent with Baron's (1990) second element of conflict previously discussed. Conflict does not necessarily occur simply because there are incompatibilities, disagreements, or differences within or between social entities. In order for conflict to occur, it has to exceed the threshold level of intensity (i.e., the point at which the conflict is of sufficient intensity that cannot be ignored) before the parties experience (or become aware of) any conflict. In other words, the incompatibilities, disagreements, or differences must be serious enough before the parties experience conflict. There are differences in the threshold of conflict awareness or tolerance among individuals. Thus, some individuals may become involved in a conflict sooner than others in similar situations.

Conflict and Competition

Ambiguity in the distinction between competition and conflict has been a source of confusion (Schmidt & Kochan, 1972). The distinction between these two terms should be delineated to understand the nature of conflict. Three major distinctions in the conceptualization of conflict and competition are presented next.

Boulding (1962) considers conflict as a subset of competition that "exists when any potential positions of two behavior units are mutually incompatible. . . . [Conflict is considered] as a situation of competition in which the parties are aware of the incompatibility of potential future positions and in which the party wishes to occupy a position that is incompatible with the wishes of the other" (p. 4). According to this conceptualization, all situations of incompatibility lead to competition, but conflict occurs when the parties become *aware* of the incompatibility and wish to *interfere* with the attainment of each other's goal attainments. In this sense, golf is a competitive game; football, a conflictual one.

Another possible distinction has been based on whether the behavior of the parties to interaction is regulated by rules and norms. According to Mack (1965), competitive behavior is so regulated, whereas conflictual behavior is not. Brickman (1974), however, persuasively argued that the presence or absence of rule structures in conflict situations has little, if anything, to do with the amount of competition present in conflict.

Conflict and competition may be distinguished neither by the presence or absence of rule structures nor by anything to do with the phenomenology of the interactants. Rather, the distinction may be approached in a manner similar to Rapoport's (1960; see also Schelling, 1980), and it may be argued that (contrary to Boulding) competition is a subset of conflict. Conflicts may be placed along a continuum of cooperative to competitive, the former occurring when there is a payoff cell or set of cells in which both parties receive satisfactory and high outcomes, and the latter occurring when only joint payoffs occur such that one party wins and the other loses (cf. Thibaut & Kelley, 1959).

In the language of game theory (e.g., Schelling, 1980), it is possible to both label and diagram three ideal points along this cooperative–competitive continuum to facilitate the categorization of conflicts. Purely cooperative conflicts (technically, "positive-sum games" or "conflicts of coordination") occur in such social situations as a lost child's trying to find his or her mother (and vice versa), a subordinate's attempting to clarify an assignment with the supervisor, and two parties' disconnected, trying to reestablish their telephone communication link. The problem is simply one of coordination—of establishing who does what in order to ensure a mutually profitable outcome for both individuals or units.

Purely competitive conflicts are technically termed "zero-sum games" or "negative-sum games," in which the positive outcomes to one party are directly and equally matched by negative outcomes to the other as a result of their joint choices from interaction. An organizational illustration is that of recruitment, where two candidates are interviewed, but only one can be hired.

Of course, in real life, including managerial settings, one hardly encounters purely cooperative or purely competitive conflict situations. Rather, most conflicts are characterized by both cooperative and competitive aspects (i.e., they are "nonzero-sum games" or "mixed-motive" conflicts). Most managerial conflicts are mixed-motive in nature. As seen later in this chapter, there are other, more functional ways of developing the taxonomy of conflict.

Classifying Conflict

The literature of organizational behavior and management has highlighted different types of conflict. Conflict may be classified on the basis of its sources or antecedent conditions. It may also be classified on the basis of organizational levels (individual, group, etc.) at which it may originate.

Antecedent Conditions

The classification of conflict is often made based on the antecedent conditions that lead to conflict. Conflict may originate from a number of sources, such as tasks, values, goals, and so on. It has been found appropriate to classify conflict on the basis of these sources for proper understanding of its nature and implications. Following is a brief description of this classification.

1. Substantive Conflict. This is caused by difference of opinion regarding task, policies, procedures, and other business-related or content issues (Guetzkow & Gyr, 1954). Substantive conflict is intellectual opposition to the ideas and is an essential step to problem solving. Engaging in substantive conflict involves evaluating opinions and ideas on the basis of evidence, logic, and critical and innovative thinking.

Jehn (1997b) characterized this type of conflict as "disagreements among group members' ideas and opinions about the task being performed, such as disagreement regarding an organization's current strategic position or determining the correct data to include in a report" (p. 288). This type of conflict has also been labeled *task conflict* (Eisenhardt et al., 1997; Jehn, 1997a; Pelled et al., 1999), *cognitive conflict* (Amason, 1996; Cosier & Rose, 1977; Holzworth, 1983), and *issue conflict* (Hammer & Organ, 1978).

2. Affective Conflict. This occurs when two or more interacting social entities, while trying to solve a problem together, become aware that their emotions and feelings regarding some or all the issues are incompatible (Guetzkow & Gyr, 1954; see also Amason, 1996). These emotions and feelings are associated with personal attacks and criticisms that lead to hostility, distrust, and cynicism. Affective conflict is also created by personality clashes, sarcasm, and making fun of one's ideas.

Pelled et al. (1999) defined it as "a condition in which group members have interpersonal clashes characterized by anger, frustration, and other negative feelings" (p. 2). This category of conflict has been labeled *psychological conflict* (Ross & Ross, 1989), *relationship conflict* (Jehn, 1997a), *emotional conflict* (Pelled et al., 1999), and *interpersonal conflict* (Eisenhardt et al., 1997).

3. Other Forms of Substantive–Affective Conflict. The preceding discussion suggests that theorists have traditionally suggested that organizational conflict has two dimensions: one consisting of disagreements about the task and one consisting of socio-emotional or interpersonal disputes. While these prior investigations provide important clues about the nature of conflict, considerably more investigations should be conducted before scholars and practitioners have a solid grasp of the phenomenon. In particular, there is a need to look beyond these traditional dimensions of task and emotional conflict, investigating other dimensions that may be influential. Such exploration is essential if we are to gain better understanding—and, in turn, a better ability to manage—conflict in the workplace.

The traditional dichotomy may be extended by adding two other kinds of conflict to it that can be classified as transforming and masquerading conflicts (Rahim & Pelled, 1998). There are several reasons for these two additional kinds of conflict to exist. First studies of conflict have often found high correlations between task and emotional conflicts. Second, previous writings have hinted at the notion that these other dimensions exist. For example, alluding to the idea of transforming conflict, Eisenhardt et al. (1997) have noted, "A comment meant as a substantive remark can be interpreted as a personal attack. . . . Personalities frequently become intertwined with issues" (p. 78). Alluding to the idea of masquerading conflict, Pelled (1996) observed that "individuals may express hostility by manufacturing useless criticisms of each other's task-related ideas" (p. 620).

The preceding theoretical discussion suggests that some conflicts are crosses between task and emotional conflicts: emotional conflict that masquerades as task conflict and task conflict that becomes emotional. Conflicts relating to this type may be labeled as cognitive–affective conflict. Following is a discussion of these conflicts.

Transforming Conflict. This conflict evolves from substantive conflict to affective conflict. In other words, this occurs when substantive conflict degenerates to affective conflict. This occurs when people involved in a substantive conflict start attacking each other personally and disagreements on business issues drift to emotional conflicts. In many cases a group discussion starts with a focus on business-related issues, but if the disagreement among members becomes intense, they may become involved in personality clashes and attack each other personally.

Masquerading Conflict. This refers to disagreements when members have emotional conflicts with each other, but disguise them as substantive conflicts. This conflict appears to be task-related on the surface but that is actually emotional in nature. Here group members who don't get along on a personal level disguise their relationship issues as criticisms of each other's business-related ideas.

4. Process Conflict. This type of conflict received relatively little attention from scholars. It is associated with how different tasks should be performed, responsibility to complete specific tasks, delegation of duties and responsibilities, and deadlines and is distinct from substantive and affective conflicts (see Jehn, 1997a; Jehn & Mannix, 2001). Process conflict can be defined as "disagreements about logistical and delegation issues such as how task accomplishment should proceed and in the work unit, who's responsible for what, and how things should be delegated" (Jehn, Greer, Levine, & Szulaqnski, 2008, p. 467).

5. Goal Conflict. This occurs when a preferred outcome or an end-state of two social entities (individuals, groups, organizations, nations) is perceived to be incompatible. In rare cases "it may involve divergent preferences over all of the decision outcomes, constituting a zero-sum game" (Cosier & Rose, 1977, p. 378). The understanding of managers A and B that only one of their preferred job design programs can be implemented for their division is an example of goal conflict.

6. Conflict of Interest. This is defined as a situation in which social entities engage in activities that are incompatible with the ones they are supposed to be engaging. This type of conflict occurs "when each party, sharing the same understanding of the situation, prefers a different and somewhat incompatible solution to a problem involving either a distribution of scarce resources between them or a decision to share the work of solving it" (Druckman & Zechmeister, 1973, p. 450). The contention of managers A and B for the same vice president's job exemplifies a conflict of interest.

7. Conflict of Values. This occurs when two interacting social entities differ in their values or ideologies on certain issues. This is also called *ideological* conflict. The ideological disagreement of supervisors A and B on the question of "compensatory hiring" is an example of value conflict. Conflict between pro-life and pro-choice groups in connection with abortion is another example of conflict of values.

8. Structural or Institutionalized Conflict. This conflict is caused by differentiation between groups and levels in an organization. There are two types of this conflict, horizontal and vertical. Horizontal conflict occurs between two subsystems at the same organizational level—between line and staff units and between sales and production departments.

Vertical conflicts are caused by disagreements between the members of the hierarchical levels relating to goals, control mechanisms, and resource availability. Conflicts between headquarters and field staffs, management and union, and franchisers and franchisees are some of the examples of this type of conflict.

9. Realistic versus Nonrealistic Conflict. The former refers to incompatibilities that have rational content (i.e., tasks, goals, values, and means and ends). Nonrealistic conflict occurs as a result of a party's need for releasing tension and expressing hostility, ignorance, or error. Whereas realistic conflict is associated with "mostly rational or goal-oriented" disagreement, nonrealistic conflict "is an end in itself having little to do with group or organizational goals" (Ross & Ross, 1989, p. 139).

Realistic and nonrealistic conflicts are similar to Haiman's (1951, p. 181) intrinsic and extrinsic conflicts. They also correspond with *real* and *induced* conflict, "the latter being cases where representatives of conflicting groups have ends to be gained (e.g., their own prestige) apart from the ends in dispute between groups. This would be the situation in which union leaders precipitated a conflict with management in order to strengthen their hold over the union membership" (Mack & Snyder, 1957, p. 220; see also Bisno, 1988, p. 31). Olson's (1968, p. 135) description of *expressive* conflict parallels nonrealistic conflict.

10. Retributive Conflict. This conflict is characterized by a situation where the conflicting entities feel the need for a drawn-out conflict to punish the opponent. In other words, each party determines its gains, in part, by incurring costs to the other party (Saaty, 1990, p. 49). Examples of retributive conflicts are Northern Ireland and Palestinian-Israeli conflicts and the Cold War between the former superpowers.

11. Misattributed Conflict. This relates to the incorrect assignment of causes (behaviors, parties, or issues) to conflict (Deutsch, 1977). For example, an employee may wrongly attribute to his or her supervisor a cut in the employee's department budget, which may have been done by higher-level managers over the protest of the supervisor.

12. Displaced Conflict. This type of conflict occurs when the conflicting parties either direct their frustrations or hostilities to social entities that are not involved in conflict or argue over secondary, not major, issues (Deutsch, 1977).

Levels of Analysis

Organizational conflict may be classified as *intraorganizational* (i.e., conflict within an organization) or *interorganizational* (i.e., conflict between two or more organizations). Intraorganizational conflict may also be classified on the basis of levels (individual, group, etc.) at which it occurs. On this basis intraorganizational conflict may be classified as intrapersonal, interpersonal, intragroup, and intergroup. These four types of conflict may be described as follows:

1. Intrapersonal Conflict. This type of conflict is also known as intra-individual or intra-psychic conflict. It occurs when an organizational member is required to perform certain tasks and roles that do not match his or her expertise, interests, goals, and values. Various types of intrapersonal or role conflict are discussed in Chapter 5.

2. Interpersonal Conflict. This is also known as *dyadic* conflict. It refers to conflict between two or more organizational members of the same or different hierarchical levels or units. The studies on superior-subordinate conflict relate to this type of conflict. The styles of handling interpersonal conflict are discussed later in this chapter and chapters 4, 6, and 9.

3. Intragroup Conflict. This is also known as intradepartmental conflict. It refers to conflict among members of a group or between two or more subgroups within a group in connection with its goals, tasks, procedures, and so on. Such a conflict may also occur as a result of incompatibilities or disagreements between some or all the members of a group and its leader(s). Intragroup conflict is discussed later in Chapter 7.

4. Intergroup Conflict. This is also known as interdepartmental conflict. It refers to conflict between two or more units or groups within an organization. Conflict between line and staff, production and marketing, and headquarters and field staffs are examples of this type of conflict. One special type of intergroup conflict is between labor and management. Different types of intergroup conflict are discussed in Chapter 8.

Conflicts classified by sources can take place at the interpersonal, intragroup, or intergroup levels. In other words, incompatibilities caused by these sources can occur in the context of two individuals, a group, or two groups.

It was indicated in the definition of organizational conflict that conflict may occur within or between social entities. This distinction between conflict within and conflict between social entities depends on a system perspective for a given problem. The classification of conflict into four types, based on the level of its origin, shows that analysis at different levels may be beneficial depending on the nature of the problem(s).

Styles of Handling Interpersonal Conflict

Interpersonal conflicts can be handled with various styles of behavior. There are four models of the styles of handling interpersonal conflict in organizations which have some similarities and differences. The styles discussed in the four models are listed in Table 2–1. Following is a description of these models:

Model of Two Styles

Deutsch (1949) first suggested the simple cooperative–competitive model in the research on social conflict. Although the cooperative–competitive dichotomy is hardly used in the conflict literature, Deutsch and his followers continue to use this conceptualization (Deutsch, 1990; Tjosvold, 1990). This view is similar to that of the game theorists who use a cooperative–competitive continuum to facilitate the categorization of conflicts (Schelling, 1980). Purely competitive

Table 2–1
Styles of Handling Interpersonal Conflict: Models of 2–5 Styles

Models	I	II	Styles III	IV	V
Two Styles					
Deutsch (1990)	Cooperation	—	—	Competition	—
Knudson, Sommers, & Golding (1980)	Engagement	—	Avoidance	—	—
Three Styles					
Putnam & Wilson (1982)	Solution-Orientation	Non-Confrontation	—	Control	—
Lawrence & Lorsch (1967a)	Confrontation	Smoothing	—	Forcing	—
Billingham & Sack (1987)	Reasoning	—	—	Verbal Aggression Violence	—
Rands, Levinger, & Mellinger (1981)	—	—	Avoid	Attack	Compromise
Four Styles					
Pruitt (1983)	Problem Solving	Yielding	Inaction	Contending	—
Kurdek (1994)	Problem Solving	Compliance	Withdrawal	Engagement	—
Five Styles					
Follett (1940)	Integration	Suppression	Avoidance	Domination	Compromise
Blake & Mouton (1964)	Confrontation	Smoothing	Avoiding	Forcing	Compromise
Thomas (1976)	Collaborating	Accommodating	Avoiding	Competing	Compromising
Rahim (1983a)	Integrating	Obliging	Avoiding	Dominating	Compromising

conflicts are technically termed "zero-sum games" or "negative-sum games," in which the positive outcomes to one party are directly and equally matched by negative outcomes to the other as a result of their joint choices from interaction. Another model of the two styles of handling marital conflict—engagement and avoidance—was suggested by Knudson, Sommers, and Golding (1980), which did not receive any prominence in theory and research.

The two-factor model does not recognize other styles, but in real life, and including managerial settings, one hardly encounters purely cooperative or purely competitive conflict situations. Game theorists recognize that most conflicts are characterized by both cooperative and competitive aspects (i.e., they are "nonzero-sum games" or "mixed-motive" conflicts). This is very similar to the compromising style.

Deutsch and his associates have suggested that a cooperative relationship is more effective than a competitive relationship in managing conflict. They have presented evidence that indicates that a cooperative relationship leads to a more functional outcome than does a competitive relationship. Unfortunately, these studies have not presented evidence of a positive relationship of cooperative style to job performance, productivity, or other independent measures of outcomes.

Model of Three Styles

Putnam and Wilson (1982) provided empirical evidence on the basis of a factor analysis of the items of their Organizational Communication Conflict Instrument that there are three styles of handling interpersonal conflict: non-confrontation (obliging), solution-orientation (integrating), and control (dominating). Hocker and Wilmot (1991) concluded after literature review that "conflict styles cluster similarly to conflict tactics—into three types (1) avoidance, (2) competitive (distributive) and (3) collaborative (integrative)" (p. 119). Lawrence and Lorsch (1967) selected twenty-five aphorisms or traditional proverbs for measuring five modes of conflict resolution, but their factor analysis identified three, instead of five, factors: forcing, smoothing, and confrontation. Weider-Hatfield (1988) concluded from her literature review that "although the conflict literature has historically embraced the 'five-style' paradigm, recent evidence indicates that individuals might select among three, not five, distinct conflict styles" (p. 364). Conclusions reached by Weider-Hatfield and Hocker and Wilmot are misleading because their reviews were restricted to communication studies.

The theoretical basis for the three-category conflict styles is not clear. Putnam and Wilson (1982) and Lawrence and Lorsch (1967) derived the three dimensions of styles from single factor analyses. Factor analysis is undoubtedly a powerful method of testing the basic dimensions of a construct as measured by a survey instrument. But in order for this analysis to be meaningful, the measurement instrument has to be designed on the basis of theory and past research, and multiple factor analyses computed with different sets of items in different samples, as suggested by Eysenck and Eysenck (1968).

The other two models of the three styles of handling conflict were developed by Billingham and Sack (1987) (reasoning, verbal aggression, and violence) and Rands, Levinger, and Mellinger (1981) (attack, avoid, and compromise). These models received some attention in theory and research in the area of marital conflict.

In order for this model to be useful in organizations, evidence of how the three styles influence organizational behavior and management is needed. Unfortunately, the researchers have not provided any evidence of the relationships between the three conflict styles and individual, group, and organizational outcomes. It appears that this model has not progressed much over the years.

Model of Four Styles

Pruitt (1983) suggested and provided some empirical evidence from laboratory studies that there are four styles of handling conflict: yielding, problem solving, inaction, and contending. These styles were based on the two-dimensional model that consists of concern for self (high or low) and concern for others (high or low). This model is much more developed than the previous two, but, like the previous two models, it does not recognize compromising as a distinct style.

Pruitt (1983) and Pruitt and Carnevale (1993) provided evidence that problem-solving style is the best for managing conflict effectively. They provided evidence to support their conclusion, mainly from laboratory studies. They have not provided any evidence of the relationships of the four styles to job performance or productivity. Another four-factor model of conflict styles (problem solving, conflict engagement, withdrawal, and compliance) was suggested by Kurdek (1994). This model received some attention in the conceptualization and operationalization of marital conflict.

Model of Five Styles

The five styles of handling interpersonal conflict in organizations were first conceptualized in 1926 by Mary P. Follett (1940). She conceptualized three main ways of handling organizational conflict—domination, compromise, and integration—as well as other, secondary ways of handling conflict, such as avoidance and suppression. Blake and Mouton (1964) first presented a conceptual scheme for classifying the modes (styles) for handling interpersonal conflicts into five types: forcing, withdrawing, smoothing, compromising, and problem solving. They described the five modes of handling conflict on the basis of the attitudes of the manager: concern for production and for people. Their scheme was reinterpreted by Thomas (1976). He considered the intentions of a party (cooperativeness, i.e., attempting to satisfy the other party's concerns; and assertiveness, i.e., attempting to satisfy one's own concerns) in classifying the modes of handling conflict into five types.

Rahim and Bonoma (1979) and Rahim (1983a) differentiated the *styles* of handling interpersonal conflict on two basic dimensions: concern for self and concern for others. The first dimension explains the degree (high or low) to which a person attempts to satisfy his or her own concern. The second dimension explains the degree (high or low) to which a person wants to satisfy the concern of others. It should be pointed out that these dimensions portray the motivational orientations of a given individual during conflict. Studies by Ruble and Thomas (1976) and Van de Vliert and Kabanoff (1990) yielded general support for these dimensions. Combination of the two dimensions results in five specific styles of handling interpersonal conflict, as shown in Figure 2–1 (Rahim & Bonoma, 1979, p. 1327). The styles of handling interpersonal conflict are described as follows.

1. Integrating Style. This style indicates high concern for self and others. This style is also known as problem solving. It involves collaboration between the parties (i.e., openness, exchange of information, and examination of differences to reach a solution acceptable to both parties). "The first rule... for obtaining integration is to put your cards on the table, face the real issue, uncover the conflict, bring the whole thing into the open" (Follett, 1926/1940, p. 38). Gray (1989) describes this as collaborating—"a process through which

Figure 2–1
The Dual Concern Model of the
Styles of Handling Interpersonal Conflict

Concern for Self

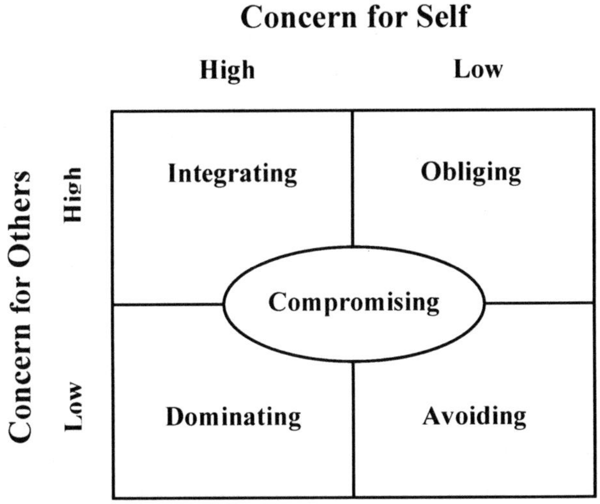

parties who see different aspects of a problem can constructively explore their differences and search for solutions that go beyond their own limited vision of what is possible" (p. 5).

Prein (1976) suggested that this style has two distinctive elements: confrontation and problem solving. Confrontation involves open communication, clearing up misunderstanding, and analyzing the underlying causes of conflict. This is a prerequisite for problem solving, which involves identification of and solution to the real problem(s) to provide maximum satisfaction of concerns of both parties.

2. Obliging Style. This style indicates low concern for self and high concern for others. This is also known as accommodating. This style is associated with attempting to play down the differences and emphasizing commonalities to satisfy the concern of the other party. There is an element of self-sacrifice in this style. It may take the form of selfless generosity, charity, or obedience to another party's order.

An obliging person neglects his or her own concern to satisfy the concern of the other party. Such an individual is like a "conflict absorber," that is, a "person whose reaction to a perceived hostile act on the part of another has low hostility or even positive friendliness" (Boulding, 1962, p. 171).

3. Dominating Style. This style indicates high concern for self and low concern for others. This is also known as competing. This style has been identified with a win–lose orientation or with forcing behavior to win one's position. A dominating or competing person goes all out to win his or her objective and, as a result, often ignores the needs and expectations of the other party. Dominating may mean standing up for one's rights and/or defending a position that the party believes to be correct.

Sometimes a dominating person wants to win at any cost. A dominating supervisor is likely to use his or her position power to impose his or her will on the subordinates and command their obedience. A person who does not possess formal position power may wield power by deceit, bluff, bringing in superiors, and so on.

4. Avoiding Style. This style indicates low concern for self and others. This is also known as suppression. It has been associated with withdrawal, buck-passing, sidestepping, or "see no evil, hear no evil, speak no evil" situations. It may take the form of postponing an issue until a better time or simply withdrawing from a threatening situation. An avoiding person fails to satisfy his or her own concern as well as the concern of the other party.

This style is often characterized as an unconcerned attitude toward the issues or parties involved in conflict. Such a person may refuse to acknowledge in public that there is a conflict that should be dealt with.

5. Compromising Style. This style indicates intermediate in concern for self and others. It involves give-and-take or sharing whereby both parties give up something to make a mutually acceptable decision. It may mean splitting the difference, exchanging concession, or seeking a quick, middle-ground position.

A compromising party gives up more than a dominating party but less than an obliging party. Likewise, such a party addresses an issue more directly than an avoiding party but does not explore it in as much depth as an integrating party.

Additional insights may be gained by reclassifying the five styles of handling interpersonal conflict according to the terminologies of game theory. Integrating style can be reclassified to a positive-sum or nonzero-sum (win–win) style, compromising to a mixed (no-win/no-lose) style, and obliging, dominating, and avoiding to zero-sum or negative-sum (lose–win, win–lose, and lose–lose, respectively) styles.

Although we have indicated that the five styles of handling interpersonal conflict can be reclassified using the taxonomy of game theory, it will be seen in Chapter 5 that the description of the styles as win–win, lose–win, win–lose, lose–lose, and no-win/no-lose may be misleading. Each of the five styles of handling interpersonal conflict may be appropriate depending on the situation. In general, integrating and, to some extent, compromising styles can be used for effectively dealing with conflicts involving strategic or complex issues. The remaining styles can be used effectively to deal with conflicts involving tactical, day-to-day, or routine problems. Thus, the selection and use of each style can be considered as a win–win style provided that it is used to enhance individual, group, and organizational effectiveness.

Integrative and Distributive Dimensions

Follett's (1940) conceptualization is the forerunner of Walton and McKersie's (1965) distinction between integrative and distributive bargaining. It has been suggested by Thomas (1976) that further insights into the five styles of handling interpersonal conflict may be obtained by organizing them according to the integrative and distributive dimensions of labor–management bargaining suggested by Walton and McKersie. These two dimensions have been described as cooperation and competition by Deutsch (1949), the principle of creating value for all and the principle of claiming value for each by Lax and Sebenius (1968) and mutual gains and concession-convergence by Rubin (1994).

The two dimensions are represented by the heavy lines in the diagonals of Figure 2–2. The integrative dimension (integrating–avoiding) represents the extent (high or low) of satisfaction of concerns received by self and others. The distributive dimension (dominating–obliging) represents the ratio of the satisfaction of concerns received by self and others. In the integrat-

Figure 2–2
The Dual Concern Model: Problem Solving and Bargaining Strategies
for Handling Interpersonal Conflict

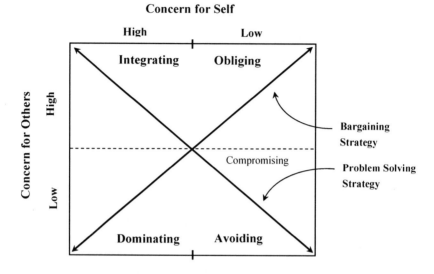

ive dimension, the integrating style attempts to increase the satisfaction of the concerns of both parties by finding unique solutions to the problems acceptable to them. The avoiding style leads to the reduction of satisfaction of the concerns of both parties as a result of their failure to confront and solve their problems. In the distributive dimension, whereas the dominating style attempts to obtain high satisfaction of concerns for self (and provide low satisfaction of concerns for others), the obliging style attempts to obtain low satisfaction of concerns for self (and provide high satisfaction of concerns for others).

Whereas the integrative dimension represents the amount of satisfaction of concerns received by both parties (i.e., self and others), the distributive dimension represents the amount of satisfaction of the concerns received by one of the parties (i.e., self or others). The compromising style represents the point of intersection of the two dimensions, that is, a middle-ground position where both parties receive an intermediate level of satisfaction of their concerns from the resolution of their conflicts.

Walton and McKersie (1965) described these two as the dimensions of labor–management bargaining. But bargaining is one of a number of strategies that can be used to manage intraorganizational conflict effectively. In order to manage various conflicts effectively, both the bargaining and problem-solving dimensions are needed. The Walton-McKersie dimensions may be reconceptualized: the distributive dimension may be considered as the dimension of bargaining, but the integrative dimension may be considered as the dimension of problem solving. The distributive dimension may be used to deal with conflict involving routine matters, but the integrative dimension may be used to deal with strategic or complex conflicts. This reconceptualization would provide more options to management practitioners and employees to manage intraorganizational conflict effectively.

Thomas (1976) recognized that the preceding design for conceptualizing the styles of handling interpersonal conflict is a noteworthy improvement over the simple cooperative–competitive dichotomy suggested by Deutsch (1949). The preceding design is also an improvement over the three styles of handling conflict proposed by Putnam and Wilson (1982). It should be noted that it is not possible to conceptualize the two independent dimensions—integrative and distributive—with the two or three styles of handling interpersonal conflict.

The two dimensional conflict model presented in Figure 2–2 is also an improvement over Pruitt's (1983) four styles of handling conflict in which no distinction is made between integrating and compromising styles. He explained his decision to ignore compromising style as follows:

> the dual concern model postulates a fifth strategy called "compromising," which is ordinarily shown in the middle of the graph because it is viewed as due to a moderate concern about self and other....it seems unnecessary to postulate a separate strategy to explain the development of compromises. (p. 173)

Van de Vliert and Kabanoff (1990) disagreed with Pruitt's decision to ignore compromising style and suggested that questionnaire "items referring to compromising and collaborating should focus on distinct behavioral characteristics of the two styles rather than on their direct or indirect consequences" (p. 206). There is substantial evidence that the integrating and compromising styles are independent of each other (Lee, 1990; Rahim, 1983a; Rahim & Magner, 1995; Ting-Toomey et al., 1991).

Further discussions on these five styles of handling interpersonal conflict are continued in Chapters 4, 6, and 9.

Summary

There is no generally accepted definition of conflict. It was defined as an interactive process manifested in incompatibility, disagreements, or dissonance within or between social entities (i.e., individual, group, and organization). Some of the elements that may be present in a conflict are opposing interests between parties, recognition of such opposed interests, and beliefs by each party that the other will thwart or has thwarted his or her interests, that conflict is a process, and that actions by one or both parties may hinder the attainment of other's goals. The threshold of conflict, which is one of the elements of conflict, indicates that the incompatibility, disagreement, or dissonance between social entities has to be significant or serious enough before the parties become aware of, and engage in, conflict. Competition is a part of conflict. Conflict may be placed along a continuum from cooperative conflict to competitive conflict. Cooperative or positive-sum conflict occurs when both parties receive satisfactory outcomes; competitive or zero-sum conflict occurs when one party wins, and the other party loses. Most managerial conflicts are characterized by both cooperative and competitive aspects, that is, mixed-motive conflicts.

Conflict can be classified on the basis of the sources or antecedent conditions that lead to conflict. Accordingly, conflict can be classified into various types: substantive conflict, affective conflict, transforming conflict, masquerading conflict, process conflict, goal conflict, conflict of interest, conflict of values, structural or institutionalized conflict, realistic versus nonrealistic conflict, retributive conflict, misattributed conflict, and displaced conflict. Conflict can also be classified according to the levels of its origin—such as intrapersonal, interpersonal, intragroup, and intergroup. The classification of conflict according to organizational levels shows that an analysis of conflict at different levels can be effective depending on the nature of the problem(s). There are four models of conflict-handling styles. The five-factor model shows that the styles of handling interpersonal conflict can be classified as integrating, obliging, dominating, avoiding, and compromising. These styles can be organized according to the integrative (integrating–avoiding) and distributive (dominating–obliging) dimensions.

The next chapter discusses the ideal outcomes of conflict management that are associated with organizational learning and effectiveness.

3

Organizational Learning and Effectiveness

Existing studies in conflict resolution, with minor exceptions, have little connection with the organization theory. These studies have generally used laboratory experiments and are based on mechanistic–reductionistic view of organizations. Strategies recommended by these studies—negotiation, mediation, and arbitration—do not involve changes in the processes and structures in the existing organizations. As a result, conflict resolution is encouraged within an existing bureaucracy that further reinforces its processes and structures.

If today's organizations want to respond effectively to the challenge of intense global competition, they have to require their supervisors and employees to learn new behaviors. Unfortunately, existing conflict resolution approaches are not suitable for changing behaviors which involves learning.

There is greater need to improve our knowledge about organizational learning and effectiveness than ever before so that organizations can effectively respond to the needs of rapidly changing environments. The issue for organizations is not whether they want to learn; they must learn as fast as they can. Therefore, one of the major objectives of managing conflict in contemporary organizations should be to enhance organizational learning that will influence long-term effectiveness.

Organizational learning is a significant construct and a number of contemporary organization theorists have indicated that the issue for the organizations is not whether they want to learn; they must learn as fast as they can (Argysis & Schon, 1996; Schein, 1993; Senge, 1990). Luthans, Rubach, and Marsnik (1995) concluded from their review of organizational learning literature that "the presence of tension and conflict seem to be essential characteristics of the learning organization. The tension and conflict will be evidenced by questioning, inquiry, disequilibrium, and a challenging of the status quo" (p. 30). Unfortunately, the literature on organizational conflict does not provide a clear link between conflict management strategies and organizational learning and effectiveness. Argyris (1994) suggests that existing theories encourage self-reinforcing and anti-learning processes which can best be described as "quasi-resolution of conflict" (p. 3). Several scholars have indicated the need for accommodating tensions and managing conflict constructively or the potential for collective learning will not be realized (Pascale, 1990; Senge, Kleiner, Roberts, Ross, & Smith, 1994). The implicit assumption here is that conflict management need to be strengthened at a macro-level for encouraging learning and effectiveness. In order to attain this objective, conflict management strategies should be designed to enhance critical and innovative thinking to learn the process of diagnosis and intervention in the right problems. Chapter 4 discusses a model of conflict management, not conflict resolution, which is designed to enhance organizational learning and effectiveness.

Defining Organizational Learning

Although the concept of organizational learning was formally introduced by Simon (1953/1976; see also Argyris, 1976) over six decades ago, it has not received much attention in the organizational literature until recently. Organizational learning involves *knowledge acquisition, knowledge distribution, information interpretation,* and *organizational memorization* (i.e., preserving information for future access and use). This enables organizational members to collectively engage in the process of diagnosis of and intervention in problems. Although there is considerable diversity in the conceptualization of organizational learning, scholars generally include Argyris and Schön's (1996) definition and classification of learning. According to them, organizational learning is a process of detection (cognitive) and correction (behavioral) of error.

Types of Learning

The literature has identified two types of organizational learning: single-loop and double-loop learning. An intervention for effective conflict management should promote double-loop, rather than single-loop, organizational learning.

Single-Loop Learning

This type of learning involves the diagnosis of, and intervention in, problems without changing the values and assumptions underlying goals, strategies, and policies. In other words, single-loop learning results in cognitive and behavioral changes within an existing paradigm (i.e., the old paradigm or mind-set). "Single-loop learning asks a one-dimensional question to elicit a one-dimensional answer. My favorite example is a thermostat, which measures ambient temperature against a standard setting and turns the heat source on or off accordingly. The whole transaction is binary" (Argyris, 1994, p. 78). Single-loop learning is similar to Senge's (1990) *adaptive* learning and Botkin, Elmandjra, and Malitza's (1979) *maintenance* learning. Argyris has given a name to this type of learning, "Model I."

Double-Loop Learning

This type of learning involves changes in the values and assumptions underlying goals, strategies, and policies. In other words, double-loop learning involves cognitive and behavioral changes outside the existing paradigm (i.e., the new paradigm or mind-set). "In the case of the thermostat, for instance, double-loop learning would wonder whether the current setting was actually the most effective temperature at which to keep the room and, if so, whether the present heat source was the most effective means of achieving it. A double-loop learning asks questions not only about objective facts but also about reasons and motives behind those facts" (Argyris, 1994, pp. 78–79). Double-loop learning is very similar to higher- or second-order learning, or "learning how to learn." This is similar to Bateson's (1972; see also Visser, 2007) *deutero-learning*. Double-loop learning is similar to Senge's *generative* learning and Botkin, Elmandjra, and Malitza's (1979) innovative learning. Argyris calls it "Model II" behavior.

It should be noted that individual learning is a necessary, but not adequate, condition for organizational learning. There must be processes and structures for transferring what is learned by individuals to the collective. In other words, organizational learning occurs when members of the collective have successfully learned from the individuals. There must also be mechanisms for preserving and accessing knowledge acquired by the collective.

As mentioned before, existing conflict resolution strategies are designed to deal with conflict within the existing structure and processes of an organization. In other words, these strategies do not involve significant changes in the functioning of the organizations. As such, existing conflict resolution strategies maintain status quo, which leads to single-loop learning.

The next chapter presents strategies for managing conflict that are designed to encourage double-loop learning (Rahim, 2002). Companies like Motorola, Xerox, General Electric, and Honda have adapted strategies of conflict management that should encourage double-loop learning to a great extent.

Organizational Effectiveness

Conflict management should be designed to encourage double-loop learning or deutero-learning, which in turn, should enhance organizational effectiveness. Unfortunately, scientific investigation regarding relationship between the two constructs is practically nonexistent. A qualitative study by Uline, Tschannen-Moran, and Perez (2003) in a high school suggests that constructive conflict can be considered as a means to promote individual and organizational learning and growth. A case study by Yeung, Lai, and Yee (2007) suggests that organizational learning leads to higher performance if learning is valued by top management and knowledge is shared through appropriate structure and a learning culture. Another study by Wong, Cheung, and Leung (2008) reported that all three forms of organizational learning—single-loop, double-loop, and deutero—contribute to performance improvement. They concluded that double-loop learning was "found to be more versatile in facilitating improvement in efficiency and effectiveness" (p. 162).

As discussed in Chapter 4, to encourage double-loop learning and consequent organizational effectiveness, a moderate amount of substantive conflict is necessary, but affective and process conflicts should be minimized, and that organizational participants should learn to use the five styles of handling conflict to deal with different conflict situations. In other words, if the variables, other than conflict, that affect organizational learning and effectiveness, are controlled, effectiveness can be maximized if conflict management strategies are implemented. This indicates that the management of organizational conflict requires proper understanding of the effect of conflict on organizational effectiveness. Goodman and Pennings (1977) have argued that effectiveness is the central theme in organizational analysis, and it is difficult to conceive of an organization theory that does not include the construct of effectiveness.

The literature on organizational behavior implicitly or explicitly suggests that organizational processes or conditions, such as leadership, conflict, communication, structure, technology, and so on, influence the effectiveness of an organization. This implies that organizational effectiveness can be conceptualized and measured. It may come as a surprise that researchers have given inadequate attention to this problem. Most of the recent textbooks on organizational behavior do not contain any systematic discussion on organizational effectiveness.

Content analysis of syllabi on organizational behavior courses for MBA students indicated that organizational effectiveness was the 31st among the 65 frequently mentioned topics (Rahim, 1981). The literature shows that "much confusion continues in the organizational literature regarding the definition, circumscription, and appropriate criteria for assessing effectiveness" (Cameron, 1986, p. 539). This confusion continues still today.

Different conceptualizations of the meanings of an organization have resulted in several approaches to the definition of organizational effectiveness. This chapter discusses four important models or approaches to organizational effectiveness: goal attainment, system resource, internal process, and strategic constituencies. Goal attainment and system resource approaches are two basic models of organizational effectiveness. Whereas the goal attainment model attempts to assess organizational effectiveness in terms of the *ends*, the system resource model focuses on the *means* for the achievement. The other two models are concerned with improving an organization's processes, such as communication, motivation, and so on (internal process); and satisfying the needs of an organization's stakeholders (strategic contingencies).

The four basic models of organization effectiveness, discussed above, have received particular attention in the literature on management and organizational behavior. Cameron (1986) has discussed four other models, which are beyond the scope of the chapter. These are competing values model (organization's emphasis is on criteria that meets constituency preferences), legitimacy model (organization survives by performing legitimate activities), fault-driven model (absence of any mistakes or traits of ineffectiveness in an organization), and high performing systems (an organization is judged excellent relative to other similar organizations) model.

Goal Attainment

This is the most widely used model by management practitioners and researchers particularly in the area of strategic management. Here the effectiveness of an organization is assessed by *ends* or *outcomes* as opposed to *means*. The advocates of this model define organizational effectiveness as *the ability of a social system to achieve its goals or objectives* (Etzioni, 1964; Georgopoulos & Tannenbaum, 1957; Price, 1968). In other words, an organization is said to be operating effectively if it attains some predetermined goals (i.e., missions, purpose, objectives). The measures of goal attainment often take the form of productivity or efficiency. Other common measures of goal attainment are return on equity, return on assets, and earning per share.

The measures of goal attainment appear to be simple, but goals may differ among organizations, they may have multiple and often conflicting goals, and they may change over time. These goals may range far beyond output or profitability. Also often differences exist between an organization's *official goals* (general purposes put forth in the charter, annual reports, public statements by top managers) and its *operative goals* (what the organization is actually trying to accomplish). Another problem of this approach relates to the difficulty in identifying the goals of an organization. Even if an organization's goals are identified, and it is found to accomplish its goals, it may be ineffective because the goals are inadequate, misleading, or detrimental. Another problem is the unavailability of goal attainment measures, such as profitability, for nonprofit organizations.

Despite these limitations of goal attainment approach it has an advantage—"the goal notion itself does provide a theoretical point of reference for reducing diversity" (Keeley, 1978, p. 272). Many theorists reject official goals as useful standards of organizational effectiveness. They generally agree that organizations can best be understood by their actual or operative goals and not the official goals. Operative goals indicate what an organization is trying to achieve that enables one to measure its effectiveness along the resulting operational dimensions.

System Resource

This model was proposed by Yuchtman and Seashore (1967) and has received widespread attention in organizational effectiveness literature. Unlike the goal attainment model, the focus of this approach is on *inputs* rather than *outputs*: it is concerned with an organization's ability to obtain an advantageous bargaining position in its environment to obtain needed resources to sustain its functioning. By "bargaining position" the scholars meant "the exclusion of any specific goal (or function) as the ultimate criterion of organizational effectiveness. Instead it points to the more general capacity of the organization as a resource-getting system" (Yuchtman & Seashore, 1967, p. 898). In other words, an organization is effective if it is able to acquire necessary resources.

This model provides a limited view on organizational effectiveness. The system-resource model has been criticized by Hall (2002) and others, who pointed out that this typology of effectiveness may, in large measure, represent an argument over semantics. As Hall points out, "resource acquisition does not just happen, it is based on what the organization is attempting to achieve—namely, its goals" (p. 239). Although it has been argued that the goal attainment and system resource approaches to organizational effectiveness are incompatible, the two can be complementary. The conceptualization of organizational effectiveness must consider not only the goals of an organization but also the processes through which it attains its objectives (Steers, 1977).

Internal Process

This model focuses on the internal organizational processes and operations (i.e., organizational health), such as interpersonal relationships, trust, commitment, and work involvement among the employees, flow of information in all directions, and so on (Argyris, 1964; Likert, 1967). Effective organizations are those with an "absence of internal strain, whose members are highly integrated into the system, whose internal functioning is smooth and typified by trust and benevolence toward individuals, where information flows smoothly both vertically and horizontally, and so on" (Cameron, 1980, p. 67). Organizations such as these are often characterized as "healthy systems."

This approach to effectiveness also provides a limited view of organizations because it ignores the relationships of internal processes to output and external environment. It can be argued that an organization may be effective even if its internal processes are less than satisfactory. For example, the existence of conflict and organizational slack may indicate inefficiency in internal processes, but conflict may be essential for innovation and change, and slack may help an organization in its long-term survival and adaptability.

Strategic Constituencies

This approach is sometimes referred to as the participant satisfaction (Keeley, 1978) or ecological model (Miles, 1980). It is concerned with the extent to which an organization is able to satisfy the needs and expectations of the strategic constituencies (stakeholders) as well as attain a satisfactory balance among them. A strategic constituency is a group of individuals, such as owners, employees, customers, suppliers, government officials, and so on, who have some interests in the organization. This model is based on the assumption that an organization will be effective if it can at least minimally satisfy the needs of different constituencies.

Although this model takes a broader view of effectiveness than the above three (Tsui, 1990), it also provides a partial view of organizational effectiveness. An organization can be effective even if it fails to satisfy the needs of all the constituencies.

What is an Appropriate Effectiveness Model?

The preceding discussion shows that the goal attainment model is widely used by the practitioners and researchers on management and administration. But the discussion also shows that each of the four models of organizational effectiveness has strengths and weaknesses. Cameron (1984) has argued that each of these models of effectiveness may be appropriate depending on the situation. A model is most appropriate for an organization if:

1. Goals are clear, consensual, time-bound, and measurable (*goal attainment*).
2. A clear connection exists between inputs and performance (*system resource*).
3. A clear connection exists between organizational processes and performance (*internal process*).
4. Constituencies have powerful influence on the organization, and it has to respond to demands (*strategic constituencies*) (Cameron, 1984, p. 276).

Measurement of Effectiveness

A literature review by Campbell (1977) found that more than thirty different criteria were used for the measurement of organizational effectiveness. These measurement criteria ranged from global to specific aspects of organizational effectiveness. It also becomes evident that some of the measurement criteria are inconsistent (i.e., an organization cannot attempt to satisfy several of these effectiveness criteria simultaneously). The review revealed that only few studies used multivariate measures of effectiveness and that the same criteria were hardly used across studies.

Steers (1975) reviewed a representative sample of seventeen studies that used multivariate models of organizational effectiveness and found no convergence on a set of measures of organizational effectiveness. Only one criterion, adaptability–flexibility, was mentioned frequently in these models, followed by productivity, satisfaction, profitability, and resource acquisition. An organizational analyst must decide the dimensions of organizational effectiveness to be measured and the method of data collection to be used.

Characteristics of the Old Paradigm

Individual Defensive Reasoning

Argyris (1994) and Argyris and Schön (1996) have persuasively argued and provided evidence that double-loop learning that is needed for increasing effectiveness is inhibited by defensive reasoning of organizational members. This type of reasoning takes place when members fail to take responsibility for their decisions and attempt to protect themselves against the complaints of errors of judgment, incompetence, or procrastination by blaming others. This psychological reaction has something to do with the mental models humans develop early in life for dealing with embarrassing or threatening situations. Other scholars have described this type of defensive behavior as executive blindness. As a result of this, "Organizational members become committed to a pattern of behavior. They escalate their commitment to that pattern out of self-justification. In a desire to avoid embarrassment and threat, few if any challenges are made to the wisdom and viability of these behaviors. They persist even when rapid and fundamental shifts in the competitive environment render these patterns of behavior obsolete and destructive to the well-being of the organization" (Beer & Spector, 1993, p. 642).

Organizational Defensive Routines

Organizational defensive routines consist of procedures, policies, practices, and actions that prevent employees from having to experience embarrassment or threat. Also, these routines prevent them from examining the nature and causes of that embarrassment or threat. Argyris (1990) has described the effects of these routines as follows:

> Organizational defensive routines make it highly likely that individuals, groups, intergroups, and organizations will not detect and correct errors that are embarrassing and threatening because the fundamental rules are (1) bypass the errors and act as if they were not being done, (2) make the bypass undiscussable, and (3) make its undiscussability undiscussable. (p. 43)

Conflict management in the old paradigm did not recognize defensive reasoning of employees and organizational defensive routines as significant factors that limit an organization's capacity to learn and respond to the environment. It is not possible to design an effective conflict management program unless the problems of defensive reactions and routines are recognized and confronted.

Problem Solving

Effective conflict management involves problem solving and learning. Unfortunately, traditional conflict resolution strategies are unable to use the problem solving process effectively. Let me explain. Existing conflict management strategies have neglected to recognize and overcome the problems of defensive reasoning of employees and organizational defensive routines. As a result, organizations do not have the culture that encourages members to engage in a real problem solving process.

Creative problem solving involves three stages: problem recognition, planning for change, and implementation (see Figure 3–1):

1. Problem Recognition involves:
    A. Problem sensing
    B. Problem formulation
2. Planning for Change involves:
    A. Recommending solutions to problems
    B. Preparing plans for intervention
3. Implementation involves:
    A. Putting plans into action
    B. Review of outcomes

The first phase of problem solving is problem recognition, which involves confronting political and other risky problems. Even if some organizational members overcome their defensive reactions, organizational defensive routines will not allow them to formulate the real problems. Organizational members who create "dissent" become the bad "guys."

Figure 3–1
Problem-Solving Process

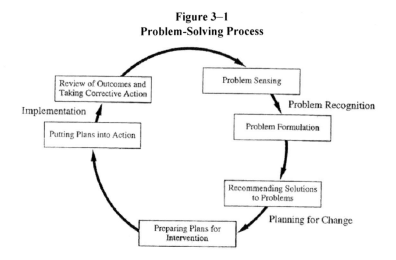

In contemporary organizations, problem formulation in the problem recognition phase is often distorted. As a result, old policies, procedures, and practices continue to be followed, although they may have been rendered ineffective due to changes in the external environment. This typically results in Type III error, which has been defined "as the probability of having solved the wrong problem when one should have solved the right problem" (Mitroff & Featheringham, 1974, p. 383). Type I error (the probability of rejecting a null hypothesis by mistake) and Type II error (probability of accepting an alternative hypothesis by mistake) are well known in statistics, but Type III error is not a statistical error. Type III error is associated with the probability of solving a wrong problem.

Organizational members may have to deal with another type of error. In poor organizations good plans for intervention may not be put into action for a variety of reasons. This results in Type IV error: the probability of not implementing a solution properly (Kilmann & Mitroff, 1979). Effective conflict management strategies should be able to minimize Type III and Type IV errors.

Mitroff's (1998) excellent book, *Smart Thinking for Crazy Times,* has provided detailed guidelines for avoiding Type III Error or E_3 to solve the right problem. These are summarized as follows:

1. **Select the Right Stakeholders.** Managers often assume that stakeholders share their opinion or try to select stakeholders who share the same opinion. To avoid E_3, Mitroff suggests that managers need stakeholders who challenge their views.

2. **Expand Your Options.** To avoid E_3, managers should look at problems from more than one perspective: *scientific/technical, interpersonal/social, existential,* and *systemic.* An individual or group can determine whether an E_3 is committed "by comparing two very different formulations of a problem. A single formulation of a problem is a virtual prescription for disaster" (Mitroff, 1998, p. 61).

3. **Phrase Problems Correctly.** Phrasing a problem incorrectly may lead to E_3. The effectiveness of the formulation of a problem depends to a great extent on the language that one uses.

4. **Extend the Boundaries of Problems.** Managers should enlarge the boundary or scope of a problem so that it is inclusive enough. In other words, "never draw the boundaries of an important problem too narrowly; broaden the scope of every important problem up to and just beyond your comfort zone" (Mitroff, 1998, p. 29).

5. **Think Systemically.** Managers should not focus on a part of the problem or ignore connection between parts. Failure to think and act systemically can lead to E_3.

Conflict Management in the New Paradigm

Traditional conflict resolution does not question whether the structure and processes of an organization are deficient which are causing dysfunctional conflict. It tries to resolve or reduce conflict between parties at the micro-level within the existing system. As discussed in the next chapter, conflict management in the new paradigm involves changes at the macro-level in an organization so that substantive conflict is encouraged; affective and process conflicts are minimized; and organizational members learn how to handle different types of conflict effectively. Recommendations by Argyris to overcome the problems of defensive reactions of organizational members and organizational defensive routines and by Mitroff to overcome the problems of Type III errors through five different ways should be given adequate consideration to make conflict management effective.

To implement the recommendations of Argyris and Mitroff, there must be changes in leadership, culture, and design in an organization. The next chapter provides detailed discussion of these changes which will be needed for effective management of conflict in the new paradigm.

Summary

Existing strategies of conflict resolution do not involve change in the structure and processes in an organization. These strategies have little or no link to organizational learning and effectiveness. Supervisors and employees in today's organizations are required to change their behaviors so that they can respond to the challenge of intense global competition. But existing conflict resolution strategies are unsuitable for bringing about these changes.

Organizational learning is a process of detection (cognitive) and correction (behavioral) of error. The literature has identified two types of organizational learning: single-loop and double-loop learning. Effective conflict management will enhance double-loop learning, which, in turn, will influence organizational effectiveness. Four models of organizational effectiveness are goal attainment, system resource, internal process, and strategic constituencies. The two basic models or approaches to organizational effectiveness are goal attainment and system resource.

Organizational learning and problem solving are hindered by defensive reactions of members and organizational defensive routines. Several ways of solving the right problems or avoiding Type III errors are: select the right stakeholders, expand your options, phrase problems correctly, extend the boundaries of problems, and think systemically. Effective conflict management to encourage double-loop learning and effectiveness will involve (1) reduction of affective and process conflicts, (2) attainment and maintenance of a moderate amount of substantive conflict, and (3) helping the organizational participants to learn the various styles of handling interpersonal conflict for dealing with different conflict situations appropriately. Conflict management in the new paradigm will involve changes in the structure and processes in an organization. The next chapter discusses the overall design or strategy for the management of organizational conflict, which involves the diagnosis of, and intervention in, intraorganizational conflict and the styles of handling interpersonal conflict.

4

Conflict Management Design

Even though conflict is often said to be functional for organizations, most recommendations relating to organizational conflict still fall within the ambit of conflict resolution, reduction, or minimization. Action recommendations from the current organizational conflict literature show a disturbing lag with the functional set of background assumptions that are endorsed. These recommendations are usually designed to deal with conflict at the dyadic or group levels and are not appropriate for macro-level changes in an organization. Insofar as it could be determined, the literature on organizational conflict is deficient (with minor exceptions) in three major areas.

1. There is no clear set of rules to suggest *when* conflict ought to be maintained at a certain level, when reduced, when ignored, and when enhanced.
2. There is no clear set of guidelines to suggest *how* conflict can be reduced, ignored, or enhanced to increase individual, group, or organizational effectiveness.
3. There is no clear set of rules to indicate how conflict involving different situations can be managed effectively.

This book addresses these issues at a *macro level* to provide a design for managing intrapersonal, interpersonal, intragroup, and intergroup conflicts that can be useful to the management practitioner and consultants as well as the academician.

Nature of Conflict Management

It will be evident in this chapter and throughout this book that the emphasis is on conflict management, away from conflict resolution. The difference is more than semantic (Boulding, 1968; Rahim, 2002). Conflict resolution implies reduction, elimination, or termination of conflict. A large number of studies on negotiation, bargaining, mediation, and arbitration fall into the conflict resolution category. In a review of literature on conflict and conflict management, Wall and Callister (1995) made the following comments:

we raised three of the most important questions in this article: is moderate conflict desirable? Is too little conflict as dysfunctional as too much? And should leaders, at times, promote conflict to attain organizational goals? Our tentative answers to these questions are no, no, and no. (p. 545)

Wall and Callister's approach to handling conflict is inconsistent with the recognition of scholars who suggest that organizational conflict has both functional and dysfunctional outcomes (Jehn, 1995; Mitroff, 1998; Pelled, Eisenhardt, & Xin, 1999). Eisenhardt, Kahwajy, and Bourgeois (1998) suggest that conflict in top management is inevitable and it is usually valuable. "Conflict at senior levels surrounding appropriate paths of action—what may be termed 'substantive,' 'cognitive,' or 'issue-oriented' conflict is essential for effective strategic choice" (p. 142). Therefore, it is concluded that Wall and Callister's recommendations fall within the realm of conflict resolution, which involves reduction or elimination of both functional as well as dysfunctional conflicts. This amounts to throwing out the baby with the bathwater.

What is needed for contemporary organizations is conflict management and not conflict resolution. Conflict management does not necessarily imply avoidance, reduction, or termination of conflict. It involves designing effective strategies to minimize the dysfunctions of conflict and enhancing the constructive functions of conflict in order to improve learning and effectiveness in an organization. As discussed in Chapter 3, studies on conflict resolution do not provide any clear link between conflict-management strategies and organizational learning and effectiveness. In order to design effective conflict management strategies, relevant literature on conflict and conflict management styles in connection with the following topics should be discussed.

Substantive Conflict

Certain types of conflicts that may have positive effects on the individual and group performance, may have to be enhanced and maintained at a moderate level. These conflicts relate to disagreements about tasks, policies, and other business issues and are called task conflict, substantive conflict, or cognitive conflict. A study by Jehn (1995) suggests that a moderate level of substantive conflict is beneficial, as it stimulates discussion and debate which help groups to attain higher levels of performance. "Groups with an absence of task conflict may miss new ways to enhance their performance, while very high levels of task conflict may interfere with task completion" (Jehn, 1997a, p. 532). Evidence indicates that substantive conflict is positively associated with beneficial outcomes. Groups that experience this conflict are able to make better decisions than those that do not. This relationship has also been found to be true at the individual level (Amason, 1996; Cosier & Rose, 1977; Fiol, 1994; Putnam, 1994; Schweiger, Sandberg, & Ragan, 1986).

Groups that report substantive conflict generally have higher performance. This conflict can improve group performance through better understanding of various viewpoints and alternative solutions (Bourgeois, 1985; Eisenhardt & Schoonhoven, 1990; Jehn, 1995, 1997a, 1997b; Jehn et al., 1999). A recent study suggests that cognitive conflict enhances students' collaborative learning in groups (Tocalli-Beller, 2003). Substantive conflict may enable group members to engage in critical and innovative thinking needed for problem solving. It should be noted that the beneficial effects of substantive conflict on performance were found only in groups performing nonroutine tasks but not groups performing standardized or routine tasks.

Although substantive conflict enhances group performance, it can diminish group loyalty, work group commitment, intent to stay in the present organization, and satisfaction (Jehn, 1997b; Jehn et al., 1999). As a result, interventions for conflict management should be able to develop cultural norms to support disagreement among group members in connection with tasks and other related management issues without generating affective conflict. Learning organizations like Honda are promoting cultures that encourage substantive conflict, which is not associated with affective conflict and negative job attitudes.

Affective Conflict

Another type of conflict, which may have negative effects on individual and group performance, may have to be reduced. This conflict is generally caused by the negative reactions of organizational members (e.g., personal attacks of group members, racial disharmony, sexual harassment, to name a few) and are called affective conflict, relationship conflict or emotional conflict. This conflict diminishes group loyalty, workgroup commitment, intent to stay in the present organization, and satisfaction (Amason, 1996; Jehn, 1995, 1997a, 1997b; Jehn et al., 1999). These result from higher level of stress and anxiety and conflict escalation.

This type of conflict "interferes with task-related effort because members focus on reducing threats, increasing power, and attempting to build cohesion rather than working on task...The conflict causes members to be negative, irritable, suspicious, and resentful" (Jehn, 1997a, pp. 531–532). Affective conflict impedes group performance by limiting information processing ability and cognitive functioning of group members and antagonistic attributions of group members' behavior (Amason, 1996; Baron, 1997; Jehn, 1995; Jehn et al., 1999; Wall & Nolan, 1986).

Transforming and Masquerading Conflicts

These two components of organizational conflict are expected to be useful in conflict management, which involves the diagnosis of and intervention in conflict. It has been suggested that a careful diagnosis of conflict is an essential first step before applying conflict management interventions (Rahim, 1985,

2002). Therefore, the development of a more refined typology of conflict should help to make such diagnosis more effective. It is expected that transforming and masquerading conflicts will be positively associated with affective conflict and, as a result, they will be negatively associated with job performance and satisfaction of employees. Therefore, these conflicts should be identified and reduced to minimize their impacts on individual and group performance, satisfaction, and other outcomes.

Process Conflict

This is another type of conflict which is negatively associated with group performance and satisfaction and it should be reduced. As discussed in Chapter 2, this type of conflict is associated with how different tasks should be performed, task assignment, responsibility to complete specific tasks, delegation of duties and responsibilities, and deadlines and is distinct from substantive and affective conflicts (see Jehn, 1997; Jehn & Mannix, 2001).

Process conflict is negatively associated with team performance, member satisfaction, and group commitment. A study by Behfar, Peterson, Mannix, and Trochim (2008) concluded that affective, substantive, and process conflict should be handled with appropriate conflict-management strategies. Their study found support for the "existing conclusions about the benefits of integrative and collaborative approaches to managing conflict and the drawbacks of contending and avoiding approaches" (p. 182).

Inverted-U Function

Several researchers have noted the positive consequences of conflict (Assael, 1969; Cosier & Dalton, 1990; Hall & Williams, 1966; Janis, 1982). Empirical studies have found that small groups are more productive when dissenters who create conflict are present than when there is no difference of opinion or conflict among members (Cartwright & Zander, 1968). Schwenk and Thomas (1983) found in their experimental study that managers who received conflicting analyses came up with higher expected profits than those managers who received single analyses. The studies included by Tjosvold and Johnson (1983) in their book indicate that conflict in organizations can be productive if it is handled in a constructive manner.

It was suggested in Chapter 1 that organizations in which there is little or no conflict may stagnate. On the other hand, organizational conflict left uncontrolled may have dysfunctional effects. Recent studies on organizational conflict suggest that a moderate amount of substantive conflict is necessary for attaining an optimum level of job performance in nonroutine tasks. Therefore, it appears that the relationship between the amount of substantive conflict and job performance approximates an inverted-U function as shown in Figure 4–1.

Figure 4–1
Relationship between the Amount of Substantive Conflict and Job Performance

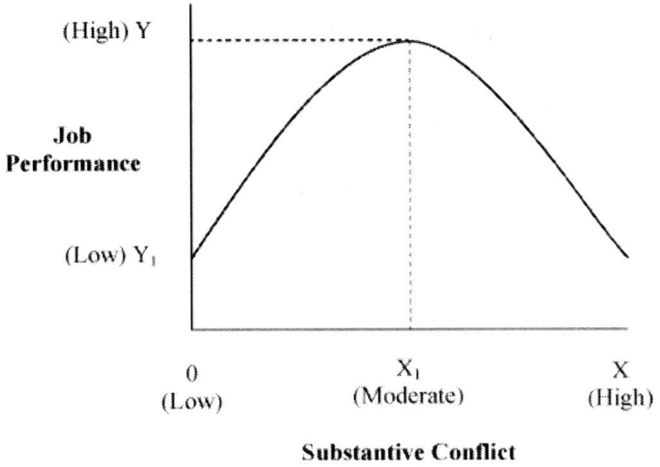

Figure 4–1 shows that a low level of job performance (OY_1) will be attained when the amount of substantive conflict is low (O) or high (OX). At a moderate amount of substantive conflict (OX_1) an optimum level of job performance (OY) can be attained. This relationship is expected to hold good when other factors that affect job performance are held constant for nonroutine tasks. This is consistent with the activation theory, which supports the inverted-U relationship between a person's activation or arousal level and his or her job performance (Berlyne, 1960; Frankenhaeuser, 1977). This is comparable to the Yerkes-Dodson phenomenon, which indicates that the relationship between the amount of motivation and level of performance is approximated by an inverted-U function (Yerkes & Dodson, 1908). Anderson's (1990) review of the literature provides strong support for the inverted-U relationship between activation and job performance. It has been acknowledged, however, that the "relationship between arousal and performance may appear linear when all the stimuli in use produce very high or very low levels of arousal" (Smith & Principato, 1983, p. 213).

Wilson and Jarrell (1981, p. 111) suggest that the view of a "humpbacked" or inverted-U shaped curve is compatible with Davis's (1975) concept of a "law of diminishing returns" for a wide range of managerial activities. A recent experimental study provided some support for the inverted-U relationship between conflict and effectiveness (Tjosvold, 1984). This study showed that constructive problem solving is encouraged at a moderate level of conflict, but it is discouraged at either a low or a high level of conflict.

In general, a moderate amount of substantive conflict may provide necessary activation or stimulation in order to optimize job performance of the organizational members or to enhance their adaptive or innovative capabilities. As such, Brown (1983) has suggested that "conflict management can require intervention to reduce conflict if there is too much, or intervention to promote conflict if there is too little" (p. 9). As will be seen later, conflict management involves more than just reducing or generating conflict to attain a moderate amount of it.

A few things should be said about the relationship presented in Figure 5–1. Empirical evidence from field studies in support of the inverted-U function is somewhat limited. Probably there are two major reasons for this. The first is the usual problem of obtaining reliable and valid measures of conflict and organizational effectiveness. The second is the problem of isolating the effect of conflict on effectiveness, after controlling for the numerous extraneous independent variables that affect organizational effectiveness. No study on this function has satisfied the requirement of proper control. Several studies on interorganizational conflict in marketing channels found positive as well as negative relationships between conflict and channel performance or efficiency (Reve & Stern, 1979). Pearson and Monoky (1976) found the level of service output to be negatively related to channel conflict. The study by Lusch (1976a) found no support for the inverted-U relationship between channel conflict and dealer operating performance. He concluded "that for the distribution of automobiles in the United States (at least for the five channels studied) channel conflict does not have a threshold effect on dealer operating performance" (p. 12). Rahim's (1990) study with a random sample of employees of a manufacturing plant found no support for the linear or inverted-U relationship between the perceptions of employees of intrapersonal, intragroup, and intergroup conflicts and supervisory rating of performance. These three and other studies on this relationship have the major limitation of control. Lusch (1976a) particularly recognized this problem and concluded that "further research should attempt to control for some of the other variables that influence retailer performance so that the impact of channel conflict can be isolated" (p. 89).

Paradox of Conflict. Guetzkow and Gyr (1954) suggested two dimensions of conflict that are useful for managing conflict—one consisting of disagreements relating to task issues and the other consisting of emotional or interpersonal issues that lead to conflict. One of the challenges of managing conflict is that these dimensions of conflict are positively correlated. Past studies have reported significant positive correlations between these conflicts which range between .34 and .88 (cf. Simmons & Peterson, 2000). Only one study by Jehn (1995) reported a negative correlation (–.17) between these conflicts. This indicates that in the process of enhancing substantive conflicts, affective conflict may also be increased. Amason and Shweiger (1997) noted that the danger of "encouraging disagreement may yield results that are no better and may well be worse than avoiding conflict altogether....The problem is that our ability to stimulate conflict outstrips our knowledge of how to manage its effects" (p. 108).

The danger of encouraging conflict and our lack of knowledge about conflict management that Amason and Shweiger discuss are out of place. Effective conflict management includes stimulation as well as resolution. This book, particular the present chapter, reports on strategies for managing different types of conflict.

Conflict Management Styles

Studies on the management of organizational conflict have taken two directions. Some researchers have attempted to measure the amount or intensity of conflict at various organizational levels and to explore the sources of such conflict. Implicit in these studies is that a moderate amount of conflict may be maintained for increasing organizational effectiveness by altering the sources of conflict. Others have attempted to relate the various styles of handling interpersonal conflict of the organizational participants and their effects on quality of problem solution or attainment of social system objectives. It becomes evident from this discussion that the distinction between the "amount of conflict" at various levels and the "styles of handling interpersonal conflict," discussed in Chapter 2, is essential for a proper understanding of the nature of conflict management.

The previous discussion was mainly based on the notion of the amount of conflict. In recent years, some researchers have used the indices of annoyance, disputes, distrust, disagreement, incompatibility, and so on to measure conflict at various levels. These are measures of the amount of conflict that are quite distinct from the styles of handling conflict. Various sources affect the amount of conflict. The management of conflict partly involves the identification and alteration of these sources to minimize affective and process conflicts and/or to attain and maintain a moderate amount of substantive conflict.

Chapter 2 presented the five styles of handling interpersonal conflict—integrating, obliging, dominating, avoiding, and compromising. Although some behavioral scientists suggest that integrating or problem-solving style is most appropriate for managing conflict (e.g., Blake & Mouton, 1964; Burke, 1994; Likert & Likert, 1976), it has been indicated by others that, for conflicts to be managed functionally, one style may be more appropriate than another depending on the situation (Hart, 1991; Rahim & Bonoma, 1979; Thomas, 1977; see also Callanan, Benzing, & Perri, 2006).

Matching Styles with Situations. Functional or effective management of conflict involves matching styles with situations. Matching can be effective when the criteria for conflict management, discussed later in this chapter, are satisfied. The situations in which each of the styles is appropriate or inappropriate are described in Table 4–1.

Table 4–1
Styles of Handling Interpersonal Conflict and
Situations Where They Are Appropriate or Inappropriate

Conflict Style	Situations Where Appropriate	Situations Where Inappropriate
Integrating	1. Issues are complex. 2. Synthesis of ideas is needed to come up with better solutions. 3. Commitment is needed from other parties for successful implementation. 4. Time is available for problem-solving. 5. One party alone cannot solve the problem. 6. Resources possessed by different parties are needed to solve their common problems.	1. Task or problem is simple. 2. Immediate decision is required. 3. Other parties are unconcerned about outcome. 4. Other parties do not have problem-solving skills.
Obliging	1. You believe that you may be wrong. 2. Issue is more important to the other party. 3. You are willing to give up something in exchange for something from the other party in the future. 4. You are dealing from a position of weakness. 5. Preserving relationship is important.	1. Issue is important to you. 2. You believe that you are right. 3. The other party is wrong or unethical.
Dominating	1. Issue is trivial. 2. Speedy decision is needed. 3. Unpopular course of action is implemented. 4. Necessary to overcome assertive subordinates. 5. Unfavorable decision by the other party may be costly to you. 6. Subordinates lack expertise to make technical decisions. 7. Issue is important to you.	1. Issue is complex. 2. Issue is not important to you. 3. Both parties are equally powerful. 4. Decision does not have to be made quickly. 5. Subordinates possess high degree of competence.
Avoiding	1. Issue is trivial. 2. Potential dysfunctional effect of confronting the other party outweighs benefits of resolution. 3. Cooling off period is needed.	1. Issue is important to you. 2. It is your responsibility to make decision. 3. Parties are unwilling to defer, issue must be resolved. 4. Prompt attention is needed.
Compromising	1. Goals of parties are mutually exclusive. 2. Parties are equally powerful. 3. Consensus cannot be reached. 4. Integrating or dominating style is not successful. 5. Temporary solution to a complex problem is needed.	1. One party is more powerful. 2. Problem is complex enough needing problem-solving approach.

Table 4–1 was prepared on the basis of a number of conflict management workshops conducted by the author for managers. In these workshops, participants were required to participate in a Management of Disagreements Exercise (see Appendix B). This essentially involves the following:

1. Participants complete and score the Rahim Organizational Conflict Inventory–II (ROCI–II) before attending the workshop.
2. The workshop leader discusses the theory of the styles of handling interpersonal conflict with superior, subordinates, and peers and interprets the participants' ROCI–II scores.
3. Participants in subgroups list the situations where each style is appropriate or inappropriate.
4. The workshop leader with the help of subgroup leaders summarizes the results of Step 3.

Table 4–1 was prepared on the basis of data collected from more than twenty workshops. The participants were from different industries and organizational levels and had different functional specializations.

Integrating Style. This is useful for effectively dealing with complex problems. When one party alone cannot solve the problem (i.e., when synthesis of ideas is needed to come up with a better solution to a problem) this style is appropriate. It is also useful in utilizing the skills, information, and other resources possessed by different parties to define or redefine a problem and to formulate effective alternative solutions for it and/or when commitment is needed from parties for effective implementation of a solution. This can be done provided that there is enough time for problem solving. Lawrence and Lorsch (1967a) found this mode (style) to be more effective than others in attaining integration of the activities of different subsystems of an organization. This style is appropriate for dealing with the strategic issues pertaining to an organization's objectives and policies, strategic planning, and so on.

This style may not be effective in some situations. It is inappropriate when the task or problem is simple or trivial; when there is no time for problem solving (i.e., immediate action is required); when the other parties do not have adequate training and experience for problem solving; or when they are unconcerned about outcomes.

Obliging Style. This style is useful when a party is not familiar with the issues involved in a conflict, or the other party is right, and the issue is much more important to the other party. This style may be used as a strategy when a party is willing to give up something with the hope of getting some benefit from the other party when needed. This style may be appropriate when a party is dealing from a position of weakness or believes that preserving a relationship is important.

This style is inappropriate if the issue involved in a conflict is important to the party, and the party believes that he or she is right. It is also inappropriate when a party believes that the other party is wrong or unethical.

Dominating Style. This style is appropriate when the issues involved in a conflict are important to the party, or an unfavorable decision by the other party may be harmful to this party. This style may be used by a supervisor if the issues involve routine matters or if a speedy decision is required. A supervisor may have to use it to deal with subordinates who are very assertive or who do not have expertise to make technical decisions. This is also effective in dealing with the implementation of unpopular courses of action.

This style is inappropriate when the issues involved in conflict are complex and there is enough time to make a good decision. When both parties are equally powerful, using this style by one or both parties may lead to stalemate. Unless they change their styles, they may not be able to break the deadlock. This style is inappropriate when the issues are not important to the party. Subordinates who possess a high degree of competence may not like a supervisor who uses this authoritarian style.

Avoiding Style. This style may be used when the potential dysfunctional effect of confronting the other party outweighs the benefits of the resolution of conflict. This may be used to deal with some trivial or minor issues or when a cooling-off period is needed before a complex problem can be effectively dealt with.

This style is inappropriate when the issues are important to a party. This style is also inappropriate when it is the responsibility of the party to make decisions, when the parties are unwilling to wait, or when prompt action is required.

Compromising Style. This style is useful when the goals of the conflicting parties are mutually exclusive or when both parties (e.g., labor and management) are equally powerful and have reached an impasse in their negotiation process. This can be used when consensus cannot be reached, the parties need a temporary solution to a complex problem, or other styles have been used and found to be ineffective in dealing with the issues effectively. This style may have to be used for avoiding protracted conflict.

This style is inappropriate for dealing with complex problems needing a problem-solving approach. Unfortunately, very often management practitioners use this style to deal with complex problems and, as a result, fail to formulate effective, long-term solutions. This style also may be inappropriate if a party is more powerful than another and believes that his or her position is right. This style also may not be appropriate when it comes to dealing with conflict of values.

Organizational members, while interacting with each other, will be required to deal with their disagreements constructively. This calls for learning how to use different styles of handling conflict to deal with various situations effectively.

Criteria for Conflict Management

In order for conflict management strategies to be effective, they should satisfy certain criteria. These have been derived from the diverse literature on organization theory and organizational behavior. The following criteria are particularly useful for conflict management, but in general, they may be useful for decision making in management.

1. Organizational Learning and Effectiveness. Conflict management strategies should be designed to enhance organizational learning (Luthans et al., 1995; Tompkins, 1995). It is expected that organizational learning will lead to long-term effectiveness. In order to attain this objective, conflict management strategies should be designed to enhance critical and innovative thinking to learn the process of diagnosis and intervention in the right problems.

2. Needs of Stakeholders. Conflict management strategies should be designed to satisfy the needs and expectations of the strategic constituencies (stakeholders) and to attain a balance among them. Mitroff (1998) strongly suggests picking the right stakeholders to solve the right problems. His comments on picking the right stakeholders to solve the right problems are relevant here:

> Humankind continually vacillates between the following two unwarranted assumptions: (1) others are fundamentally like us and will react as we do to a situation, and (2) others are so completely different from us that there is no basis for mutual understanding whatsoever....Both are pernicious because they dehumanize us and those to whom we would relate. In both cases, the fundamental error is taking the narcissistic self as the primary, if not the only, stakeholder in all situations. (p. 50)

Sometimes multiple parties are involved in a conflict in an organization and the challenge of conflict management would be to involve these parties in a problem solving process that will lead to collective learning and organizational effectiveness. It is expected that this process will lead to satisfaction of the relevant stakeholders.

3. Ethics. Mitroff (1998) is a strong advocate of ethical management. He concluded that if we are unable to define a problem correctly, which leads to ethical decisions beneficial to human beings, then we have not defined the problem adequately.

As will be seen in Chapter 9, a wise leader must behave ethically, and to do so the leader should be open to new information and be willing to change his or her mind. By the same token subordinates and other stakeholders have an ethical duty to speak out against the decisions of supervisors when consequences of these decisions are likely to be serious. To manage conflicts ethically, organizations should institutionalize the positions of employee advocate, customer and supplier advocate, as well as environmental and stockholder advocates. Only if these advocates are heard by decision-makers in organizations may we hope for an improved record of ethically managed organizational conflict (Rahim, Garrett, & Buntzman, 1992). The disastrous outcomes in corporations like Enron and Worldcom probably could be avoided if this process was legitimized and it was made a part of their organizational cultures.

Conflict Management Strategy

Existing literature on conflict management is deficient on strategies needed to manage conflict at the macro-level that can satisfy the preceding criteria. There is a need to design new conflict management strategies based on contemporary literature that are likely to satisfy the three criteria. These strategies are:

1. Minimize Conflict. The following conflicts should be minimized to reduce their adverse impacts on individual and group effectiveness.

A. Affective Conflict. This conflict should be minimized at all levels in the organization through effective conflict management.
B. Process Conflict. This conflict should be minimized at all levels in the organization through effective conflict management.
C. Substantive Conflict. This conflict should be minimized for routine or standardized tasks.

2. Increase Conflict. A moderate amount of substantive conflict should be attained and maintained for nonroutine tasks. Although substantive conflict enhances group performance, like affective conflict, it can diminish job attitudes. As a result, interventions for conflict management should be designed to develop cultural norms to support disagreement among group members in connection with tasks and other related management issues without generating affective conflict.

3. Learn Conflict Management Strategies. As discussed, there are various styles of behavior, such as integrating, obliging, dominating, avoiding, and compromising, which can be used to deal with affective, substantive, and process conflicts. Scholars have generally ignored the issue of effective handling of these three types of conflict to enhance group performance and satisfaction.

Organizational members would require training and on-the-job experience to select and use the styles of handling interpersonal conflict so that various conflict situations can be appropriately dealt with. In general, managing conflict to enhance learning and effectiveness would require the use of integrating or problem solving conflict-handling strategy and not bargaining strategy (Rahim, 2002; see Behfar, Peterson, Mannix, & Trochim, 2008; Gray, 1989). A study by Rahim (2010) shows that a functional strategy is associated with relatively greater use of the integrating style than the avoiding style *plus* relatively greater use of the obliging style than the dominating style. A dysfunctional strategy is associated with the opposite conditions, i.e., greater use of the avoiding and lower use of the integrating styles *plus* greater use of the dominating style and lower use of the obliging style. A functional strategy is essential to deal with a conflict involving complex issues.

Contingency Approach

Management scholars now agree that there is no one best approach to make decisions, to lead, and to motivate. The *contingency approach* (also called situational approach), which is the hallmark of contemporary management, has replaced the simplistic "one best" approach (Pennings, 1992). Consider, for example, the decision theory of leadership, which states that each of the five leadership styles (1 = *Autocratic* ... 5 = *Participative*) is appropriate depending on the situation. The theory considers two situations: the *quality of the decision* (i.e., the extent to which it will affect important group processes) and *acceptance of the decision* (i.e., the degree of commitment of employees needed for its implementation). The theory suggests that when the decision quality and acceptance are both low, the leader should use the autocratic style. On the contrary, if the decision quality and acceptance are both high, the leader should use the participative style. Therefore, it appears that effective leadership depends on matching leadership styles with situations. Failure to match these two variables leads to ineffective leadership.

Taking the lead from the contingency approach, it is possible to develop a contingency theory of conflict management. For example, in a conflict situation characterized by low decision quality and acceptance, the dominating style may be justified. In the reverse condition (high decision quality and high decision acceptance), using the integrating style is the most appropriate to use.

The strategies of conflict management presented in this chapter are consistent with the contemporary leadership theories in organizations: Fiedler's (1967) contingency theory of leadership, House's (1971) path-goal theory of leadership, and Vroom and Yetton's (1973) decision theory of leadership. According to these theories, there is no one best style for dealing with different situations effectively. Whether a particular leadership style is appropriate or inappropriate depends on the situation.

The theory of conflict management presented earlier is flexible in terms of the situations or factors to be considered in selecting and making use of a conflict style (see Table 4–1). A style is considered appropriate for a conflict situation if its use leads to effective formulation and/or solution to a problem.

Conflict Management Process

The management of organizational conflict involves the diagnosis of, and intervention in, conflict. Diagnosis provides the basis for intervention. This process is shown in Figure 4–2.

Figure 4–2
The Process of Managing Conflict

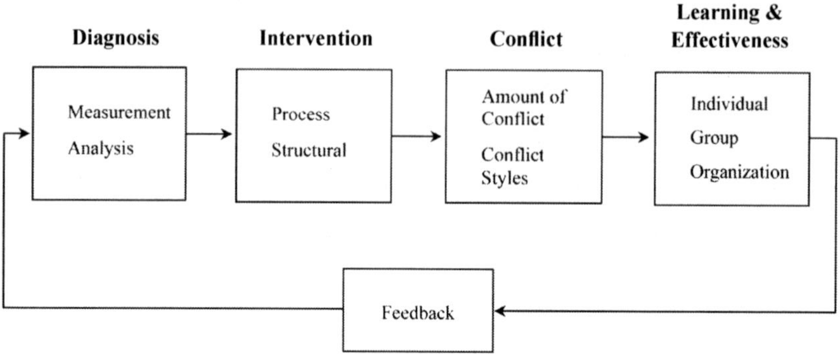

Diagnosis	Intervention	Conflict	Learning & Effectiveness
Measurement Analysis	Process Structural	Amount of Conflict Conflict Styles	Individual Group Organization

Feedback

Diagnosis

As discussed in Chapter 3, the first step in the problem-solving process is *problem recognition,* which involves *problem sensing* and *problem formulation.* The field of management has developed solutions to numerous problems, but it has neglected to investigate and develop the process of problem recognition. Problem finding or recognition requires appropriate diagnosis of the problems, which is neglected in contemporary organizations. As a result, very often interventions are recommended without proper understanding of the nature of the problem(s). This can lead to ineffective outcomes.

Identification or diagnosis of the problems of conflict in an organization must precede any intervention designed to manage the conflict. Several writers specifically suggested the need for the diagnosis of conflict through some formal and informal approaches (Brown, 1979; DuBrin, 1972). Proper diagnosis of the causes and effects of different types of conflict in an organization is important because its underlying causes and effects may not be what they appear on the surface. We also need to know (1) whether an organization has too little, moderate, or too much affective, process, and substantive conflicts and (2) whether the organizational members are appropriately selecting and using the five styles of handling conflict to deal with different situations. If an intervention is made without a proper diagnosis of conflict, then there is the probability that a change agent may try to solve a wrong problem. This may lead to Type III error (Mitroff, 1998; Mitroff & Featheringham, 1974). The management of organizational conflict involves a systematic diagnosis of the problems in order to minimize the Type III error.

The preceding discussion is consistent with the literature of organization development, which indicates that organizational diagnosis is essential for effective change program (see French & Bell, 1999; Burke, 1994). The diagnostic aspect of conflict management has been particularly neglected by the management researchers and practitioners. A comprehensive diagnosis involves the measurement of conflict, its sources, and effectiveness and analysis of relations among them.

Measurement. A comprehensive diagnosis involves these measurements:

1. The amount of conflict at the intrapersonal, interpersonal, intragroup, and intergroup levels;
2. The styles of handling interpersonal, intragroup, and intergroup conflicts of the organizational members;
3. The sources of (1) and (2); and
4. Individual, group, and organizational learning and effectiveness.

Analysis. The analysis of data collected above should include:

1. The amount of conflict and the styles of handling conflict classified by departments, units, divisions, and so on, and whether they are different from their corresponding national norms.
2. The relationships of the amount of conflict and conflict styles to their sources.
3. The relationships of the amount of conflict and conflict styles to organizational learning and effectiveness.

The results of diagnosis should indicate whether there is any need for intervention and the type of intervention necessary for managing conflict. The results of diagnosis should be discussed, preferably by a representative group of managers who are concerned with the management of conflict, with the help of an outside expert who specializes in conflict research and training. A discussion of the results should enable the managers to identify the problems of conflict, if any, that should be effectively managed.

The preceding approach may be used to conduct a comprehensive diagnosis of conflict, but not every organization requires such a diagnosis. A management practitioner or consultant should decide when and to what extent a diagnosis is needed for a proper understanding of a conflict problem.

As discussed in Chapter 3, two instruments—the Rahim Organizational Conflict Inventory–I (ROCI–I) and the Rahim Organizational Conflict Inventory–II (ROCI–II)—were designed by the author for measuring the amount of conflict at individual, group, and intergroup levels and the five styles of handling interpersonal conflict (Rahim, 1983a,d). Each instrument uses a 5-point Likert scale, and the responses to items are averaged to create subscales. A higher score indicates a greater amount of conflict or greater use of a conflict-handling style. The ROCI–II measures integrating, obliging, dominating, avoiding, and compromising styles, which can be used to calculate the Problem Solving (PS) and Bargaining (BA) dimensions.

PS = IN – AV
BA = DO – OB

Since the ROCI–II measures the five styles with a 5-point scale, the subscales for PS and BA dimensions range between + 4 and – 4. A positive value for the PS subscale indicates a party's perception of the extent to which the concerns of both parties are satisfied. A negative value indicates a party's perception of the extent to which the satisfaction of concerns of both the parties is reduced. Whereas a score of + 4 represents maximum satisfaction of concerns received by both parties, a – 4 score represents no satisfaction of concerns received by both parties as a result of the resolution of their conflict.

A value in the BA subscale indicates a party's perception of the ratio of satisfaction of concerns received by self and the other party. A value of + 4 indicates maximum satisfaction of concerns received by self and no satisfaction of concerns received by the other party. A value of – 4 indicates no satisfaction of concerns received by self and maximum satisfaction of concerns received by the other party. The percentile and reference group norms of the five styles of handling interpersonal conflict are in Chapter 6. These data on norms are important for diagnosis.

A number of studies have shown that cooperative styles, such as integrating, obliging, and compromising are correlated with positive outcomes and non-cooperative styles, such as dominating and avoiding and correlated with negative outcomes (cf. Burke, 1969; Korbanik, Baril, & Watson, 1993; Rahim, Magner, & Shapiro, 2000; Johnson, 1989). Therefore, for managing conflict a positive score on the PS subscale and slightly negative score on the BA subscale are appropriate.

Data collected through the questionnaires should not be the sole basis of a diagnosis. In-depth interviews with the conflicting parties and observation are needed to gain a better understanding of the nature of conflict and the type of intervention needed.

Intervention

A proper diagnosis should indicate whether there is any need for intervention and the type of intervention required. An intervention may be needed if there is too much affective and process conflicts, or too little or too much substantive conflict, and/or the organizational members are not handling their conflict effectively. The national norms of conflict reported by Rahim (2004) could provide some rough guidelines to decide whether an organization has too little or too much of a particular type of conflict. In addition to this, data from in-depth interviews are needed to determine the effectiveness of the styles of handling interpersonal conflict of the organizational members.

There are two basic approaches to intervention in conflict: *process* and *structural* (Rahim & Bonoma, 1979). Beer and Walton (1987) described these as human-process and technostructural approaches of intervention for organization development. A process refers to the sequence of events or activities that are undertaken to bring about some desired outcome. There are certain processes in an organization, such as communication, decision making, leadership, etc., which are necessary for making the social system work. Structure refers to the stable arrangement of task, technological, and other factors so that organizational members can work together effectively. In order to accomplish the goals of an organization, both process and structure require proper integration.

Process. This intervention attempts to improve organizational effectiveness by changing the intensity of affective, process, and substantive conflicts and members' styles of handling interpersonal conflict. The process approach is mainly designed to manage conflict by helping the organizational participants learn how to match the uses of the styles of handling interpersonal conflict with different situations. In other words, this intervention enables the organizational members to make effective uses of the five styles of handling interpersonal conflict depending on the nature of the situations.

Changes in the levels of affective, process, and substantive conflicts will require changes in organizational processes, such as culture and leadership. Changes in culture and leadership processes will also support the organizational members' newly acquired skills of conflict management.

Applied behavioral scientists have developed organizational development strategies and techniques for improving the organizational effectiveness (Beer & Walton, 1987; Burke, 1994; French, Bell, & Zawacki, 1989; Golembiewski, 1998), which may be adapted for managing organizational conflict. French and Bell (1999) defined organization development as a:

> long-term effort, led and supported by top management, to improve an organization's visioning, empowerment, learning, and problem-solving processes, through an on-going, collaborative management of organization culture—with special emphasis on the culture of intact work teams and other team configurations—using the consultant-facilitator role and the theory and technology of applied behavioral science, including action research. (p. 26)

Traditionally, the conflict resolution theorists emphasized the areas of agreement or commonality existing between conflicting entities by suppression or avoidance of the areas of disagreement. This probably encourages single-loop learning. Organizational development interventions, on the contrary, are designed to help the organizational participants to learn mainly the integrative or collaborative style of behavior through which to find the "real" causes of conflict and arrive at functional solutions. This approach is needed for encouraging double-loop learning. For example, Watkins and Golembiewski (1995) have suggested how organization development theory and practice might change to create collective learning. Organizational development strategies focused on learning are especially useful in managing strategic conflict where integrating style is more appropriate than other styles.

Lectures, videos, cases, and exercises can be used for learning conflict management. Appendixes A and B contain several cases and exercises on conflict, such as transactional analysis, management of differences, team building, intergroup problem solving, and organizational mirroring, which can be used to train organizational members in conflict management. Argyris (1994) has indicated that cases from managers' own organizations can be used to overcome defensive reactions of the supervisors and employees.

Other intervention techniques can be useful to bring about a change in learning and innovation in an organization. These include cultural assimilator training developed by Fiedler, Mitchell, and Triandis (1971), which can be adapted as part of the reframing process. An organizational consultant can use observation and interview data to construct causal cognitive maps that link ineffective organizational performance to managerial policies and practices. Also role playing along with psychoanalytic reframing techniques, such as generative metaphors, storytelling, and reflective/inquiry skills training are useful in challenging managers and employees to discard their old ways of thinking and to see the relevance of organizational learning orientation. Another technique that may be useful for managing strategic conflict is Mitroff and Emshoff's (1979) dialectical inquiry. This is based on the Hegelian dialectic, which involves a process of change through the conflict of opposite forces.

As suggested by French and Bell (1999) learning new behavior requires support from top management (which probably requires transformational leadership) and collaborative organizational culture. Following is a discussion of the nature of leadership and culture that can support effective conflict management.

Leadership. Senge (1990) maintains that a different set of leadership roles will be needed with more emphasis on leaders as teachers, stewards, and designers. These leaders, "articulate a clear and challenging vision for their firm based on their insights into key industry trends that can be the catalyst for redefining the foundation of competition....they focus on developing the people around them, motivating them to want to learn and take greater responsibility....they lead in 'unlearning'—the conscious effort to challenge traditional assumptions about the company and its environment" (Slater, 1995, p. 33). General Electric's former CEO Jack Welch and Chrysler's former CEO Lee Iacoca fit this description of leadership.

To some extent this type of leadership fits Bass's (1985) description of transformational leadership that has three distinct factors: charisma, intellectual stimulation, and individualized consideration. Transformational leaders encourage their subordinates to engage in critical and innovative thinking that are needed for problem solving. These leaders, sometimes referred to as charismatic leaders, use their personal power to inspire employees to new ways of thinking and problem solving. Substantial evidence now exists indicating that transformational leadership (as measured by the Multifactor Leadership Questionnaire; Bass, 1985) is positively associated with unit performance (Bass & Yammarino, 1991; Hater & Bass, 1988; Keller, 1992).

Conflict and tension will go up as more people challenge the old ways of thinking and doing things. As result, the problems are surfaced (problem recognition), which leads to recommendations for change in the process and structure (solving problems), and implementation of recommendations.

Organizational Culture. Conflict management to support organizational learning and long-term effectiveness would require cultures that support experimentation, risk taking, openness, diverse viewpoints, continuous questioning and inquiry, and sharing of information and knowledge. This implies that employees would be encouraged to take responsibility for their errors and not blame others for their mistakes or incompetence.

Such a culture would encourage substantive or task-related conflict and discourages affective and process conflicts. For example, Honda Corporation encourages its employees to explicitly surface and handle conflict in a constructive way. Honda holds sessions in which employees can openly (but politely) question supervisors and challenge the status quo. "This is not an empty ritual but a vital force in keeping Honda on its toes. It sustains a restless, self-questioning atmosphere that one expects to see in new ventures—yet Honda is into its fourth generation of management. Its founders retired in 1970" (Pascale, 1990, p. 26).

Conflict management requires experimentation and risk taking. Garvin (1993, 1999) indicated that effective programs require an incentive system that encourages risk taking. An organization may have to reward failures; otherwise organizational members will learn to do what is safe and avoid risk-taking behaviors. B. F. Skinner's operant conditioning, which refers to voluntary learning of behavior through positive reinforcement, is particularly appropriate here. This was acknowledged by Schein (1993): "This is the kind of learning symbolized by the use of the carrot instead of the stick, the creation of incentives to do the right thing, and the immediate rewarding of correct behavior. In this model, errors and wrong behavior are not punished but are ignored so that the learner remains focused on improving and refining correct behavior" (p. 86). Managers need to know how to use reinforcements to elicit conflict management behaviors that are not only associated with effective performance and creativity, but also with risk taking for improving long-term performance.

Kerr (1995) in updating his classic article, "On the Folly of Rewarding A, While Hoping for B," discussed numerous reward systems which are ineffective because they "are fouled up in that the types of behavior rewarded are those which the rewarder is trying to discourage, while the behavior desired is not being rewarded at all" (p. 7). This situation has not changed during the last two decades and is unlikely to change to a significant extent in the future (Dechant & Veiga, 1995, p. 16).

Structural. This intervention attempts to improve the organizational effectiveness by changing the organization's structural design characteristics, which include differentiation and integration mechanisms, hierarchy, procedures, reward system, etc. This approach mainly attempts to manage conflict by altering the perceptions of the intensity of conflict of the organizational members at various levels.

Conflicts, which result from the organization's structural design, can be managed effectively by appropriate change in such design. Evidence indicates that there is no one best design for all organizations. Whether a mechanistic (bureaucratic) or organic (organismic) design is appropriate for an organization or one or more of its subsystems depends on the organization's environment (stable or dynamic). Studies by Lawrence and Lorsch (1967; see also Lawrence, 2001) and Morse and Lorsch (1970) led to the development of the contingency theory of organization design, which suggests that mechanistic design is appropriate for departments which respond to the stable environment, but organic design is appropriate for departments which are responsible for unstable environment. The greater the congruence between the design and environment, the more effective is the management of conflict and the greater is the organizational effectiveness. Organizational development interventions generally recommend the adoption of organic–adaptive structures, which encourage effective management of conflict.

Although Duncan and Weiss (1979) indicated about three decades ago the need for designing organizations for encouraging organizational learning, scholars have not yet provided adequate attention to this issue. Many organizations have responded to competitive pressures by creating flatter, decentralized, and less complex designs than others. The shift is reflected in new organizational forms, such as the modular organization, virtual corporation, and the horizontal organization. One of the recent *Business Week* reports by Byrne (1993, pp. 78–79) discussed seven of the key elements of the horizontal corporation:

1. Organize around process, not task.
2. Flatten hierarchy.
3. Use teams to manage everything.
4. Let customers drive performance.
5. Reward team performance.
6. Maximize supplier and customer contact.
7. Inform and train all employees.

Many organizations have responded to competitive pressures by downsizing. Unfortunately, downsizing does little to alter the single-loop learning and consequently the basic way work gets done in a company. To do that takes a different model, the organic design. This design is flatter, decentralized, and less complex than others. Some of the biggest corporations, such as GE, Xerox, DuPont, and Motorola are moving in this direction. Unfortunately changes in organization design, without corresponding changes in culture, may not alter single-loop learning and consequently the basic ways of doing work.

An organizational consultant may decide to use both process and structural intervention approaches for managing conflict. It should be noted that although process intervention is primarily designed to alter the styles of handling conflict of the organizational members through education and training, such an intervention might also affect their perception of the amount of conflict. On the other hand, the structural intervention is primarily designed to alter the amount of conflict by changing certain structural design characteristics; such an intervention may also affect the styles of handling conflict.

Major Research Challenges

In the area of managing conflict in complex organizations, there are several research challenges. The major ones are listed as follows:

1. Several studies investigated the relationships of intragroup affective, process, and substantive conflicts to job performance and satisfaction. We need studies to investigate the relationships of (1) the three types of conflict to individual job performance and satisfaction and of (2) the three types of conflict to intergroup collaboration and satisfaction.
2. We need to investigate the mediating or moderating effects of the conflict-handling styles on the relationship between the three types of conflict and job performance and satisfaction.
3. We need to know more about the effects of affective, process, and substantive conflicts on productivity under different conditions of task (e.g., structured vs. unstructured) and technology (unit, mass, continuous process).
4. There are two qualitative studies that discuss how the five styles of handling conflict should be used to deal with different situations effectively (Rahim, 1997; Thomas, 1977). More studies are needed to assess the effectiveness of each style to deal with different situations.
5. There are several antecedents of conflict and styles of handling conflict. More studies are needed to clearly identify the process and structural factors that influence conflict and conflict-handling styles.
6. There are several studies on the relationship between personality and the styles of handling interpersonal conflict (for a review see Moberg, 1998; Antonioni, 1998). More studies are needed to establish clear links between personality and styles.
7. There are some cross-cultural studies on the styles of handling conflict (Ting-Toomey et al., 1991). We need to have more cross-cultural studies on styles and the effects of substantive, affective, and process conflicts on job performance and satisfaction.

Information generated from these studies would help to improve the management of conflict in contemporary organizations. In other words, the conflict management theory presented in this chapter is likely to be refined as relevant studies are published from time to time.

Summary

Organizational conflict must not necessarily be reduced, suppressed, or eliminated, but managed to enhance organizational learning and effectiveness. The criteria for conflict management include enhancing organizational learning and effectiveness, satisfying the needs of stakeholders, and promoting ethical management. Strategies for conflict management at the individual, group, and intergroup levels involve (1) reduction of affective and process conflicts, (2) reduction of substantive conflict for routine tasks, (3) attainment and maintenance of a moderate amount of substantive conflict at each level for nonroutine tasks, and (4) helping the organizational participants to learn the various styles of handling conflict for dealing with different conflict situations effectively.

The studies of organizational conflict have taken two directions. One group of studies used the measures of the amount or intensity of conflict. Implicit in these studies is that dysfunctional conflicts may have to be minimized and that moderate amount of functional conflicts may have to be attained by altering the sources of these conflicts. Other studies have looked at the various styles of handling conflict of the organization members, such as integrating, obliging, dominating, avoiding, and compromising. For conflicts to be managed functionally, one style may be more appropriate than another depending on the situation.

The management of organizational conflict involves the diagnosis of, and intervention in, conflict. A proper diagnosis should include the measures of the amount of conflict, the styles of handling conflict, sources of conflict, and learning and effectiveness. It should also indicate the relationships of the amount of conflict and conflict styles to their sources and learning and effectiveness.

Intervention is needed if there is too much affective and process conflicts or there is too much substantive conflict for routine tasks or too little or too much substantive conflict for nonroutine tasks and if conflicts are not handled effectively to deal with different situations. There are two types of intervention: process and structural. The process approach is mainly designed to manage conflict by enabling organizational participants to learn the various styles of handling conflict and their appropriate uses. The process approach to intervention requires an organizational culture that supports conflict and learning.

The structural approach is designed to manage conflict by changing the organization's structural design characteristics. The effectiveness of a department can be improved by matching its structural design with the needs of its relevant environment. A structural intervention aims mainly at attaining and maintaining a moderate amount of functional conflict and reducing the incidence of dysfunctional conflict by altering the sources of these conflicts. The next chapter discusses intrapersonal conflict and its management.

5

Intrapersonal Conflict

As discussed in Chapter 2, organizational conflict was classified as intrapersonal, interpersonal, intragroup, and intergroup on the basis of levels. This chapter describes the nature, dynamics, sources, and management of intrapersonal conflict. Psychologists have studied conflict at the intrapersonal level extensively. They define conflict as "a situation in which a person is motivated to engage in two or more mutually exclusive activities" (Murray, 1968, p. 220; see also Bazerman, Tenbrumsel, & Wade-Benzone, 1988; Mosak & LeFevre, 2003). According to communication scholar Roloff (1987), this conflict "occurs when there is incompatibility or inconsistency among an individual's cognitive elements [which] implies that a new cognitive element is at variance with a prior explanation or expectation. Thus intrapersonal conflict reflects a challenge to a person's basis for prediction and control resulting in greater uncertainty" (p. 489).

An individual is in an intrapersonal conflict if he or she has difficulty making a decision because of uncertainty he or she is pushed or pulled in opposite directions, that is, the alternatives are both attractive and/or unattractive. Each organizational member is required to face the challenge of coping with this type of conflict almost every day. Kurt Lewin's (1948) field theory falls in this category. He conceptualized conflict as a situation where oppositely directed, simultaneous forces of about equal strength occur in a person.

Types of Intrapersonal Conflict

According to Lewin (1948) there are three types of intrapersonal conflict. Following is a discussion of these three types.

Approach–Approach Conflict

This occurs when a person has to choose between two attractive alternatives. A manager is confronted with an approach–approach conflict if he or she has to recommend one of two subordinates for promotion who are equally competent for the position. A job seeker who has two attractive job offers has to cope with this conflict.

A situation like this may produce a state of unstable equilibrium. As soon as an individual approaches one of the goals, it becomes more attractive and the choice becomes easier the closer he or she moves toward the goal. The conflict is resolved as the individual moves toward the goal and it becomes more attractive than the other.

Approach–Avoidance Conflict

This type of conflict involves only one goal. It occurs when a person has to deal with a situation that possesses both desirable as well as undesirable aspects, that is, when a person feels similar degrees of attraction towards and repulsion from a goal. A faculty member may be in this type of conflict if he or she wants to join a top school where the prospect of tenure is uncertain.

The closer an individual comes to the goal, the greater the anxiety and fear, but withdrawal from the goal increases the strength of desire and a cycle of anxiety develops. This is the process through which one is brought back to the original point of equilibrium.

Double Approach–Avoidance. This conflict is characterized by a situation in which one is confronted with two goals that each has positive and negative features. Because individuals tend to approach and avoid each of the goals, this process is called double approach–avoidance.

An example of this type of conflict is deciding to live in the country that has its advantages and difficulties. Deciding to live in the city will similarly present both advantages and the inconvenience of city life.

Avoidance–Avoidance Conflict

This conflict occurs when each of the competing alternatives possesses negative consequences, that is, they are equally repulsive. A manager will be in this type of conflict if he or she has to decide between accepting a pay cut or quitting his or her job. The person is possibly distressed in his or her attempt to decide upon the lesser of the two evils. This conflict is also called double-avoidance conflict.

Perceived incompatibilities or incongruencies frequently occur when an organizational participant is required to perform a task that does not match her or his expertise, interests, goals, and values. Such a conflict also occurs if there is a significant mismatch between the role that a person expects to perform and the role that is demanded of the person by the organization. The latter has been classified as *role conflict* by some researchers (e.g., Kahn, Wolfe, Quinn, Snoak,

& Rosenthal, 1964; Rizzo, House, & Lirtzman, 1970). For our purposes role conflict is a part of intrapersonal conflict.

Role

The concepts of role and role conflict have been developed by researchers in several disciplines. Since a number of studies have been conducted on role conflict, a considerable part of this chapter is devoted to the explanation of the nature of role and role conflict.

Common to most definitions of role is the view that an individual behaves with reference to the expectations that others have about the way he or she should behave (see Stark, 2007). Generally, this term is utilized to represent behavior and attitudes expected of the occupant of a given position or status. There are at least three uses of the term.

1. First, role is used to mean a normative status that includes the behavior, attitudes, and values attributed by society to a person occupying a given position.
2. Second, role is used to mean an individual's conceptualization of his or her situation with reference to his or her and others' positions in the society.
3. Third, role is used to refer to the behavior of a person occupying a social position.

Role Conflict

This type of conflict occurs when a role occupant is required to perform two or more roles that present incongruent, contradictory, or even mutually exclusive activities. Role conflict was defined by Pandey and Kumar (1997) "as a state of mind or experience or perception of the role incumbent arising out of the simultaneous occurrence of two or more role expectations such that compliance with one would make compliance with the other(s) more difficult or even impossible" (p. 191). Kahn et al. (1964) conducted a nationwide study on role conflict and ambiguity. The study involved a survey of 725 subjects representing male wage and salary workers of the United States during 1961 and an intensive series of case studies of 53 selected firms from 6 industrial locations. The researchers defined role conflict as "the simultaneous occurrence of two (or more) sets of pressures such that compliance with one would make more difficult compliance with the other" (Kahn et al., 1964, p. 19) and further identified four distinct types of role conflict.

Intrasender Conflict

This type of conflict occurs when a role sender requires a role receiver (i.e., the focal person) to perform contradictory or inconsistent roles. For example, a role sender may request the role receiver to do something that cannot be done without violating a rule, yet the role sender attempts to enforce the rule.

Intersender Conflict

A role receiver experiences this type of conflict if the role behavior demanded by one role sender is incongruent with the role behavior demanded by another role sender(s). A person who often experiences role conflict, for example, is a foreman, who receives instruction from a general foreman that may be inconsistent with the needs and expectations of the workers under the former.

Interrole Conflict

This type of conflict occurs when an individual occupies two or more roles whose expectations are inconsistent. A corporation president is expected, in that role, to take part in social engagements to promote the image of the corporation. This may be in conflict with his or her role as a parent, in which he or she is expected to spend more time with his or her children to be an ideal parent.

Intrarole (Person-Role) Conflict

This type of role conflict occurs when the role requirements are incongruent with the focal person's attitudes, values, and professional behavior. For example, intrarole conflict occurs when an organizational member is required to enter into price-fixing conspiracies, which are not congruent with his or her ethical standards.

Role Overload and Underload

These four types of role conflict may lead to another complex form of conflict called role overload. It "involves a kind of person-role conflict and is perhaps best regarded as a complex, emergent type combining aspects of intersender and person-role conflicts" (Kahn et al., 1964, p. 20). This occurs when an organizational member is required to perform a number of appropriate roles sent by different role senders, which, taken as a set, are too much to be accomplished by him or her.

Role overload can be classified as quantitative and qualitative. French and Caplan (1972) originally conceptualized *quantitative* and *qualitative* role overload as specific types of role conflict. The former refers to situations in which role occupants are required to perform more work than they can within a specific time period. The latter refers to situations in which role occupants believe they do not possess the skills or competence necessary to perform an assignment.

Role overload is quite prevalent in organizations. Managers particularly experience quantitative overload because they work under continuous time pressure. Because of this, they may set up priorities and perform the roles that they consider more important than others. A large number of managers deal with this problem by working overtime.

While role overload is a significant problem in contemporary organizations, role underload is also another problem that organizations have to deal with. Two types of role underload are *quantitative* and *qualitative*. Quantitative underload refers to a situation where employees do not have much work to do, and, as a result, they spend part of their time doing very little work. Qualitative underload refers to a situation where an employee's training and experience are inadequately used at work. This happens in many routine repetitive jobs.

Role Ambiguity

A concept closely related to role conflict is role ambiguity. It refers to the lack of clarity in understanding what expectations or prescriptions exist for a given role. An organizational member requires information about the expectations from his or her role, the means of achieving the role, and consequences of performing the role. Role ambiguity occurs when the information either does not exist or is not properly communicated if it does exist (Kahn et al., 1964).

It is interesting to note that Peterson et al.'s (1995) twenty-one-nation study reported lower role ambiguity in Asian and African countries (which are high on power distance and low on individualism) than in many Western countries (which are low in power distance and high in individualism). This suggests that national culture influences the perception of role ambiguity.

A Model of Role Conflict and Ambiguity

Figure 5–1 portrays a slightly modified version of Kahn et al.'s (1964, p. 30) model of role conflict and ambiguity. The model can be used to present the notion of role episode and the factors that are involved in adjustment to role conflict and ambiguity.

The model presents role conflict through a series of events or a role episode. Two boxes in the figure are headed "role senders" and "focal person." The role senders communicate their expectations or influence to the focal person to reinforce or modify his or her behavior. The box on the left represents the expectations of the role senders (Section I) and the means by which these are communicated (Section II). The box on the right represents the perception of these communications by the focal person (Section III) and his or her response to the influence attempt (Section IV).

The figure illustrates that the episode begins with a role sender's expectations, that is, the perceptions and evaluations of the focal person's role behavior. The sender then moves into the next phase (i.e., sent role), which takes the form of role pressure communicated to the focal person. The direction of the arrow between sent role and received role indicates the communication flow from the role sender(s) to the focal person.

Figure 5.1
A Model of Role Conflict and Ambiguity

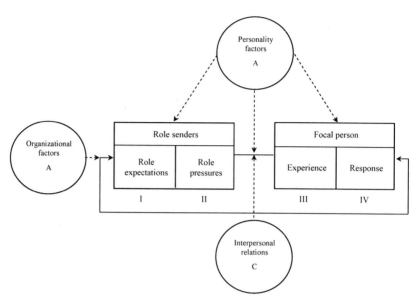

Source: Kahn, R. L., Wolf, M. D., Quinn, R. P., Snoak, J. D., & Rosenthal, R. A. (1964). Organizational stress: Studies in role conflict and ambiguity. New York: Wiley, p. 30. Reprinted with permission.

The focal person receives the sent role and begins an interpretation process. Role conflict occurs at this stage if the sent role is different from the role expected by the focal person. The next phase is the role behavior, that is, the response by the focal person, which may take the form of either compliance or noncompliance with the sent role. The loop connecting the focal person and role sender indicates the feedback mechanism through which the role sender knows how much of the focal person's response is consistent with the sent role. This becomes an input to the process by which the role sender indicates another cycle of role sendings.

The direction of arrows in the broken lines connecting the three circles and the episode indicates that organizational factors (A) may affect an episode. The personality factors (B) of the role senders and the focal person and the interpersonal relations (C) between them may affect an episode as well as be affected by it. Some of the major factors that affect role conflict are discussed in detail under the heading "sources" of intrapersonal conflict, later in this chapter.

A number of studies on organizational behavior have used role conflict as a univariate construct. Miles and Perreault (1976; see also King & King, 1990;

Pandey & Kumar, 1997) suggested the need for studying role conflict as a multivariate construct consisting of five types of conflict, previously discussed. This is needed to gain proper understanding of the factors that affect different types of role conflict and the effects of these conflicts on individual, group, and organizational effectiveness.

Consequences of Role Conflict

A number of studies have attempted to relate role conflict to personal and organizational outcomes. Kahn et al. (1964) concluded from their study that "the emotional costs of role conflict for the focal person include low job satisfaction, low confidence in the organization, and a high degree of job-related tension. A very frequent behavioral response to role conflict is withdrawal or avoidance of those who are seen as creating the conflict" (p. 380). Role ambiguity was found to be as prevalent as role conflict, and the consequences are similar.

Role conflict has been found to be associated with lack of job involvement and organizational commitment, tension and anxiety, intent to leave the job, lack of confidence in the organization, and inability to influence decision making (Behrman & Perreault, 1984; Brief & Aldag, 1976; Fisher & Gitelson, 1983; House & Rizzo, 1972; Jackson & Schuler, 1985; Johnson & Stinson, 1975; Miles, 1975; Miles & Perreault, 1976; Rizzo et al., 1970; Sohi, 1996).

A recent study in India found person-role conflict, but not within-role and inter-role conflicts, to be negatively associated with job involvement. The three subscales of role conflict were positively associated with organizational conflict (intergroup, intragroup, intrapersonal conflicts) but negatively associated with role efficacy (role making, role centering, and role linking) (Pandey & Kumar, 1997). Several studies have reported deleterious effects of role conflict and role ambiguity on job performance of organizational members (e.g., Kahn & Byosiere, 1992; McGrath, 1976; Sohi, 1996). A recent study by Fried, Ben-David, Tiegs, Avital, and Yeverechyahu (1998) questioned the independence of role conflict and role ambiguity with respect to their relations to job performance. Their data indicated that role conflict and ambiguity have an interactive effect (role conflict × role ambiguity) on the supervisory ratings of job performance. Thompson and Werner (1997) reported negative relationships of role conflict to the three dimensions of organizational citizenship behavior (interpersonal helping, personal industry, and individual initiative).

A study by Netemeyer, Johnston, and Burton (1990), in a structural equations framework, shows that role conflict and role ambiguity may influence intent to a leave job indirectly through other variables, such as job satisfaction and organizational commitment. Sales (1969) investigated the consequences of role overload and found that it can contribute to the cause of coronary disease.

A meta-analysis of work demand stressors and job performance by Gilboa, Shirom, Fried, and Cooper (2008) reported a low but significant negative mean correlation between job performance measures (general performance, self-rated performance, and supervisor-rated performance) and role conflict, role ambiguity, and role overload. They also reported that the negative correlation between job performance and role overload was higher for managers than nonmanagers.

The studies just cited above deal only with the negative or dysfunctional aspects of role conflict. However, a study by Babin and Boles (1996), which used structural equations model, reported a positive relationship between role conflict and performance in retail service providers. Unfortunately, these studies (with the exception of the Babin & Boles study) did not attempt to investigate the functional aspects of role conflict that can enhance individual and/or organizational effectiveness. Implicit in these reported studies is the notion that role conflict is dysfunctional and should be reduced or eliminated. Although several studies have found adverse effects of role perceptions on a number of attitudinal, behavioral, and psychosomatic outcomes, the relationship between role conflict and organizational effectiveness has yet to be established. Two major problems are associated with the studies on role conflict and individual and organizational effectiveness. These are the failure to control the factors, other than role conflict, that affect organizational effectiveness and the failure to develop valid measures of organizational effectiveness. As emphasized in Chapter 3, organizational conflict of any type must not necessarily be reduced or eliminated but managed to increase organizational effectiveness. The next section deals with this important issue.

Managing Intrapersonal Conflict

The management of intrapersonal conflict involves matching the individual goals and role expectations with the needs of the task and role demand to optimize the attainment of individual and organizational goals. It was suggested in Chapter 4 that the management of conflict involves diagnosis of, and intervention in, conflict. Following is a discussion on the diagnosis of, and intervention in, intrapersonal conflict.

Diagnosis

The diagnosis of intrapersonal conflict can be performed by self-report, observation, and interview methods. The ROCI–I uses self-report to measure intrapersonal conflict of organizational members. Rizzo et al. (1970) designed a questionnaire to measure role conflict and role ambiguity that is frequently used in organizational studies. They used the self-report of incompatibility and inconsistency in the requirements of the role of an individual to measure role conflict and ambiguity. Tracy and Johnson (1981) concluded from their study that this measure of role conflict and role ambiguity represent generalized role stress and role clarity/comfort, respectively.

Measurement. A comprehensive diagnosis of intrapersonal conflict involves the measurement as follows:

1. The amount of intrapersonal conflict.
2. The sources of such conflict.
3. Learning and effectiveness of the individual employees.

Analysis. An analysis of the preceding diagnostic data should be performed to derive the following:

1. The amount of intrapersonal conflict existing in various organizational levels, units, departments, or divisions and whether they deviated from the national norms significantly.
2. Relationship between intrapersonal conflict and its sources.
3. Relationships of intrapersonal conflict to learning and effectiveness.

National Norms. As discussed in Chapter 4, data for the national norms of intrapersonal, intragroup, and intergroup conflicts were collected on the ROCI–I from 1,188 managers. Tables 5–1 and 5–2 were prepared on the basis of this sample. Table 5–1 shows the national percentile norms of managers. The percentile score of an individual shows his or her relative position on the intrapersonal conflict subscale compared with other members in the normative group. For instance, a subject scoring at the 65th percentile on this scale is as high or higher than 65 percent of the normative group. His or her score is exceeded by only 35 percent of this group.

Table 5–2 shows the sample size (N), means (M) of reference group norms, standard deviations (SD) of intrapersonal conflict, classified by organizational level, functional area, and education, and the results of one-way analyses of variance (F-ratio). The results of one-way analyses of variance show differences in intrapersonal conflict among the executives of top, middle, and lower organizational levels. There was an inverse relationship between organizational level and intrapersonal conflict. There were also some differences in intrapersonal conflict among executives of different functional areas. There were no significant differences in conflict among the executives with different educational levels.

The normative data should enable a management practitioner or a behavioral science consultant to decide whether the members of an organization or one or more of its subsystems are experiencing too little, too much, or a moderate amount of intrapersonal conflict. The normative data should be used with caution because they provide some crude indicators of what may be the normal level of conflict in an organization.

Tables 5–3 and 5–4 provide additional percentile and reference group norms, respectively. Normative data were collected from students on the three types of conflict ($N = 676$) and the five styles of handling interpersonal conflict ($N = 712$). These data were collected from employed students of schools of busi-

Table 5–1
National Managerial Percentile Norms of Intrapersonal Conflict

Mean Scores	Percentiles	Mean Scores
5.00		5.00
4.85		4.85
4.70		4.70
4.55		4.55
4.40		4.40
4.25		4.25
4.10	99	4.10
3.95	98	3.95
3.80	97	3.80
3.65	96	3.65
3.50	94	3.50
3.35	92	3.35
3.20	90	3.20
3.05	88	3.05
2.90	86	2.90
2.75	81	2.75
2.60	76	2.60
2.45	71	2.45
2.30	62	2.30
2.15	53	2.15
2.00	43	2.00
1.85	23	1.85
1.70	18	1.70
1.55	12	1.55
1.40	8	1.40
1.25	4	1.25
1.10	3	1.10
1.00	2	1.00

Note: $N = 1,188$

ness administration at Youngstown State and Western Kentucky universities who were registered in the author's management courses during 1978 to 1983 and 1983 to 1999, respectively. The average age and work experience of MBA students were 26.56 ($SD = 5.27$) and 4.96 ($SD = 4.58$) years, respectively. The average age and work experience of the undergraduate students were 23.5 ($SD = 3.92$) and 3.74 ($SD = 3.64$) years, respectively.

Table 5–2
National Managerial Reference Group
Norms of Intrapersonal Conflict

Variable	N	M	SD	F
Organizational Level				69.77*
Top	196	1.86	.56	
Middle	407	2.16	.61	
Lower	547	2.46	.70	
Functional Area				6.57*
Production	216	2.34	.65	
Marketing	27	2.28	.83	
Finance & Accounting	36	2.04	.54	
Personnel	24	2.01	.53	
General Management	252	2.06	.68	
R&D	198	2.35	.66	
Engineering	196	2.41	.70	
Other	214	2.26	.72	
Education				1.50
High school	136	2.18	.58	
2-year college	231	2.26	.70	
Bachelor's degree	529	2.25	.69	
Master's degree	208	2.35	.75	
Other	57	2.21	.68	
Total Sample	1,188	2.26	.69	

Note: $* p < .05$.

Sources. The sources of intrapersonal conflict are mainly structural; they are situationally imposed. The diagnosis of intrapersonal conflict must identify these sources so that they can be altered to minimize this conflict.

Misassignment and Goal Incongruence. If a person is assigned to do a task for which he or she does not have the appropriate expertise, aptitude, and commitment, then the person may experience qualitative role overload. There are notable examples of misassignment in the military organization; for example, a truck driver is assigned the task of a cook, or a bookkeeping clerk is required to perform the task of a machine operator. Argyris's (1964, 1974) research on personality and organization theory shows that the needs of the individual and the goals of the organization are generally antithetical.

Table 5–3
Collegiate Percentile Norms of Intrapersonal Conflict

| Mean Scores | Percentiles | | Mean Scores |
	MBA (n = 172)	Undergraduate (n = 504)	
5.00			5.00
4.85	99		4.85
4.70	98	99	4.70
4.55	97	98	4.55
4.40	94	97	4.40
4.25	93	96	4.25
4.10	90	94	4.10
3.95	88	91	3.95
3.80	87	88	3.80
3.65	86	85	3.65
3.50	84	81	3.50
3.35	81	76	3.35
3.20	76	71	3.20
3.05	69	64	3.05
2.90	66	58	2.90
2.75	59	52	2.75
2.60	52	45	2.60
2.45	45	40	2.45
2.30	41	31	2.30
2.15	30	23	2.15
2.00	22	17	2.00
1.85	11	8	1.85
1.70	8	4	1.70
1.55	5	2	1.55
1.40	4	1	1.40
1.25	3		1.25
1.10	2		1.10
1.00	1		1.00

Argyris's (1974, p. 7) research shows that only top management felt any absence of conflict between their own needs and the goals of the organization. This possibly suggests that there is an inverse relationship between organizational level and perception of intrapersonal conflict. Evidence of this relationship for managers can be found in Table 5–2. At the higher organizational level, the employees have greater freedom to do the things they want to do to satisfy their individual needs as well as those of the organization. Unfortunately, no

Table 5–4
Collegiate Reference Group Norms of Intrapersonal Conflict

Variable	N	M	SD	F
Organizational Level				7.48*
Top	11	2.21	.87	
Middle	100	2.52	.09	
Lower	131	2.69	.78	
Nonmanagement	222	2.88	.76	
Worker	133	2.97	.84	
Education				2.09
Undergraduate	502	2.81	.75	
MBA	172	2.71	.85	
Gender				.06
Male	402	2.80	.76	
Female	263	2.78	.81	
Total sample	676	2.26	.69	

Note: * $p < .05$.

study specifically investigated the relationship between organizational level and conflict.

Inappropriate Demand on Capacity. If a person cannot properly satisfy all the demands of his or her position even by working at the maximum capacity, then this leads to quantitative role overload. If a person's capacity (skill, commitment, role expectation) significantly exceeds the demands of the position, the person will not find his or her work challenging. A person may find his or her job challenging and motivating when the role demand slightly exceeds the individual's role expectation. Inadequate role demand or qualitative role underload is a common problem for young graduates, who often find their jobs not as challenging as the employers painted them to be (Newton & Keenan, 1987).

Organization Structure. The structure of an organization has a major influence on role conflict (Kahn et al., 1964). Organizations generate a high degree of role conflict by creating conflicting goals, policies, and decisions. A number of earlier studies found multiple lines of authority to be associated with role conflict and loss of organizational effectiveness (Evan, 1962; Kaplan, 1959; LaPorte, 1965).

Low role conflict is associated with organizational practices that promote "personal development, formalization, adequacy of communication, planning, horizontal communication, top management receptiveness to ideas, coordina-tion of work flow, adaptability to change and adequacy of authority" (Rizzo et al., 1970, p. 161). House and Rizzo (1972) found that organizational practices, such as formalization, planning activity, provision for horizontal coordination, selection based on ability, and adherence to chain of command are all nega-tively related to role conflict and ambiguity. Morris, Steers, and Koch (1979) reported that participation in decision making and formalization (i.e., extent to which written rules and procedures regarding an employee's job are available) were negatively associated with role conflict. Supervisory span (i.e., number of subordinates for whom the supervisor is charged with formal responsibility) and span of subordination (i.e., number of individuals who typically assign work to an employee) were positively associated with role conflict.

Supervisory Style. This may be one of the major generators of role conflict. Rizzo et al. (1970) found role conflict to be lower when "supervisors are de-scribed as more frequently engaging in emphasizing production under condi-tions of uncertainty, providing structure and standards, facilitating teamwork, tolerating freedom, and exerting upward influence" (p. 161). House and Rizzo (1972) found negative relationships of role conflict to formalization, supervisory supportiveness, and team orientation.

Newton and Keenan (1987) reported that social support from supervisors was negatively associated with qualitative role underload and positively associated quantitative role overload. Supervisory support was negatively associated with role conflict, but it was not associated with role ambiguity.

Position. Role conflict is associated with positions that carry greater su-pervisory responsibility (Newton & Keenan, 1987). A classic position that is exposed to more role conflict than others is that of the foreman (Charters, 1952; Roethlisberger, 1965; Rosen, 1970). A foreman is often caught in the middle between the inconsistent demands from superiors and subordinates. Another classic position in an organization that is exposed to more role conflict is the salesperson. Kahn et al. (1964) found that organization members who were required to engage in boundary-spanning activities (i.e., make frequent outside contacts) experienced more role conflict. The studies by Miles and Perreault (1976), Organ and Greene (1974), and Rogers and Molnar (1976) provide further support for this relationship. Kahn et al. found a slight difference in the degree of role conflict reported by intra- and inter-organizational boundary spanners. But Keller, Szilagyi, and Holland (1976) in their field study found no relationship between boundary-spanning activity and role conflict and ambiguity.

Personality. Rotter (1966) theorized that consistent individual differences ex-ist between the personality dispositions of internal and external locus of control. Individuals who have high internal locus of control (internalizers or internals) believe that events in their lives are primarily influenced by their own behavior and actions. Individuals who have high external locus of control (externalizers or externals) believe that events in their lives are primarily influenced by other people or events outside their control. Szilagyi, Sims, and Keller's (1976, p. 267) field study reported that internals generally perceived less role conflict than externals. It should be noted, however, that while correlation coefficients were statistically significant, they were low.

Another type of personality that is likely to affect both the perception of, and response to, role conflict is Type A. Newton and Keenan (1987) reported that Type A behavior was negatively associated with qualitative role underload and positively associated with quantitative role overload.

This section provided an approach to a comprehensive diagnosis. This should not be taken to mean that every organization needs or can afford such a diagnosis. The results of diagnosis should indicate whether there is any need for intervention and the type of intervention required. It should, at the minimum, indicate whether too much of this conflict exists and whether its effects are functional or dysfunctional. If it is felt that the effects of intrapersonal conflict on individual effectiveness are negligible or nonsignificant, there is no need for an intervention in such conflict. If the effects of intrapersonal conflict on individual effectiveness are found to be significantly negative, an intervention may be needed to reduce this conflict to enhance effectiveness.

Intervention

As discussed in Chapter 4, two types of intervention, process and structural, are available for the management of conflict. These have been presented here for the management of intrapersonal conflict.

Process. The technique of role analysis is presented in this chapter as a process intervention for managing intrapersonal conflict. Although this technique has been classified as a process intervention, it also contains some components of structural intervention.

Technique of Role Analysis. This method of intervention was first applied by Dayal and Thomas (1968) to help a new organization in India grow and increase its effectiveness. Role analysis is an intervention designed to improve overall organizational effectiveness by intervening at individual, group, and intergroup levels.

Application of this technique involves five distinct steps. A model of role analysis is utilized to examine the purpose of the role, its prescribed and discretionary elements, and its relationship with other roles. The role analysis should ideally start with the top manager of the system being changed. The formal steps of the technique are listed as follows:

1. *Purpose of role.* The focal role occupant (i.e., individual whose role is being analyzed) initiates the discussion relating to his or her role. The group members or their representatives discuss the purpose of the role (i.e., how the role fits in with the goals of the organization and/or subsystems).

2. *Role perception.* The focal role occupant lists the activities that he or she feels occupy the role. Participants discuss the items and ask for explanations, and, thus, new items are added and ambiguous or contradictory items are dropped. The participants help the role incumbent to analyze the prescribed and discretionary components of the role. This frequently "enables the individual to clarify the responsibility he must take on himself for decisions, the choices open to him for alternative courses of action, and new competencies he must develop in his assigned role" (Dayal & Thomas, 1968, p. 487).

3. *Expectations of role occupant.* The focal role occupant lists his or her expectations from the group members. Members of the group discuss these expectations to clarify role interdependencies; a mutually acceptable solution is reached describing expectations and obligations.

4. *Expectations from role occupant.* Each participant presents a list of expectations from the focal role, which represents the group's views of the participant's obligation to the group member in performing his or her role. Here much of the process in step 3 is repeated for each participant.

5. *Role profile.* The focal role occupant is responsible for writing down the main points of the discussion, called a role profile. This consists of (1) prescribed and discretionary activities, (2) obligation of this role to other roles in the group, and (3) expectations of someone in his or her role to other roles in the group.

This technique can be used to analyze and differentiate individual, group, and intergroup roles and to help the individuals in managing tasks and role interdependencies more systematically. The latter is attained through the analysis of role relationships and reassignment of tasks that provide a better match between the needs of the individual and the task goals. From the foregoing analysis, it appears that role analysis may not only affect conflict at the individual level but also at the group and intergroup levels.

Structural. This section presents job design as a structural intervention for managing intrapersonal conflict.

Job Design. This involves the planning of the job, including its contents, the methods of performing the job, and how it relates to other jobs in the organization. Job design method can follow two approaches. The classical approach involves structuring the task activities to make full use of the division of labor and specialization. This job engineering is still a popular job design strategy. The second approach involves changing the job to make it satisfying. This is called job enrichment.

Herzberg's two-factor theory provided real impetus to job enrichment (Herzberg, Mausner, & Snyderman, 1959). Herzberg's approach to job enrichment involves improvement of the motivation factors, such as achievement, recognition, responsibility, advancement, and opportunity for growth. This approach is based on the assumption that job enrichment increases job satisfaction, which, in turn, increases motivation and better performance. Herzberg et al. (1959) suggested that improvement in the hygiene factors (salary, company policies, working conditions, etc.) does not lead to increase in employee motivation. The theory has been criticized on the grounds of (1) failure to provide the evidence of existence of two factors, such as motivation and hygiene, (2) assuming that motivating factors increase motivation of all employees, and (3) failure to specify how motivating factors can be measured for existing jobs (Hackman & Oldham, 1976).

Another approach to job enrichment, recently developed by Hackman and Oldham (1980), is shown in Figure 5–2. Their approach attempts to make jobs more meaningful by increasing or adding certain core job characteristics, such as skill variety, task identity, task significance, autonomy, and feedback. This approach attempts to remedy some of the problems in Herzberg et al.'s approach.

Figure 5–2
A Model for Job Redesign

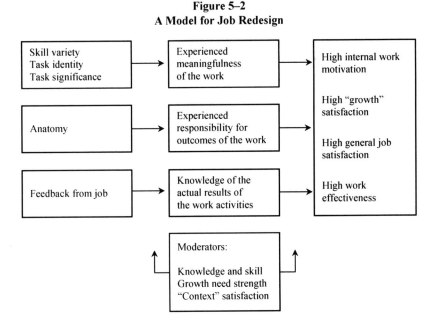

Source: Hackman, J. R., & Oldman, G. R. (1980). *Work redesign.* Reading, MA: Addison-Wesley, p. 90. Reprinted with permission.

Building on the works of Turner and Lawrence (1965), Hackman and Oldham (1975) identified five core dimensions that must be considered in enriching a job. These dimensions are positively related to motivation, satisfaction, and quality of work and negatively related to turnover and absenteeism. It is expected that these five dimensions will negatively relate to intrapersonal conflict. The five core dimensions can be described as follows:

1. *Skill variety.* This refers to the degree to which a job requires a variety of activities that involve the use of a number of different skills and talents of employees.

2. *Task identity.* This refers to the degree to which the job requires an employee to perform a complete piece of work, that is, doing a job from beginning to end with a visible outcome.

3. *Task significance.* This refers to the degree to which the job has an impact on the lives or work of other people, within or outside the organization.

4. *Autonomy.* This refers to the degree to which the job provides freedom, independence, and discretion to the employee in scheduling his or her work and in determining the procedures to be used in carrying it out.

5. *Feedback.* This refers to the amount of information that results from the performance of a job by an employee about how well she or he is performing.

As shown in Figure 5–2, the core dimensions influence three critical psychological states. The jobs that are high on skill variety, task identity, and task significance influence experienced meaningfulness of the work. Psychological states, such as experienced responsibility for outcomes of the work, and knowledge of the actual results of the work activities are influenced by job autonomy and feedback, respectively. According to this theory, higher level of psychological states lead to positive personal and work outcomes, such as high internal work motivation, high growth satisfaction, high general job satisfaction, and high work effectiveness. Hackman and Oldham (1975) devised the following equation for computing an overall index, the Motivation Potential Score (MPS):

$$MPS = \left(\frac{\text{Skill Variety} + \text{Task Identity} + \text{Task Significance}}{3} \right) \times \text{Autonomy} \times \text{Feedback}$$

The MPS was hypothesized to be positively related to personal and work outcomes. But because individual employees differ, the researchers suggested that every employee does not respond to the MPS identically. Three factors moderate the relationship between the core job characteristics and outcomes. These are:

1. *Knowledge and skill* of the employees to perform job well.

2. *Growth need strength,* i.e., need for learning, self-direction, and personal growth of the employees.

3. *"Context" satisfactions,* i.e., the level of satisfaction, particularly with job security, compensation, coworkers, and supervision.

The employees who report higher on one or more of the above moderators should respond more positively to jobs that score high on MPS. "The 'worst possible' circumstance for a job that is high in motivating potential, for example, would be when the job incumbent is only marginally competent to perform the work, has low needs for personal growth at work, and is highly dissatisfied with one or more aspects of the work context. The job clearly would be too much for that individual, and negative personal and work outcomes would be predicted" (Hackman & Oldham, 1980, p. 88).

The researchers designed an instrument called the Job Diagnostic Survey (JDS) for measuring each of the variables in the job characteristics model (Hackman & Oldham, 1975). On the basis of the employees' responses to the JDS, it is possible to compute the MPS for employees. This is used to predict the extent to which the characteristics of a job motivate employees to perform such a job. A number of studies have found moderate to strong support for this theory (Hackman & Oldham, 1976; Orpen, 1979). In a study of seventy-seven nursing aides and assistants in a large university hospital, Brief and Aldag (1976) found negative relations between role conflict and the perceptions of five core task dimensions, but only the relations between role conflict and task identity and autonomy were statistically significant.

The Job Descriptive Model appears to be a useful conceptual framework for studying the effects of job design on work behavior and performance of individual employees. The model is in its early stage of development; therefore, further studies are necessary to investigate the effects of job design on conflict. We particularly need longitudinal field experiments to assess the effects of job design interventions on different types of conflict discussed in this chapter.

Summary

Kurt Lewin (1948) defined conflict as a situation in which opposing and simultaneously occurring forces of about equal strength occur in a person. The four types of this conflict are approach–approach conflict, approach–avoidance conflict, double approach–avoidance, and avoidance–avoidance conflict. Perceived incompatibilities or incongruencies frequently occur when an organizational participant is required to perform a role or task that does not match his or her expertise, interests, goals, and values.

Role conflict occurs when the focal person is expected to perform incompatible or inconsistent role expectations communicated by his or her role senders. Kahn et al. (1994) identified four types of role conflict—intrasender, intersender, interrole, and intrarole conflicts. Role overload is a complex form of conflict that combines aspects of intersender and intrarole conflict. Two types of role overload are quantitative and qualitative. Kahn et al. presented role conflict through a series of events or a role episode. A concept related to role conflict is role ambiguity, which refers to the lack of understanding of what expectations or prescriptions exist for a given role. The consequences of role conflict include job dissatisfaction, lack of job involvement, lower organizational commitment, tension and anxiety, propensity to leave organizations, lack of confidence in the organization, and inability to influence decision making.

The management of intrapersonal conflict involves diagnosis and intervention. The diagnosis should essentially indicate whether there is too much intrapersonal conflict in an organization and whether its effects on individual effectiveness are dysfunctional. The sources of intrapersonal conflict are misassignment and goal incongruence, inappropriate demand on capacity, organization structure, supervisory style, position, and personality. These sources may be altered to reduce or generate conflict. Intervention is needed when the effect of intrapersonal conflict on organizational participants becomes dysfunctional. Two major intervention techniques, such as role analysis and job design, are available for the management of intrapersonal conflict. The next chapter discusses interpersonal conflict and its management.

6

Interpersonal Conflict

Interpersonal conflict refers to the manifestation of incompatibility, inconsistency, or disagreement between two or more interacting individuals. As discussed in Chapters 2 and 4, there are several styles of handling interpersonal conflict: integrating, obliging, dominating, avoiding, and compromising. This chapter discusses the styles of handling conflict of an organizational member with his or her superior(s), subordinates, and peers. It does not deal with the amount of conflict between two organizational members. This is because most of the literature on interpersonal conflict in organizations deals with the styles of handling interpersonal conflict rather than the amount of such conflict. A number of studies on interpersonal conflict deal mainly with superior–subordinate conflict.

Prisoner's Dilemma

The Prisoner's Dilemma (PD) is a well-known strategy in game theory, and it is possible to describe interpersonal conflict through the language of this theory. It was originally developed at RAND Corporation in 1950 (cf. Poundstone, 1992). In the classical version of the game, PD is presented as follows.

Suppose two individuals, A and B, have been arrested on the suspicion that they committed a serious crime. Although they are guilty, there is insufficient evidence for conviction of the serious crime but enough for a lesser one. The accused are separated and not allowed to communicate with each other. The district attorney (DA) wants them to confess to the crime and makes the following offer to each. "If you confess your crime and your accomplice does not do the same, I will reduce your sentence to one year and use your testimony to make sure that your accomplice goes to prison for ten years. But if your accomplice confesses while you remain silent, he/she will get a reduced sentence of one year while you spend ten years in prison. If both of you confess I will reduce sentence of each for five years."

Should A and/or B confess or not confess to the DA the crimes they have committed? What are the outcomes of their decisions? There are four possibilities. Figure 6–1 shows the payoff matrix based on years in prison. It shows the dilemma for the prisoners:

1. If both A and B confess, they will be convicted of the serious offense, but their sentence will be reduced from ten to five years. As a result, they will be worse off than if they held out and did not confess.
2. If A does not confess, but B confesses, A will get a maximum sentence of ten years, and B will get the minimum sentence of one year. As a result, B is better off than A.
3. If A confesses, but B does not confess, A will get a reduced sentence of one year and B will get the maximum sentence of ten years. As a result, A is better off than B.
4. If both of them hold out and do not confess, they can be convicted only for the lesser offense and sentenced for one year. The prisoners can be better off if they never cooperate with the police and do not confess their crime.

    The payoff matrix helps us to understand some of the dilemmas that may be present in interpersonal conflicts. The PD game has applications in social and business situations (Dixit & Nalebuff, 2008).

Consider two firms, say Coca-Cola and Pepsi, selling similar products. Each must decide on a pricing strategy. They best exploit their joint market power when both charge a higher price; each makes a profit of ten million dollars per month. If one sets a competitive low price, it wins a lot of customers away from the rival. Suppose its profit rises to twelve million dollars, and that of the rival falls to seven million. If both set low prices, the profit of each is nine million dollars. Here, the low-price strategy is akin to the prisoner's confession, and the high-price akin to keeping silent.

Figure 6–1
Prisoner's Dilemma:
Payoff Matrix Based on Years in Prison for A and B

A

	Confess	Not Confess
B Confess	5, 5	10, 1
B Not Confess	1, 10	1, 1

Call the former cheating, and the latter cooperation. Then cheating is each firm's dominant strategy, but the result when both "cheat" is worse for each than that of both cooperating.

Obviously, the management of interpersonal conflict in organizations is much more complex than the payoff matrix. As was mentioned in Chapter 2, there are other more effective ways of developing the taxonomy of interpersonal conflict and its management.

A Model of Conflict

Over the years a number of models have been developed to illustrate the dynamics of different types of organizational conflict. Instead of developing a separate model for each type of organizational conflict, an integrated model has been developed that can be used to illustrate the dynamics of interpersonal, intragroup, and intergroup conflicts.

Various models present organizational conflict as a process. Goldman (1966) presented a cycle of conflict based on (1) an initiating event, (2) an influencing event, and (3) a concluding event. Pondy (1967) presented a model of organizational conflict that identified five stages of conflict episode: (1) latent conflict, (2) perceived conflict, (3) felt conflict, (4) manifest conflict, and (5) conflict aftermath. Walton and Dutton (1969) presented a model of interdepartmental conflict that focused on the (1) determinants of conflict, (2) attributes or manifestations of conflict, and (3) consequences of the relationship patterns of organizational effectiveness. Thomas's (1976) process model of conflict episode includes (1) frustration, (2) conceptualization, (3) behavior, and (4) outcome.

Figure 6.2 presents a theoretical model of organizational conflict, especially interpersonal, intragroup, and intergroup conflicts. This model is based on the voluminous literature on the subject, especially the ones reviewed earlier. The model can be used in formulating and testing hypotheses and thereby validating the model itself. This model will enable an organizational interventionist to manage conflict effectively.

Antecedent Conditions

The model begins with the antecedent conditions or sources of conflict, which can be classified as process and structural. Extensive treatments of these two sources of conflict are provided in this and the following two chapters. The model also shows that individual differences in personality, gender, power bases, educational level, and so on, may also affect conflict.

Perceptual and Behavioral Changes. Conflict may affect the perceptions and behavior of parties toward each other. If the conflict becomes intense, the parties move away from a congenial and trusting relationship and redirect their

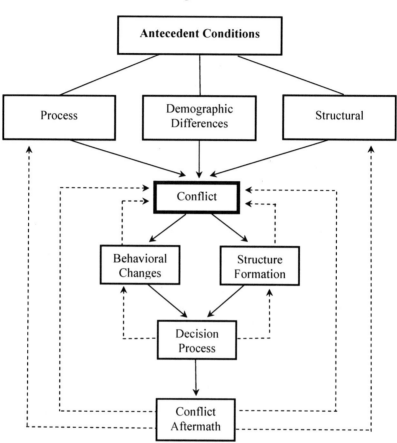

Figure 6–2
A Model of Organizational Conflict

energies toward the goal of winning. Since the immediate goal of each party is to win or control the situation, the interest in the solution of the problem(s) becomes less important. In other words, the parties may become less prepared to contribute to organizational goals effectively.

One possible consequence of win–lose conflict is the distortion in the perception of the parties. The perceptual distortion may become progressively greater, and each party may consider the other party an enemy, and they may describe each other with negative stereotypes. Thus, it will be more difficult for the parties to gather and evaluate information objectively to deal with their conflict constructively.

Structure Formation. As the conflict intensifies, the parties may restrict free communication and interaction. They may decide to communicate with each other only through writing; that is, the parties may formulate a structure of interaction that discourages free exchange of information. All contacts between the parties become formal, rigid, and carefully defined. In a bureaucratic organization, the parties may use existing rules and procedures to deal with the situation(s). In some situations, a party may come up with different interpretation of a rule so that a decision can be made in her or his favor.

Decision Process. When win–lose conflict is intensified, the parties may be unable to use problem-solving methods to make decisions to deal with their disagreements. Instead, they may establish a medium of negotiation that is generally bargaining. When two large powerful social entities are involved, the bargaining sessions may be extremely formal and lengthy. If conflict is intensified, "there is little room for compromise, and there is a dearth of imagination and creativity. Emphasis is placed on proving how tough and unyielding one is, so as to persuade the adversary that one cannot be pushed around" (Pruitt & Rubin, 1986, p. 93).

If a conflict is intense, the parties may attempt to make greater use of the win–lose method to deal with their conflict. If both parties are equally powerful, they may use a dominating style to handle their disagreements. If they fail to reach an agreement, they may change their style from dominating to compromising to resolve the conflict. If there are differences in power between the parties, the more powerful party may use a dominating style to impose a solution on the less powerful party. To deal with the situation, the less powerful party may be forced to use an avoiding style, that is, accept the decision given by the more powerful party without protest. If the conflicting parties fail to reach a decision, a mediator or arbitrator may be selected by the parties to break the deadlock.

In the case of conflict within a group, a decision is often made by majority vote or by the group leader. This process of decision making may lead to the formation of subgroups within a group, which may lead to further intensification of conflict.

In the case of superior–subordinate conflict, the decision is often made by the superior and communicated to the subordinate. In many cases the organizations allow subordinates to go to a higher-level executive to discuss their grievances. Many organizations allow the lower-level employees to take their problems to grievance committees.

In the case of conflict between two colleagues at the same organizational level, the superior of the two parties is often called upon to make a decision to resolve the conflict. The same decision process may be used when two departments or units fail to resolve their conflicts in a reasonable manner.

Conflict Aftermath. Conflict management process generally leaves a legacy which will influence attitudes of the parties toward each other and their future relationships. If bargaining and compromising styles are exclusively utilized as a method of conflict resolution, both parties may perceive themselves as partly losers after the cessation of conflict. If one party is clearly a loser after a resolution, this party may have antagonistic feelings toward the other party, which may affect the generation and resolution of another conflict. The resolution of a win–lose conflict not only may affect the behavior and attitudes of the parties for each other but also may affect organization structure. For example, the conflicting parties or their superior may formulate more rules and procedures or clarify the existing ones to deal with future conflict between the parties.

If the parties use an integrating or problem-solving style to deal with their conflict, this may reduce the psychological distance between them. They may be more prepared to deal with their disagreements in a more constructive manner that involves exchange of information and open communication. A problem-solving approach for the management of conflict may lead to greater commitment to the agreement reached between parties.

Consequences of Interpersonal Conflict

One would expect the outcomes of interpersonal conflict that fully satisfy the outcomes of both parties to be functional for an organization. Previous studies generally indicate that a problem-solving or integrating style by the members of an organization leads to greater satisfaction and effectiveness of the organizational members.

Individual and Group Performance

A study by Aram, Morgan, and Esbeck (1971) suggested that team collaboration was positively related to satisfaction of individuals' needs, but not to job performance. However, there are other studies which contradict the finding of this study relating to job performance. A recent study that tested a structural equations model of power bases, conflict-management styles, and job performance shows, among others, that problem solving style (i.e., using more integrating and less avoiding styles), not bargaining style (i.e., using more dominating and less obliging styles), positively influence job performance at the group level (Rahim, Antonioni, & Psenicka, 2001). Vigil-King's (2000; see also Behfar, Peterson, Mannix, & Trochim, 2008) study shows that teams that use more integrative conflict-management styles are likely to have higher performance than teams using less integrative styles. A study by Rahim (2010) shows that an effective strategy is associated with greater use of the integrating and lower use of avoiding styles *plus* greater use of the obliging and lower use of the dominating styles. An ineffective strategy is associated with greater use of the avoiding and lower use of the integrating styles *plus* greater use of the dominating style and lower use of the obliging style.

Lawrence and Lorsch (1967a) indicated that a confrontation (integrating) style was used to deal with intergroup conflict to a significantly greater degree in higher- than lower-performing organizations. Likert and Likert (1976) strongly argued, and provided some evidence to suggest, that an organization that encourages participation and problem-solving behaviors attains higher level of effectiveness.

Individual and Organizational Outcomes

Misquita (1998) reported that when subordinates perceived that their supervisors were handling conflict with an integrating style, their organizational commitment increased. If the subordinates perceived that their supervisors were using avoiding and dominating styles, their organizational commitment reduced. Weider-Hatfield and Hatfield's (1995) two studies explored the relationship between the five styles of handling conflict and their perceptions of organizational effectiveness, using a human resource model as a guide. Results showed that subordinates' use of the integrating style was positively associated with six individual and organizational outcomes (job satisfaction, global equity, system outcomes, job outcomes, performance outcomes, and interpersonal outcomes). Also, the compromising style was positively associated with interpersonal outcomes, the dominating style was negatively associated with job satisfaction, and dominating and avoiding styles were negatively associated with interpersonal outcomes.

Recent studies on the integrating style of handling conflict show consistent results. Use of this style results in high joint benefit for the parties, better decisions, and greater satisfaction of the partner (Tutzauer & Roloff, 1988; Wall & Galanes, 1986). Similar conclusions were reached in studies by Korbanik, Baril, and Watson (1993) and Johnson (1989). Burke (1969) suggested that, in general, a confrontation (integrating) style was related to effective management of conflict and that forcing (dominating) and withdrawing (avoiding) were related to the ineffective management of conflict.

The contingency theory of conflict management discussed in Chapter 4 suggests that all five styles of handling conflict are useful depending on situations. The situations where each style is appropriate or inappropriate were presented in Table 4–1. This approach to conflict management is consistent with the contingency or situational theories of leadership discussed in Chapter 4. According to these theories, effective leaders select and use the styles of handling conflict depending on the situation so that their goals are effectively attained. For example, an integrating or participative style is appropriate for a leader when he or she is faced with a complex problem that requires input and commitment from subordinates for effective formulation and implementation of solutions. A dominating style may be appropriate when the task or problem is simple or routine.

Negotiation

Fisher and Ury (1981), in their excellent book, *Getting to YES: Negotiating Agreement Without Giving In*, make a very good point that everybody is a negotiator. Whenever we have a conflict with another party, we are required to negotiate. Negotiation skills are essential for managing interpersonal, intragroup, and intergroup conflicts. Since managers spend more than one-fifth of their time dealing with conflict, they need to learn how to negotiate effectively. Sometimes they are required to negotiate with their superiors, subordinates, and peers, and, at other times, they are required to mediate conflict between their subordinates.

Fisher and Ury (1981; see also Fisher, Ury, & Patton, 1991; Thompson & Leonardelli, 2004) have forcefully argued that a method called *principled negotiation* or *negotiation on merits* can be used to manage any conflict. Principled negotiation requires problem solving and the use of an integrating style of handling conflict. Fisher and Ury's four principled negotiation components involve separating the people from the problem; focusing on interests, not positions; inventing options for mutual gains; and insisting on using objective criteria. A brief exposition of these components is as follows.

Separate the People from the Problem

If the parties can concentrate on substantive conflict instead of on affective conflict, they may be able to engage in the problem-solving process. Unfortunately, "emotions typically become entangled with the objective merits of the problem....Hence, before working on the substantive problem, the 'people problem' should be disentangled from it and dealt with separately" (Fisher & Ury, 1981, p. 11). Separating the people from the problem does not mean ignoring or suppressing these emotions, but emotional issues should be dealt with separately before the parties will be ready to concentrate on the substantive issues. Wilmot and Hocker (2007) suggest that for parties in interpersonal conflicts, "long-term relational or content goals can become superordinate goals that reduce conflict over short-term goals, but only if you separate 'the people' from 'the problem'" (p. 258).

The conflicting parties should come to work with, and not against, each other to deal with their common problem. They should remain focused on solving the problem(s) so that they can reach an agreement that is mutually acceptable. Focusing on the problem instead of on the other party helps to maintain their relationship.

Focus on Interests, Not Positions

This component is designed to overcome the problem of focusing on stated positions of the parties because the goal of conflict management is to satisfy their needs, desires, concerns, and fears. Fisher, Ury, and Patton (1991) cite the following story to illustrate the point.

> Consider the story of two men quarrelling in the library. One wants the window open and the other wants it fully closed. They bicker back and forth as to how much to leave it open: a crack, halfway, three quarters of the way. No solution satisfies them. Enter the librarian. She asks one why he wants the window open: "To get some fresh air." She asks the other why he wants it closed: "To avoid a draft." After thinking a minute, she opens wide a window in the next room, bringing in fresh air without a draft. (p. 40)

The librarian, instead of focusing on the stated positions of the parties, mediated the dispute by first finding out the underlying reasons behind them.

A position is what a party wants, that is, a specific solution to an interest. If a bargainer starts with a position, he or she may overlook many creative alternative solutions for satisfying the interests. Being locked into positions is contrary to an open-ended problem solving approach which is necessary to identify the multiple interests of each party. If the parties can focus on common interests that may involve redefining negotiating goals and the process may lead to maximizing what is attained by both sides.

Fisher and Ury (1981) argue, "When you do look behind opposed positions for the motivating interests, you can often find an alternative position which meets not only your interests but theirs as well" (p. 43). This is especially true in organizations where members are very often concerned about productivity, efficiency, cost, and so on.

Invent Options for Mutual Gain

Bargainers rarely see the need for formulating options or alternative solutions so that parties may be benefited. As was mentioned before, during period of intense conflict, the parties may have difficulty in formulating creative solutions to problems that are acceptable to both parties. "Often negotiators become wedded to their position, believing only their solution will work. This can stifle creativity. Instead, the negotiator should brainstorm multiple solutions, with interests of the opposing party in mind" (Lens, 2004, p. 510). It would help if some sessions are arranged where the parties could engage in brainstorming designed to generate as many ideas as possible to solve the problem at hand. Fisher and Ury suggest that the negotiators need to overcome the following four obstacles to generating new ideas:

1. Fixed-pie Assumption. Negotiation is not a zero-sum game, i.e., negotiators should not assume an either/or situation.

2. Premature Judgments. Negotiators should not commit prematurely to a specific course of action as it will be difficult for them to change course that will lead to better outcomes.

3. Searching for a Single Answer. Negotiators should engage in a decision-making process in which they can select from a large number of options.

4. A Assumes that B is Responsible for Satisfying A's Interests. Each negotiator should consider how potential outcomes can serve the other party's interests. This should enable the negotiators to invent options for mutual gains.

Insist on Using Objective Criteria

To manage conflict effectively, a negotiator should insist that result be based on some objective criteria. Brett (1984) presented the classic example of "the tale of the mother with two children and with one piece of cake. Because both children are clamoring for the entire piece, the wise mother tells one child he can cut the cake into two pieces and tells the other child she can make the first choice" (p. 673). Examples of objective criteria include market value, attainment of specific goals, scientific judgment, ethical standards, and so on.

Once the negotiators start searching for objective standards for managing conflict effectively, the principal emphasis of the negotiation changes from negotiations over positions to alternative standards. "Once a standard is agreed on, there need be no further negotiations over the issue because the settlement terms are implicit in the objective standards" (Brett, 1984, p. 674).

Learning to communicate effectively with the other party is very important in principled negotiation. Wilmot and Hocker (2007) suggest that the following statements may be used if one wants to use the integrating style of handling interpersonal conflict:

Collaborative Principle	Sample Statement
People	This is a problem you and I haven't had to face before. I am sure we can work it out.
Interests	What is it that you are most hoping for? or Let's figure out where we agree, and that will give us a base to work from.
Options	I'd like to postpone making a decision about filing a grievance until our next meeting. Today I want to explore all the options that are available to us in addition to filing a grievance. Is that all right with you?
Criteria	I can't be satisfied with getting my way if you're disgruntled. Let's get an example of market value from an objective source. (p. 262)

As discussed before, principled negotiation involves the use of the integrating style of handling conflict. The integrating style is appropriate to use in situations involving complex issues. Organizational members should be trained to use principled negotiation to handle these situations effectively. This type of negotiation is not effective for dealing with trivial or simple issues.

The BATNA Principle

Of all the principles discussed in *Getting to YES,* probably negotiation scholars remember BATNA concept most. For a negotiator, BATNA, which is an acronym for "Best Alternative To a Negotiated Agreement," and it is the alternative that negotiators can turn to if current negotiations fail and an agreement cannot be reached.

Fisher and Ury (1981) suggest the following process in determining one's BATNA:

- Develop a list of actions you might take if no agreement is reached,
- Improve some of the more promising ideas and convert them into practical options; and
- Select, tentatively, the one option that seems best (p. 108).

BATNAs can be determined for any conflict situation—simple or complex—involving negotiation. While you are determining your own BATNA, you should consider the alternatives available to the other party.

Hard versus Soft Negotiating Style

Principled negotiation is different from the positional or "hard" bargaining where the negotiator wants to win at all costs. Also, principled negotiation does not use "soft" bargaining techniques that may result in undue concessions to the opponent. Table 6–1 portrays styles of negotiation involved in hard, soft, and principled negotiation.

Managing Interpersonal Conflict

The management of interpersonal conflict involves changes in the attitudes, behavior, and organization structure, so that the organizational members can work with each other effectively for attaining their individual and/or joint goals. The management of interpersonal conflict essentially involves teaching organizational members the styles of handling interpersonal conflict to deal with different situations effectively, and setting up appropriate mechanisms so that unresolved issues are dealt with properly. The management of interpersonal conflict, which involves diagnosis and intervention, is discussed as follows.

Table 6.1

Comparing Hard, Soft, and Principled Negotiation Styles

Hard	Soft	Principled
Parties are adversaries.	Parties are friends.	Parties are problem-solvers.
The goal is winning.	The goal is agreement even if it leads to losses.	The goal is to reach an effective solution
There is only one solution to the problem you like.	Search for a solution the other party is likely to accept.	There are alternative solutions to the problem.
Personal attacks and threats are appropriate.	Friendly gestures and concessions are appropriate.	The focus is on interests, not positions.
Distrust is assumed.	Trust is assumed.	Proceed independent of trust.
Misleading and distorting positions are appropriate.	Positions are changed easily to satisfy the other party.	Positions are based on fair and objective standards.
Compromise is never acceptable.	Concessions are made to encourage good relationship and to avoid conflict.	Compromise is appropriate when based on principle, not pressure.

Source: Adapted from Fisher, R., Ury, W., & Patton, B. (1991). *Getting to yes: Negotiating agreement without giving in.* New York: Penguin Books, pp. 9, 13.

Diagnosis

The diagnosis of interpersonal conflict can be performed by such methods as self-reports, observation, and interviews. The Rahim Organizational Conflict Inventory–II (ROCI–II) may be used to measure how an organizational member handles interpersonal conflict with superior(s) (Form A), subordinates (Form B), and peers (Form C).

Measurement. A comprehensive diagnosis of interpersonal conflict involves the measurement of the following:

1. The styles of handling interpersonal conflict used by the organizational members to deal with different situations;
2. Factors that affect the styles of handling conflict; and
3. Effectiveness of the individual members of an organization.

Analysis. An analysis of the preceding diagnostic data should provide the following information:

1. The styles of handling interpersonal conflict utilized by the members of various units, departments, or divisions and whether they deviated from the national norms significantly;

2. Whether organizational members are using appropriate behavioral styles to deal with different situations effectively; and

3. Relationships of the styles to situations and individual effectiveness.

National Norms. As reported in Chapter 2, data for the national norms of the styles of handling interpersonal conflict with superior(s), subordinates, and peers were collected on the ROCI–II (Forms A, B, and C) from 1,219 executives. Tables 6–2 and 6–3 were prepared on the basis of these data. Table 6–2 shows the national percentile norms of managers. The percentile score of an individual shows his or her relative position on one of the five subscales of the styles of handling interpersonal conflict with superior(s), subordinates, and peers compared with other managers in the normative group. For example, a manager scoring at the 70th percentile on a scale is as high or higher than 70 percent of the normative group. His or her score is exceeded by only 30 percent of the normative group.

Table 6–3 shows the sample size (N), means (M) (reference group norms), standard deviations (SD) of the five styles of handling interpersonal conflict, classified by referent role, organizational level, functional area, and education, and the results of one-way analyses of variance (F-ratio).

The results of the analyses of variance show that there were significant differences in each style of handling conflict with superior(s), subordinates, and peers. This suggests that the styles of handling conflict of an organizational member are, to some extent, determined by the hierarchical relationship that exists between the parties involved in conflict. There were also differences in obliging and avoiding styles among the executives across organizational levels, in the obliging style across the functional area, and in the dominating and avoiding styles across the educational categories.

The normative data are useful in determining whether the members of an organization are making too little, too much, or moderate use of each style of handling interpersonal conflict. These data, of course, cannot indicate whether the styles are used to deal with different situations effectively.

As discussed in the previous chapter, additional percentile and reference group norms computed from the collegiate samples are presented in Tables 6–4 and 6–5, respectively.

One-way analyses of variance show that the five styles of handling conflict differed among the three-referent roles; integrating, obliging, and compromising styles differed among the five organizational levels; dominating and compromising styles differed between undergraduate and graduate students; and dominating and compromising styles differed between males and females. These normative data are useful for undergraduate and graduate courses on organizational behavior, organizational psychology, and conflict management where students can compare their individual conflict management styles with corresponding percentile and reference group norms. The students generally enjoy this sort of feedback.

Table 6–2

National Managerial Percentile Norms of the Five Styles of Handling Conflict with Supervisor, Subordinates, and Peers

Percentiles

Mean Scores	Form A (n = 452)					Form B (n = 363)					Form C (n = 404)					Mean Scores
	IN	OB	DO	AV	CO	IN	OB	DO	AV	CO	IN	OB	DO	AV	CO	
5.00	99		99			99		99			99					5.00
4.85	91	99	98	99	99	90	99	98	99	99	89	99	99		99	4.85
4.70	86	97	97	98	98	82	98	97	98	98	83	98	98	99	98	4.70
4.55	80	95	96	95	97	72	97	95	97	97	76	97	97	98	97	4.55
4.40	68	90	95	95	96	63	95	92	94	96	64	96	94	97	96	4.40
4.25	55	83	93	92	95	49	90	87	91	86	55	93	90	96	94	4.25
4.10	42	72	88	89	91	35	83	77	89	76	39	87	86	95	90	4.10
3.95	21	60	82	86	78	15	77	74	88	69	12	82	79	91	73	3.95
3.80	13	53	74	82	63	7	65	71	80	62	7	76	66	90	56	3.80
3.65	7	45	60	78	57	4	48	57	76	42	4	63	62	88	49	3.65
3.50	5	35	56	74	51	3	37	47	68	39	2	47	58	83	42	3.50
3.35	4	23	51	66	35	1	23	42	58	35	1	38	45	76	29	3.35
3.20	3	14	38	62	31		17	36	52	31		23	36	73	26	3.20
3.05	3	8	29	55	26		11	29	39	26		17	30	63	22	3.05
2.90	2	6	25	49	21		6	18	34	20		10	24	56	18	2.90
2.75	1	4	20	39	15		4	15	23	15		7	17	44	14	2.75
2.60		3	16	31	12		3	11	20	10		3	10	37	10	2.60
2.45		2	8	21	9		2	8	16	9		2	8	26	8	2.45
2.30		1	7	19	6		1	5	9	7		1	6	23	6	2.30
2.15			5	16	5			4	1	2			2	19	5	2.15
2.00			3	10	4			2					1	10	4	2.00
1.85			1	6	1			1						7	1	1.85
1.70				3										4		1.70
1.55				2										3		1.55
1.40				1										2		1.40
1.25														1		1.25
1.10																1.10
1.00																1.00

Note: N = 1,219. Forms A, B, and C measure how an organizational member handles her or his conflict with supervisor, subordinates, and peers. Each manager completed one of the three forms. IN = Integrating, OB = Obliging, DO = Dominating, AV = Avoiding, and CO = Compromising

Table 6–3
National Managerial Reference Group Norms of the Styles of Handling Interpersonal Conflict with Supervisor, Subordinates, and Peers

Variable	N	Integrating M	SD	F	Obliging M	SD	F	Dominating M	SD	F	Avoiding M	SD	F	Compromising M	SD	F
Referent Role				4.66*			77.47*			24.19*			5.63*			17.44*
Superior (Form A)	452	4.18	.43		3.60	.53		3.27	.68		2.88	.78		3.51	.64	
Subordinates (Form B)	363	4.26	.39		3.21	.49		2.94	.67		2.78	.68		3.31	.69	
Peers (Form C)	404	4.24	.38		3.24	.51		3.16	.66		2.72	.71		3.59	.66	
Organizational Level				.46			8.29*			1.69			3.63*			1.32
Top	176	4.24	.49		3.22	.59		3.20	.70		2.67	.75		3.43	.68	
Middle	501	4.23	.49		3.36	.53		3.14	.67		2.79	.74		3.46	.68	
Lower	515	4.21	.38		3.41	.53		3.10	.69		2.84	.71		3.51	.65	
Functional Area				1.81			2.22*			1.36			1.44			0.75
Production	253	4.16	.39		3.37	.54		3.08	.68		2.84	.73		3.46	.66	
Marketing	32	4.23	.38		3.39	.53		3.26	.59		2.69	.67		3.59	.63	
Finance & Accounting	28	4.24	.44		3.34	.55		2.94	.68		2.79	.79		3.32	.69	
Personnel	35	4.30	.36		3.48	.47		3.23	.57		2.67	.64		3.59	.63	
General Management	287	4.27	.45		3.27	.57		3.17	.70		2.70	.76		3.50	.67	
R & D	200	4.22	.39		3.45	.55		3.16	.66		2.81	.72		3.52	.68	
Engineering	181	4.24	.39		3.38	.51		3.06	.63		2.84	.69		3.44	.63	
Other	197	4.22	.38		3.37	.54		3.17	.75		2.87	.76		3.45	.72	
Education				.93			1.36			5.75*			5.41*			0.57
High school	145	4.19	.36		3.37	.49		3.01	.72		2.97	.67		3.50	.65	
2-year college	233	4.21	.42		3.32	.53		3.03	.64		2.91	.76		3.44	.70	
Bachelor's degree	572	4.25	.39		3.40	.54		3.15	.68		2.76	.71		3.50	.66	
Master's degree	202	4.21	.44		3.32	.56		3.30	.65		2.67	.76		3.44	.69	
Other	64	4.20	.50		3.38	.67		3.14	.74		2.77	.80		3.45	.70	
Total sample	1,219	4.22	.40		3.36	.55		3.13	.68		2.80	.73		3.48	.67	

$* p < .05.$

Table 6–4
Collegiate Percentile Norms of the Styles of Handling Conflict with Supervisor, Subordinates, and Peers

Mean Scores	Form A (n = 709)					Percentiles Form B (n = 298)					Form C (n = 441)					Mean Scores
	IN	OB	DO	AV	CO	IN	OB	DO	AV	CO	IN	OB	DO	AV	CO	
5.00	99					99					99					5.00
4.85	95	99				96					95					4.85
4.70	91	98		99		94			99		92			99		4.70
4.55	87	96	99	98	99	90	99	99	98	99	88	99	99	98	99	4.55
4.40	81	92	98	97	98	84	98	98	95	98	81	98	98	97	98	4.40
4.25	74	87	97	95	97	76	96	96	91	97	74	96	97	96	96	4.25
4.10	64	79	94	91	96	66	92	93	84	92	60	87	96	95	94	4.10
3.95	36	59	91	81	91	29	81	88	77	73	20	76	88	91	88	3.95
3.80	27	44	82	75	78	19	74	75	74	53	13	63	83	90	84	3.80
3.65	19	38	75	71	62	12	67	71	60	45	7	49	77	88	79	3.65
3.50	15	31	64	66	47	8	54	48	54	37	5	35	67	83	74	3.50
3.35	11	22	59	43	42	5	36	44	44	23	3	23	57	76	65	3.35
3.20	8	14	53	36	28	3	22	21	37	18	2	17	51	73	56	3.20
3.05	6	9	40	23	23	2	16	16	28	13	1	10	46	63	48	3.05
2.90	5	6	30	12	18	1	8	13	22	10		7	33	56	40	2.90
2.75	3	3	25	11	14		3	5	15	6		4	26	44	32	2.75
2.60	2	2	19	9	9		2	3	13	5		3	19	37	25	2.60
2.45	1	1	14	3	6		1	1	10	3		2	14	26	21	2.45
2.30			9	2	4				4	1		1	8	23	13	2.30
2.15			7	1	2				2				6	19	11	2.15
2.00			5		1				1				4	10	9	2.00
1.85			2										2	7	3	1.85
1.70			1										1	4	1	1.70
1.55														3		1.55
1.40														2		1.40
1.25														1		1.25
1.10																1.10
1.00																1.00

Note: N = 712. Forms A, B, and C measure how an organizational member handles his or her conflict with supervisor, subordinates, and peers. Some of the students completed all the three forms; others, who did not have any subordinates, completed Form A and/or C. IN = Integrating, OB = Obliging, DO = Dominating, AV = Avoiding, and CO = Compromising

Table 6–5
Collegiate Reference Group Norms of the Styles of Handling Interpersonal Conflict with Supervisor, Subordinates, and Peers

Variables	N	Integrating			Obliging			Dominating			Avoiding			Compromising		
		M	SD	F	M	SD	F	M	SD	F	M	SD	F	M	SD	F
Referent role				10.06*			25.60*			9.45*			6.82*			22.83*
Superior (Form A)	709	3.96	.51		3.76	.50		3.25	.67		3.18	.74		3.62	.54	
Subordinates (Form B)	298	4.02	.39		3.38	.43		3.45	.65		3.01	.67		3.68	.49	
Peers (Form C)	441	4.09	.36		3.38	.51		3.34	.69		3.09	.69		3.82	.44	
Organizational level				2.79*			4.24*			1.46			1.14			3.60*
Top	29	3.95	.40		3.31	.51		3.56	.56		2.86	.69		3.54	.62	
Middle	204	3.99	.50		3.54	.57		3.35	.61		3.14	.65		3.64	.53	
Lower	291	4.09	.46		3.60	.46		3.35	.65		3.15	.70		3.76	.52	
Non-management	596	3.98	.44		3.56	.52		3.29	.73		3.15	.73		3.72	.47	
Worker	144	4.02	.53		3.70	.60		3.28	.69		3.14	.79		3.61	.54	
Education				.06			1.87			5.20*			.56			15.27*
Undergraduate	1,150	4.01	.53		3.60	.56		3.24	.65		3.09	.76		3.59	.59	
MBA	301	4.01	.43		3.56	.51		3.34	.68		3.13	.70		3.72	.48	
Gender				.00			.27			7.38*			2.97			16.39*
Male	864	4.01	.45		3.57	.52		3.36	.66		3.09	.73		3.65	.53	
Female	564	4.01	.45		3.56	.53		3.26	.70		3.16	.70		3.76	.46	
Total sample	1,451	4.02	.40		3.50	.55		3.35	.68		3.09	.73		3.71	.67	

Note: The difference between the number of respondents ($N = 712$) and the total sample ($N = 1,451$) means that 712 students completed 1,451 forms. One-way analyses of variance show that there were significant differences in all the five conflict styles for referent role; integrating, obliging, and compromising styles for organizational level; dominating and compromising styles for education; and dominating and compromising styles for gender.

Sources. A number of studies, which were cited in later chapters, have investigated the sources of intraorganizational conflict in general. However, the factors that affect the styles of handling conflict have not been adequately investigated. Several factors, such as personality, bases of power, organizational climate, and referent role affect not only interpersonal but also intragroup and intergroup conflicts. Instead of discussing their effects on different types of conflict in separate chapters, their effects have been presented in an integrated fashion in this chapter.

Personality. After a thorough review of the experimental studies on personality and conflict, Terhune (1970) concluded that "personality effects do seem influential and highly important in cooperation–conflict behavior . . . certainly the researcher should not be discouraged if personality effects do not just 'pop out' on first analysis, especially in complex situations" (p. 230).

Kilmann and Thomas's (1975) field study with a collegiate sample explored the relations between the five modes (styles) of handling interpersonal conflict and the four dimensions of Jungian (Jung, 1923) personality: sensing–intuition, thinking–feeling, introvert–extravert, and judging–perceiving, as measured by the Myers-Briggs Type Indicator (Myers, 1962). The results showed that the extroverts are more likely to strive for collaborative or integrative style of handling conflict than introverts. Chanin and Schneer's (1984) experimental study found that whereas the feelers handle conflict through compromising and obliging styles, the thinkers handle conflict through dominating and integrating styles. Another laboratory experiment by Schneer and Chanin (1987) reported that the individuals with high need for dominance and low need for affiliation choose to use dominating style, whereas individuals with low need for dominance and high need for affiliation choose to use the obliging style. Jones and White's (1985) laboratory experiment found a positive correlation between need for affiliation and preference for compromising style and a negative correlation between need for affiliation and preference for integrating style. The study also reported a positive correlation between deference (need to accept someone else's leadership) and dominating style and a negative correlation between aggression and compromising style.

Other field studies show that personality dimensions such as sensation–seeking (i.e., thrill and adventure seeking, experience seeking, disinhibition, and boredom susceptibility) (Pilkington, Richardson, & Utley, 1988), self-monitoring (i.e., social sensitivity), and Type A behavior (Baron, 1989) may be associated with the styles of handling interpersonal conflict. For example, sensation seeking was associated with the styles of handling conflict of females only; high sensation seekers used more dominating and less obliging styles than the low sensation seekers. Among non-managers, Type Bs were more likely to handle conflict with peers through compromising style than Type As or employees categorized as intermediate. These differences were not found among managers. High and moderate self-monitors reported a greater likelihood of handling conflict with others through integrating and compromising styles than low self-monitors.

The studies previously reviewed and earlier field studies by Bell and Blakeney (1977), and Jones and Melcher (1982) found low correlations between personality and the styles of handling interpersonal conflict. Several negotiation scholars reported weak relationships between personality and negotiation outcomes (Neale & Northcraft, 1991, Pruitt & Carnevale, 1993). After reviewing negotiation literature, Wall and Blum (1991) reached a similar conclusion regarding negotiator personality and negotiation outcomes:

> Currently, we find a mixed bag of main, interactive, and insignificant effects, but we detect no consistent stream of research supporting a significant impact for any trait. This absence is quite sobering, given that it is detected in laboratory studies. If individual differences fail to produce an effect under very controlled conditions or are washed out by other factors studied in the lab, it is quite doubtful they would yield effects in real bargaining. (pp. 127–128)

These low correlations may be partly attributed to the failure of the researchers to control the hierarchical relationship between the parties involved in conflict and the situations or issues involved in conflict. Jones and White (1985) suggest that the low correlations between personality and conflict styles are understandable. This is because "[personality] and resulting behaviors interact in complex ways that traditionally have resisted both strong and simple associations. It is likely that individuals will have varying predispositions for using the different modes because of personality differences" (p. 163).

Wall and Blum's (1991) conclusions may be premature. Antonioni (1998; see also Moberg, 1998) argues that it would be inappropriate to assume that individual differences are not important for understanding how individuals handle interpersonal conflict. His study used a collegiate and a managerial sample to explore the relationships of the Big Five Personality factors as measured by NEO–FFI (Costa & McCrae, 1985) and the five styles of handling conflict with peers as measured by the ROCI–II. Results suggest that extroversion, conscientiousness, openness, and agreeableness are positively associated with integrating style. Extroversion was positively associated with dominating style, while agreeableness and neuroticism were negatively associated with dominating style. Extraversion, openness, and conscientiousness were negatively associated with avoiding, while agreeableness and neuroticism were positively associated with avoiding.

This study shows that individual differences should not be neglected in conflict management research. Future studies should particularly investigate "whether personality factors limit an individual's choice of conflict management style, and thus limit positive outcomes as well" (Antonioni, 1998, p. 353).

Two studies by Hammock and Richardson (1991) suggest that self-reported responses indicating dominating style is positively associated with self-reported aggression and behavioral aggression. Results also showed that integrating and obliging styles are negatively associated with aggressive behavior. The two studies by Hammock and Richardson show consistent results predicted by theory.

Although the results of a number of studies on the relationships of personality and conflict styles are inconsistent, there is great deal of interest in this type of research. Recent studies that investigated this relationship are by Cole (1996), Frederickson (1998), Roberts (1997), Sorenson and Hawkins (1995), Trubisky, Ting-Toomey, and Lin (1991) and others. It is not possible to review the findings of these and other studies due to limitation of space.

Bases of Power. A number of studies have been conducted to investigate the effects of French and Raven's (1959) bases of power (coercive, reward, expert, legitimate, and referent) of the superior on the work performance and satisfaction of the subordinates (see Rahim, 2009, for a review of these studies). However, the organization theorists neglected to examine the effects of a superior's bases of power on interpersonal conflict and the selection and use of the styles of handling such conflict by subordinates.

Raven and Kruglanski (1970) reviewed numerous studies to examine the relationship between social power and social conflict and concluded that the "power analysis provided a richer basis for the analysis of dyadic conflict" (p. 105). They also concluded that the analysis becomes complex when it is applied to other types of conflicts. Stern and Gorman (1969) suggested, in connection with intrachannel conflict, that "the exercise of power is a major conflict response as well as a cause of conflict" (p. 161). In a study of automobile manufacturers and their dealer network, Lusch (1976b) indicated that coercive source of power increased, and noncoercive sources of power (reward, expert, legitimate, and referent) decreased, manufacturer–dealer conflict.

Jamieson and Thomas (1974) examined students' perception of their teachers' bases of power and their own modes of handling conflict with teachers. The students (at the high school and undergraduate levels) reported somewhat less accommodating (obliging) and somewhat more competing (dominating) styles with teachers who used more coercive power. Coercive power was positively correlated with the competing (dominating) style at the graduate level. Referent power induced accommodating (obliging) style at the high school and undergraduate level and collaborating (integrating) style at the graduate level. A recent study by Rahim, Antonioni, and Psenicka (2001) tested a structural equations model of the five French and Raven bases of supervisory power (coercive, reward, legitimate, expert, and referent), styles of handling conflict with supervisor (problem solving and bargaining), and job performance. Employees ($N = 1,116$) completed questionnaires on power and conflict styles, and their job performance was evaluated by 398 of their respective supervisors. The data were aggregated for the subordinates associated with a given manager ($N = 398$) to make sure that independent observation assumption is not violated.

The LISREL analysis of data indicates that legitimate power influenced refer-ent power positively and coercive power negatively, and reward and legitimate powers positively influenced expert power, which in turn, positively influenced referent power. Referent power, in turn, positively influenced problem solving (i.e., using more integrating and less avoiding styles) and negatively influenced bargaining (i.e., using more dominating and less obliging styles) conflict-man-agement styles, and finally, problem-solving style, but not bargaining style, positively influenced job performance.

Organizational Culture. Likert and Likert (1976) persuasively argued and provided some evidence that a positive organizational climate, such as System IV, can provide for a more functional management of conflict than Systems I, II, or III. Likert (1967) classified his Systems I, II, III, and IV as exploitive–authori-tative, benevolent–authoritative, consultative, and participative organizations, respectively. It is expected that a more positive climate will enable the members to confront their disagreements and disputes in a constructive fashion so that problems are identified and corrective measures taken. Therefore, dysfunctional conflicts experienced by the organization members are reduced.

In recent years, the concept of organizational culture has received increas-ing attention from management scholars and practitioners. Schein (1990) has rightly indicated that "climate is only a surface manifestation of culture and thus research on climate has not enabled us to delve into the deeper causal aspects of how organizations function" (p. 109). An organization's culture refers to the shared assumptions, attitudes, values, beliefs, expectations, and norms. Schein has provided case examples of organizational culture in two corporations. These show the effect of culture on conflict management, which, in turn, influences the long-term growth and adaptability of the organizations. In Company A it was "assumed that ideas will not be implemented unless everyone involved in implementation has been convinced through debate of the validity of the idea. . . . By way of contrast [in Company B] one finds at the artifact level a high degree of formality . . . a total absence of cross-divisional or cross-functional meetings and an almost total lack of lateral communication. Memos left in one department by an outside consultant with instructions to be given to others are almost never delivered" (Schein, 1990, pp. 113–114). These case examples show the relationship between culture and conflict management. Whereas in Company A employees are encouraged to manage conflict with debate and discussion with superiors, subordinates, and peers, in Company B conflict is resolved through suppression or avoidance. As a result, Company B "finds itself in a world that requires rapid decision making, yet its systems and procedures are slow and cumbersome. To be more innovative in marketing it needs to share ideas more, yet it undermines lateral communication" (Schein, 1990, p. 115).

In a field study in five countries, Ting-Toomey et al. (1991; see also Trubisky et al., 1991) provided evidence that national culture influences the styles of handling interpersonal conflict. Their study with the ROCI–II shows that the U.S. respondents indicated greater use of the dominating style than Japanese and Korean respondents. The Chinese and Taiwanese respondents reported greater use of obliging and avoiding styles than the U.S. respondents. Another study reported similar differences in conflict-handling styles of the U.S. and Chinese managers (Morris et al., 1998).

Referent Role. Organizations plant the seeds of conflict by allowing different statuses to different people. In superior–subordinate communication, subordinates frequently say what is acceptable rather than what they know is true. This is especially true when superiors are authoritarian and regard their subordinates as inferiors. Therefore, it is natural to assume that an individual would probably make more of an effort to use an obliging style with a superior than with a subordinate or peer.

Since subordinates are likely to withdraw from a conflict situation (Kahn, Wolfe, Quinn, Snoak, & Rosenthal, 1964), it would be expected that individuals would be more likely to use the avoiding style with superiors than with peers and more with peers than subordinates. A study by Phillips and Cheston (1979) reported that a forcing (dominating) approach is the most common in handling differences with subordinates than with peers and much less with superiors. The compromising approach is the most common to those conflict situations in which both parties have equal power (peers). Therefore, it would be expected that the compromising style would be more likely to be used as a means of conflict management in dealing with peers than in dealing with either superiors or subordinates.

A study by Rahim (1985) with the ROCI–II shows how managers handle their interpersonal conflict with superiors, subordinates, and peers. The executives are primarily obliging in dealing with their superiors, integrating with subordinates, and compromising with peers. To a lesser extent, executives are compromising and dominating with superiors and avoiding with subordinates. Probably these are the backup styles used by managers when their primary styles fail to resolve a conflict with superiors and subordinates. For example, if a manager fails to resolve a conflict with his or her superior by using an obliging style, he or she may be inclined to use a compromising or even dominating style to deal with the conflict. Several studies in the U.S. reported that referent role influences the choice of conflict management styles (Oh, 1997; Ahose, 1995).

Lee's (1990) study, which used both observational methods and self-reports with the ROCI–II, found consistent differences in four conflict styles when the participants (Korean managers) interacted with superiors, subordinates, and peers. This study provided further empirical evidence that, in organizations, the styles of handling interpersonal conflict are a function of the parties' hierarchical relationships. Studies by Lee (1996) with central government employees in South Korea, by Kozan (1989) with Turkish and Jordanian managers, and by Munduate, Ganaza, and Alcaide (1993) with Spanish managers and employees show that referent role or relative status of employees influences their styles of handling conflict.

Musser (1982) presented a decisional model to show how a subordinate actually chooses a behavioral style to deal with high-stakes conflict with a superior(s). A subordinate selects one of the five styles of handling conflict (strategies) depending on his or her response to each of the variables, such as the subordinate's desire to remain in the organization, subordinate's perceived congruence between the superior's and his or her own attitudes and beliefs, and the subordinate's perceived protection from arbitrary action. A study by Renwick (1975) attempted to determine whether organizational status (superior–subordinate) influenced the conflict-handling modes likely to be adopted. Her findings were that organizational status did not affect the likelihood with which each of the five modes of conflict resolution would be used. This discrepancy may possibly be attributed to the single-item instrument she used to measure the five conflict modes.

Gender. There were a number of field studies relating to gender differences on the styles of handling interpersonal conflict. Rahim (1983a) investigated the differences in the styles of handling interpersonal conflict of men and women and found women to be more integrating, avoiding, and compromising and less obliging than men managers. A study by Cole (1996) in Japanese cultural contexts indicated that males used more dominating styles than females, while females used more avoiding and compromising styles than males. These findings are somewhat consistent with the results reported by Kilmann and Thomas (1975) and Baron (1989).

A study with 234 administrators (Female = 117, Male = 117) from 12 state universities in Ohio reported that women were more compromising with their superiors than men. There were no gender differences among the remaining four styles (Neff, 1986). Several studies have compared the conflict-handling modes of men and women in organizations. Renwick (1977) used a single-item instrument to measure the modes of fifty-five men and forty women in business organizations. She found no significant differences between women and men in their modes of handling conflict. Shockley-Zalabak (1981) also attempted to investigate the differences in conflict-handling modes of men and women with Hall's (1969) Conflict Management Survey. The respondents were thirty-eight males and thirty-one females in five business organizations. Her finding was similar to that of Renwick, that is, there were no statistically significant differences in conflict-handling modes between men and women. Dune's (1989) study challenged laboratory data that "women are more conciliatory during negotiations and less comfortable with tasks associated with conflict management than men" (p. 1033).

Like personality, the relationships of gender to the styles of handling interpersonal conflict are weak and inconsistent. A similar conclusion was reached by Wall and Blum (1991). Their literature review shows that there is marginal and inconsistent relationship between gender and negotiation outcomes. After an extensive review of the literature on gender differences in conflict-handling styles, Nicotera and Dorsey (2006) concluded the following: "There is no *there* there. Conflict style is *not* driven by biological sex, regardless of how many studies try to find the effect; it simply is not there....the search for gender *differences* in organizational communication and in conflict communication particularly, has little promise to produce any meaningful findings" (p. 312). Therefore, it can be concluded that there is no need for further research to find gender differences in the styles of handing interpersonal conflict.

A diagnosis should particularly indicate whether the organizational participants are relying too much on one or more behavioral styles (e.g., dominating or avoiding) to deal with interpersonal conflict. A diagnosis should also indicate whether the organizational members are selecting and using appropriate behavioral styles to deal with different situations.

Intervention

Intervention is necessary when the organizational members have difficulty in dealing with different situations with appropriate behavioral styles. The behavioral and structural intervention strategies for the management of interpersonal conflict are presented as follows.

Process. The objective of a process intervention is to help the organizational members to enhance their integrating style of handling conflict by changing their attitudes and behavior. If the diagnosis indicates that the members of an organization or one or more of its subsystems are having difficulty in the selection and use of integrating style, and/or they are making frequent use of obliging, dominating, and avoiding styles, a transactional analysis training may be useful for them.

Transactional Analysis. Developed by Berne (1961, 1964) and provided a clear and popular presentation by Harris (1969), James and Jongeward (1971), and Harris and Harris (1985), transactional analysis provides better understanding of social transactions that involve interactions between two individuals. Goldman (1991; see also Stewart, 2007) suggests that transactional analysis is "a tactical tool available to a negotiator [that] provides a model for controlling our own behavior and for better understanding and influencing the behavior of others" (p. 114). A transactional analysis intervention can enable the members of an organization to improve their communication skills and consequently the styles of handling conflict with superiors, subordinates, and peers.

The three aspects of transactional analysis are *structural analysis, transactional analysis proper*, and *life positions*. The following is a discussion of these three aspects.

1. *Structural, or personality,* analysis is the study of ego states. Human beings interact with each other in terms of three psychological states: Parent (P), Adult (A), and Child (C). The three ego states exist in each individual. Berne (1972) defined ego states as "coherent systems of thought and feeling manifested by corresponding patterns of behavior" (p. 11). The three ego states can be described as follows:

a. *Parent ego state* reflects the attitudes, values, and behavior of authority figures, especially parents. This state may include prejudicial, critical, manipulative, or nurturing attitudes and behavior.

b. *Adult ego state* represents the rational part of personality. It is based upon reason, collecting and processing information for problem solving, and discussion on the basis of evidence and information. It assumes that human beings are equal, important, and reasonable.

c. *Child ego state* reflects the experiences and conditions of early childhood. In this state, the individual thinks, feels, and behaves just the way she or he did as a child.

The next section discusses how these ego states affect the interactions among individuals.

2. *Transactional analysis proper.* The three ego states are present in every individual and affect the interactions of a person with others. When Person A communicates with Person B, Person A is in a distinct ego state and can direct her or his message to any of the three ego states of Person B. The basic unit of communication is called a transaction. Transactions may be classified as complementary, crossed, or ulterior.

a. *Complementary transaction* occurs when they are parallel; that is, a message sent from one ego state (e.g., Parent) receives an expected response from the appropriate ego state of the other party (e.g., Child). In other words, "when stimulus and response on the P–A–C transaction diagram make parallel lines, the transaction is complementary and can go on indefinitely. It does not matter which way the vectors go (Parent–Parent, Adult–Adult, Child–Child, Parent–Child, Child–Adult) if they are parallel" (Harris, 1969, p. 70). Examples of these transactions are shown in Figure 6–3.

b. *Uncomplimentary, or crossed, transaction* occurs when a message from one ego state (e.g., Parent) receives a response from a different ego state (e.g., Adult) than intended. This happens when stimulus and response cross on the P–A–C transaction diagram. As a result, there may be a communication breakdown or conflict. Examples of these transactions are shown in Figure 6–4.

c. *Ulterior transaction* occurs when the overt stimulus indicates a transaction at one level (Adult–Adult), but the underlying intent of it may place the transaction at another level (Parent–Child). An example of this transaction is given in Figure 6–5.

Figure 6–3
Complementary Transactions

(a) Parent–Parent

    S: College students nowadays
do not want to work hard
for grades.

    R: Where will it all end.

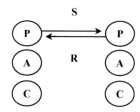

Fig. 6–3(a) Parent–Parent Transaction

(b) Adult–Adult

    S: Congratulations on your
passing the CPA exam.

    R: Thank you.

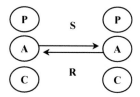

Figure 6–3(b) Adult–Adult Transaction

(c) Child–Child

    S: I don't know how to
Complete this project.

    R: I always have to be your
Helper.

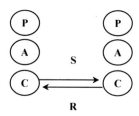

Figure 6–3(c) Child–Child Transaction

(d) Parent–Child

    S: Let me help you with your
Project.

    R: Gee, I'd like that.

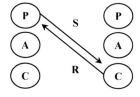

Figure 6–3(d) Parent–Child Transaction

Figure 6–4
Complementary Transactions

(a) S: Why are you late today, John?

 R: Don't be so critical.

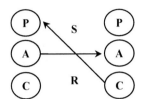

Figure 6–4(a) Crossed Transaction

(b) S: You stayed away from the
  meeting again.

 R: If you take care of your own
  problems, you wouldn't notice.

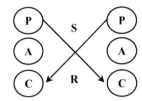

Figure 6–4(b) Crossed Transaction

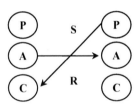

(c) S: I have to complete a
  schedule tonight that is due
  tomorrow morning.

 R: You will never learn to do things
  ahead of time.

Figure 6–4(c) Crossed Transaction

Figure 6–5
Ulterior Transaction

 S: (Subordinate) There may be
  another way of solving the problem.

 R: (Superior) You should try the present
  method, which worked before, to
  solve the problem.

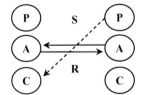

 Ulterior (U): I don't like your
  challenging my authority. You must
  do things exactly in the way I told
  you to do them.

Although Adult–Adult transaction is the most desirable one, other complementary transactions can operate with some success. For example, if the supervisor desires to play the role of parent, and the subordinate desires the role of child, they may develop a relationship that is reasonably effective. But the problem is that the employee fails to grow and mature. Therefore, it has been suggested that Adult–Adult transactions obtain the best results for the individual and the organization.

3. *Life positions.* In a transaction, a person tends to be dominated by one of the four life positions (Harris, 1969). Early in his or her childhood, a person develops a dominant philosophy of relating to others. This tends to remain with the person for a lifetime unless major experiences occur to alter it. These positions can also be used to analyze a series of transactions between two parties. Thus, if an individual is communicating primarily from one ego state, it can correspond to one of these four positions:

Primarily From	To	Position Being Assumed
Parent	Child	I'm OK–You're not OK.
Child	Parent	I'm not OK–You're OK.
Adult	Adult	I'm OK–You're OK.
Child	Child	I'm not OK–You're not OK.

In transactional analysis, the emphasis is on authentic communications and relationships. It is expected that because of this intervention the organizational members will learn to handle their interpersonal conflict more effectively. It is expected that transactional analysis intervention not only can affect the way organizational members handle their dyadic conflict but also can affect their intragroup and intergroup conflicts.

Although a number of companies have used transactional analysis, the effectiveness of this technique has yet to be assessed scientifically. Some companies that used this technique reported that it was moderately successful (Rettig & Amano, 1976).

Structural. Several structural interventions are available for the management of interpersonal conflict. Appeal to authority and the use of ombudsmen are two structural arrangements that are presented in this chapter for the management of conflict between two organizational members. These arrangements are necessary to deal with conflicts between two parties when they fail to resolve their disagreements.

Appeal to Authority. Organizations allow members to appeal to a common superior if two or more members, at the same organizational level, fail to resolve their disagreements. The common supervisor can make a decision that will be binding on the two parties involved in conflict, and the supervisor has the right to enforce her or his decisions. This system can work effectively if the supervisor is respected by the conflicting individuals, understands the complexity of the problems, and is able to make a good decision. "When the decision-maker cannot understand the issues, or when the conflicting parties do not believe he does or don't respect his authority, his ability to resolve conflict is sharply curtailed. People will not accept the superior's judgement....Of course, hierarchical superiors can resort to their own dominance to force acceptance, but this sharply undermines the efficiency of the system" (Hampton, Summer, & Webber, 1982, p. 642).

Some organizations allow members to appeal to a higher-level manager if they feel that the immediate supervisor has not handled a matter fairly. This system may work satisfactorily provided that there are few complaints against the immediate supervisors, the higher-level manager devotes adequate time to understand the problem and make a good decision, and the immediate supervisor does not hold a grudge against the complainant. Too many complaints against an immediate supervisor signal the existence of problems associated with the supervisor. Therefore, the higher-level manager should diagnose the problems and take appropriate corrective action. Some organizations allow the lower-level members to take their disagreements to grievance committees.

Corporate Ombudsman. The *APA Dictionary of Psychology* defines ombudsman as "a person and or program responsible for investigating consumer complaints and grievances and acting as a consumer advocate in resolving problems" (VandenBos, 2007, p. 644). The first ombudsman was appointed in Sweden in 1809 to deal with complaints from citizens about their government. This has been an intriguing mechanism for managing conflict in government (Ambrož, 2005; Stewart, 1978). In recent years, it has been increasingly used in institutions of higher education. These institutions are employing ombudsmen so that teacher–student conflict, especially relating to grades, can be effectively dealt with and so that formal grievance procedures are not needed.

An ombudsman is a mediator who ensures fair and just application of the rules and procedures of an organization for the management of conflict between two or more parties. An ombudsman can help to mediate conflict between parties by collecting and providing information on the relevant issues and providing the parties with expert advice and opinion when the parties ask for them. Ombudsmen do not have any authority to make decisions that are binding on the parties, but they can make recommendations.

Kolb's (1988) study indicates that application of this structural mechanism for conflict management in corporations is a recent phenomenon. She found two types of corporate ombudsman: helping and fact-finding. In managing conflict, whereas the helping ombudsman tries to formulate unique, individualized solutions for employee conflict, the fact-finding ombudsman tries to determine whether appropriate rules and procedures were followed and whether there is a satisfactory explanation for a complaint. An effective corporate ombudsman should both help as well as fact-find to manage conflict effectively.

This type of structural mechanism is appropriate for managing routine conflicts. It should not be used in a way that undermines the formal hierarchical relationships in organizations. This sort of third-party intervention is not appropriate for managing intergroup and other strategic conflicts. Reasons for this are explained in detail in Chapter 8.

Summary

Interpersonal conflict relates to disagreements, differences, or incompatibilities between an individual and his or her superior(s), subordinates, or peers. The PD game helps us to conceptualize some of the dilemmas that are present in an interpersonal conflict, but this type of conflict in organizations is much more complex than what we see in the payoff matrix. A more realistic taxonomy is the five styles of handling interpersonal conflict: integrating, obliging, dominating, avoiding, and compromising. The model of conflict begins with the antecedent conditions or the sources of conflict and includes behavioral changes, structure formation, decision process, and conflict aftermath.

Although it has been generally accepted that the integrating or problem-solving style is the best for dealing with interpersonal conflict, all five styles are appropriate depending on situations. Negotiation skills are important in managing conflict. Four principles of negotiation are to separate the people from the problem; focus on interests, not positions; invent options for mutual gain; and insist on using objective criteria.

For the management of interpersonal conflict, a diagnosis should particularly indicate whether the organizational members are handling their conflict appropriately depending on situations. The factors that affect the styles are personality, bases of power, organizational culture, and referent role. Some of these sources may be altered through appropriate interventions, which, in turn, will affect the conflict styles of organizational members. The process and structural interventions for the management of interpersonal conflict are transactional analysis, appeal to authority, and ombudsman. The next chapter discusses intragroup conflict and its management.

7

Intragroup Conflict

Although numerous studies on group dynamics were conducted since the completion of the Hawthorne studies, scholars have not given enough attention to the study of intragroup conflict in organizations. Organizations are increasingly turning to groups with the hope of improving productivity by increasing motivation, creativity, and performance. However, group members may differ in their opinions regarding tasks that should be performed and this may lead to conflict.

Intragroup conflict refers to the incompatibility, incongruence, or disagreement among the members of a group or its subgroups regarding goals, functions, or activities of the group. "An intragroup problem exists whenever a group member perceives a difference between what is presently occurring between him or her and the group and what he or she desires to occur" (Jarboe & Witteman, 1996, p. 316). Unless a substantial number of the members of a group or its subgroups are involved in conflict, it is not classified as intragroup conflict.

The study of groups in organizations has received significant attention for several reasons. First, groups are the building blocks of an organization. Second, groups provide the primary mechanism for the attainment of organizational goals. Third, groups provide psychological and other support to the individual members.

There are numerous definitions of groups (Shaw, 1981; Forsyth, 1983). These definitions have mainly focused on the following criteria: objectives, interaction, and interdependence. To make the discussion of conflict within a group meaningful, the definition of a group should include the following:

1. A group must consist of two or more members.
2. A group must possess a stable structure; that is, a collection of individuals that changes (e.g., passengers in an airplane) cannot be considered a group.
3. The members should be interdependent.
4. The members should interact with each other.
5. The members should work toward the attainment of a common goal(s).

Types of Groups

Different kinds of groups are found in organizations. Groups can be broadly classified as formal or informal. Following are a classification and discussion of these groups:

Formal Groups

The formal groups are formed by the organization for the purpose of attaining certain goals. These groups can be classified as task or project groups.

Task Group. Groups that are formed around certain tasks or functions and remain in existence for a long period of time are called task or functional groups.

Types of Task Groups. Fiedler (1967) further classified task groups into three types according to the nature of task interdependencies among group members in attaining their group objectives. The three types of task groups are interacting, coaching, and counteracting.

Interacting group. In this group, the performance of a task by a member depends on the completion of the task assigned to another member. A production team on the assembly line, where the output of one worker becomes the input of another worker, is an example of an interacting group.

Coaching group. This is a group in which the members perform their functions relatively independently of each other. Examples of this type of group are faculty groups whose members perform their teaching and research functions relatively independently of each other.

Counteracting group. This is composed of persons who work together for the purpose of negotiating and reconciling conflicting opinions and purposes. This type of group is exemplified by a labor–management negotiating team.

Project Groups. Groups formed for the purpose of completing specific projects or tasks are called project groups or task forces. This group remains in existence for a limited period of time—a phase-out takes place after the goals of the project or tasks are attained.

Informal Groups

These groups are formed by the organizational members without any direction from management. These groups exist to satisfy certain needs not met by the formal groups. Sometimes the goals of the formal and informal groups are not consistent; that is, they are in conflict. Two types of the informal groups are interest and friendship groups.

Interest Groups. These groups are formed by the organizational members to satisfy their common interest. For example, employees may join an interest group to serve on the United Way campaign, to discuss computer software, or to seek redress of their grievances from management.

Friendship Groups. These groups are formed by employees to satisfy their social needs, such as friendship, support, esteem, and belongingness. For example, employees may join such a group to play golf or cards, to watch movies, or to discuss political events. These groups may exist beyond the formal organization because they satisfy certain human needs.

It is important to recognize that informal groups are an important part of organizational life. Greenberg and Baron (2008, p. 293) recognize that informal friendship groups can have beneficial effects on organizational functioning.

The discussion in this chapter mainly relates to the interdependent task groups, such as interacting and coaching groups. A counteracting group, which contains two distinct parties (e.g., labor and management or line and staff), is discussed in the next chapter.

Effects of Intragroup Conflict

Several earlier studies reported the relationship between intragroup conflict and individual and organizational outcomes. Julian and Perry (1967), in their experimental study, found that both quality and quantity of team performance were considerably higher in competitive than cooperative conditions. Hoffman and Maier (1961) found that experimental groups with heterogeneous members and consequent conflicts of interest and opinion produced better solutions to standardized sets of solutions. Torrance (1954) reported that aircraft crews who perceived a greater amount of conflict were more effective than crews who reported less conflict. A field study that investigated the relationship between intragroup conflict and job performance was by Rutland (1983). This study with mountain-climbing groups found support for the hypothesis that conflict is positively associated with job performance. Pelz and Andrews (1976) found that scientists who were exposed to discussion with differently oriented colleagues tended to be more productive.

It is generally agreed by organization theorists that cooperation or lack of conflict generally induces positive relations among group members, but groups may not be able to attain a higher level of performance. Some of these problems are discussed under "cohesiveness and groupthink," later in this chapter.

More recent studies have tried to investigate the relationship between intragroup conflict and individual and group outcomes. A study by Baker, Tjosvold, and Andrews (1988) reported that project managers who used both cooperative and confirming (conveying that the other party is accepted as effective and avoiding insults and blaming) approaches to conflict "received high marks from project team members on a conflict constructiveness measure and on a management effectiveness measure. Quite clearly the combination of these two approaches was highly productive within the engineering group studied" (p. 1275). Unfortunately, this study did not deal with the difficult issue of the relationships of the amount and/or the styles of handling intragroup conflict to group productivity or task performance. Wall and Nolan's (1986) experimental study with task-oriented groups reported the following:

1. Inequity was negatively associated with satisfaction with group and posi- tively associated with conflict. Greater inequity was associated with affective conflict than substantive (task) conflict.
2. Lower inequity was associated with integrative, rather than distributive or avoidance, styles of conflict management. The least amount of inequity was associated with substantive conflict managed with integrative styles.
3. Satisfaction was more positively associated with integrative styles than either distributive or avoidance styles of conflict management. The greatest amount of satisfaction with the group was associated with substantive conflicts that are managed with an integrative style. Substantive conflict was positively associated with the use of an integrative style, and affective conflict was positively associated with the avoidance style of conflict management.
4. There was no relationship between the number of conflict episodes and the quality of outcome, that is, the group's final product (which was operation- ally defined as the grade the individuals received for their final project).

Unlike the study by Baker et al. (1988), Wall and Nolan (1986) attempted to investigate the relationships of conflict and conflict styles to the group's final product. Wall and Nolan indicated that their "results were contrary to the general position one finds in the literature" (p. 1048). This study does not either confirm or disconfirm the relationship between intragroup conflict and individual or group performance.

Robey, Farrow, and Franz (1989) reported a field study at five periods over twenty-two months that tested a model of group participation, influence (of individual members who affect decisions related to the final design of infor- mation system), conflict (manifest disagreement among group members), and conflict management (extent to which disagreements are replaced by agreement and consensus) in information system development projects. Results indicated that participation positively affected influence, that influence positively af- fected conflict and conflict management, and that conflict negatively influenced conflict management. This study did not attempt to measure the final output of the project groups.

A field study by Schnake and Cochran (1985) investigated the effects of two goal-setting dimensions (goal clarity and goal difficulty) on intra- and inter-departmental conflicts and the effects of these conflicts on internal work motivation and intrinsic job satisfaction. Results indicate that lower levels of goal difficulty and goal clarity are associated with higher levels of intra- and inter-departmental conflict and that higher levels of conflict are associated with lower levels of internal work motivation and intrinsic job satisfaction. The results of the study should be viewed with caution because of the problems of common method variance.

A field study by Rahim (1990) with manufacturing employees reported positive relationship between conflict (sum of intrapersonal, intragroup, and intergroup conflict) and job burnout (sum of emotional exhaustion, depersonalization, and personal accomplishment). But the relationship between conflict and supervisory rating of job performance (sum of performance, conformance, dependability, and personal adjustment) was nonsignificant.

Blau's (1963) study of two government agencies suggested a negative relationship between competitive behavior and performance in situations of cooperative group norms. Rahim's (1983e) study with a collegiate sample indicated a low to moderate degree of inverse relationship between intragroup conflict and three dimensions of perceptual measures of organizational effectiveness, such as productivity, adaptability, and flexibility. The correlation between intragroup conflict and organizational climate, as measured by Likert's (1967) Profile of Organizational Characteristics, was negative. The study also indicated a moderate negative correlation between intragroup conflict and job satisfaction. Dewar and Werbel (1979) found a weak negative correlation between overall conflict and job satisfaction.

Findings from Recent Studies

Affective Conflict. Recent studies show that affective conflict negatively influences group performance, group loyalty, work-group commitment, job satisfaction, and intent to stay in the present organization (Amason, 1996; Jehn, 1994; Jehn, Northcraft, & Neale, 1999). De Dreu and Weingart's (2003) meta-analysis also confirmed the inverse relationship between affective conflict and group performance and members' satisfaction with their teams. After reviewing relevant literature, Behfar, Peterson, Mannix, and Trochim (2008) concluded that there are three principal reasons for the dysfunctions of affective conflict:

1. It limits the information processing ability of the group because group members spend their time and energy focusing on each other rather than on the group problems.
2. It limits group members' cognitive functioning by increasing their stress and anxiety levels.
3. It encourages antagonistic or accusatory attributions for other group members' behavior, which can create a self-fulfilling prophesy of mutual hostility and conflict escalation.

There was at least one study by Pelled, Eisenhardt, and Xin's (1999) that found no relationship between affective conflict and group performance. As noted in Chapter 4, a greater use of the problem solving plus a lower use of the bargaining conflict-handling strategy should be effective in minimizing the negative outcomes of affective conflict.

Process Conflict. As discussed in Chapter 2, this is another type of conflict, first presented by Jehn (1997a), is associated with group performance and satisfaction. Although it is now accepted that process conflict is an important concept, it is one of the least investigated and understood than affective and substantive conflicts. It was long recognized by scholars that managing team issues such as who should do what work, logistics, delegation, and how task performance should proceed is essential for avoiding dysfunctions of this type of conflict. There is no study on how process conflict should be managed to improve team performance and satisfaction. As discussed in previous section on affective conflict, a greater use of the problem solving plus a lower use of the bargaining conflict-handling strategy should be effective in minimizing the negative outcomes of process conflict.

A small number of studies have reported negative relationships of process conflict to team performance and satisfaction (Jehn, 1997a; Jehn et al., 1999). Another study reported that high levels of process conflict can reduce the positive functions of substantive conflict and increase dysfunctions of affective conflict (Behfar, Mannix, Peterson, & Trochim, 2002). A recent study by Jehn and Mannix (2001) reported that high-performing groups increased process conflict from the beginning to the middle to the end of the group interaction, but lower-performing groups had higher process conflict at the beginning and at the end of the group interaction compared to the middle. After reviewing the literature on team conflict, Behfar and Thompson (2007) suggested that "empirical findings regarding process conflict and its functional and dysfunctional impact on performance are limited and somewhat contradictory" (p. 17).

Substantive Conflict. As discussed in Chapter 4, a study by Jehn (1995) indicates that a moderate level of substantive conflict is functional, as it stimulates discussion and debate, that help groups to attain a higher level of performance. This conflict can improve group performance through better understanding of various viewpoints and alternative solutions (Bourgeois, 1985; Eisenhardt & Schoonhoven, 1990; Jehn, 1997a, 1997b; Jehn et al., 1999). "Groups with an absence of task conflict may miss new ways to enhance their performance, while very high levels of task conflict may interfere with task completion" (Jehn, 1997a, p. 532). Groups that experience substantive conflict are able to make better decisions than those that do not. This relationship has also been found to be true at the individual level (Amason, 1996; Cosier & Rose, 1977; Fiol, 1994; Schweiger, Sandberg, & Ragan, 1986). It should be noted that the beneficial effects of substantive conflict on performance were found only in groups performing nonroutine tasks, but not groups performing standardized or routine tasks.

Although substantive conflict enhances group performance, like affective conflict, it can diminish group loyalty, work-group commitment, intent to stay in the present organization, and satisfaction (Jehn, 1997a; Jehn, Northcraft, & Neale, 1999). As a result, interventions for conflict management should be able to develop cultural norms to support disagreement among group members in connection with tasks and other related management issues without generating affective conflict.

Although it is generally accepted that a moderate amount of substantive conflict is functional for groups, a recent meta-analysis shows that it may have a negative impact on the group performance and satisfaction of individual members (De Dreu & Weingart, 2003). However, the literature on organizational conflict long recognized that substantive conflict can be functional or dysfunctional depending on how it is managed (Rahim, 1985, 2002; see also Rahim, 2010). Without effective conflict management, stimulation of substantive conflict may be ineffective (Nemeth, Connell, Rogers, & Brown, 2001). Further evidence of the role of conflict management can be found in DeChurch and Marks's (2001) study, which shows the importance of conflict management in improving the positive functions of substantive conflict. Their study with project groups shows that the relationship of substantive conflict to group performance was positive when conflict was managed actively (i.e., greater use of the dominating and integrating and lower use of the avoiding and obliging conflict-handling styles), but the relationships were negative when it was managed passively. Similarly, relationship between substantive conflict and group satisfaction was positive when agreeable conflict-management style (i.e., greater use of the integrating and obliging styles and less use of the dominating and avoiding styles) was used. Therefore, the conclusion is that substantive conflict can be functional depending how conflict-handling styles were used to deal with the disagreements among group members.

It appears that the existing studies on organizational conflict have neglected to investigate the moderating or mediating effect of the styles of handling conflict on the relationships of substantive conflict to job performance and member satisfaction. Future studies need to indicate how different conflict-handling styles should be used to deal with intragroup conflict (e.g., substantive conflict, process conflict, affective conflict, transforming conflict, and masquerading conflict). In other words, effective conflict-management is needed to minimize the dysfunctions of process, affective, transforming, and masquerading conflicts and to enhance the functions of substantive conflict.

Managing Intragroup Conflict

The management of intragroup conflict involves effectively channeling the energies, expertise, and resources of the group toward the formulation and/or attainment of group goals. Specifically, this involves altering the sources of conflict so that affective, process, transforming, and masquerading conflicts are minimized, a moderate amount of substantive conflict is attained and maintained, and group members are trained to learn the styles of handling conflict to deal with various conflicts effectively. Since the styles of handling conflict were discussed in detail in the previous chapter, this chapter mainly deals with the amount of intragroup conflict. The diagnosis of, and intervention in, intragroup conflict are discussed next.

Diagnosis

The diagnosis of intragroup conflict and the styles of handling such conflict can be performed by such methods as self-report, observation, interviews, and company records. The ROCI–I can be used to measure the amount of conflict in each group. The items of ROCI–II, Form C, can be slightly altered to measure the styles of handling conflict of the group members.

Measurement. A comprehensive diagnosis of intragroup conflict should involve the following measurements:

1. The amount of intragroup conflict and the styles of handling such conflict.
2. Factors that affect intragroup conflict and the styles of handling such conflict.
3. Learning and effectiveness of group(s).

Analysis. The analysis of the preceding diagnostic data should indicate:

1. The amount of intragroup conflict and the styles of handling such conflict in different groups, departments, units, and so on and whether the amount of conflict deviated from the national norms.
2. Relationships of the amounts of intragroup conflict and the styles of handling such conflict to their sources.
3. The relationships of the amounts of intragroup conflict and the styles of handling such conflict to group learning and effectiveness.

National Norms

Data for the national norms were collected on the ROCI–I from 1,188 executives, as described before in Chapter 3. Tables 7–1 and 7–2 are prepared on the basis of this sample. Table 7–1 shows the national percentile norms of these managers. The percentile score of a manager shows his or her relative position on the intragroup conflict subscale.

Table 7–1
National Managerial Percentile Norms of Intragroup Conflict

Mean Scores	Percentiles	Mean Scores
5.00		5.00
4.85		4.85
4.70		4.70
4.55		4.55
4.40		4.40
4.25		4.25
4.10		4.10
3.95	99	3.95
3.80	98	3.80
3.65	97	3.65
3.50	96	3.50
3.35	93	3.35
3.20	91	3.20
3.05	89	3.05
2.90	85	2.90
2.75	82	2.75
2.60	70	2.60
2.45	62	2.45
2.30	54	2.30
2.15	41	2.15
2.00	30	2.00
1.85	13	1.85
1.70	9	1.70
1.55	6	1.55
1.40	4	1.40
1.25	2	1.25
1.10	1	1.10
1.00		1.00

Note: $N = 1,188$.

Table 7–2 shows the sample size (N), means (M) (reference group norms), and standard deviations (SD) of the intragroup conflict as reported by 1,188 executives, classified by organizational level, functional area, and education, and the results of one-way analyses of variance (F–ratio).

The results of one-way analyses of variance show that there were significant differences in the perception of intragroup conflict among the executives of

Table 7–2
National Managerial Reference Group Norms of Intragroup Conflict

Variable	N	M	SD	F
Organizational level				6.23*
Top	196	2.34	.52	
Middle	407	2.29	.50	
Lower	547	2.42	.63	
Functional area				.94
Production	216	2.38	.58	
Marketing	27	2.35	.57	
Finance & Accounting	36	2.24	.62	
Personnel	24	2.18	.54	
General management	252	2.36	.55	
R&D	198	2.40	.58	
Engineering	196	2.39	.58	
Other	214	2.33	.58	
Education				1.39
High school	136	2.41	.62	
2-year college	231	2.40	.61	
Bachelor's degree	529	2.35	.56	
Master's degree	208	2.31	.53	
Other	57	2.45	.61	
Total sample	1,188	2.36	.58	

*$p < .05$.

three organizational levels. The lower-level executives reported more intragroup conflict than did top executives, and the top executives reported more conflict than did the middle executives. There were no differences in the perception of intragroup conflict among these executives classified by functional area and educational categories.

Tables 7–3 and 7–4 provide additional percentile and reference group norms, respectively. As discussed in Chapter 6, these normative data were collected from students ($N = 676$) in two universities.

A one-way analysis of variance shows that there were significant differences in interpersonal conflict among organizational levels. The normative data are useful for undergraduate and graduate courses on organizational behavior, organizational psychology, and conflict management where students can compare their perceptions of intragroup conflict with corresponding percentile and reference group norms.

Table 7–3
Collegiate Percentile Norms of Intragroup of Conflict

| | Percentiles | | |
Mean Scores	MBA (n = 172)	Undergraduate (n = 504)	Mean Scores
5.00			5.00
4.85			4.85
4.70			4.70
4.55			4.55
4.40			4.40
4.25			4.25
4.10			4.10
3.95			3.95
3.80	99		3.80
3.65	98	99	3.65
3.50	96	97	3.50
3.35	90	96	3.35
3.20	88	93	3.20
3.05	87	90	3.05
2.90	82	84	2.90
2.75	78	78	2.75
2.60	63	64	2.60
2.45	55	55	2.45
2.30	44	47	2.30
2.15	34	37	2.15
2.00	28	28	2.00
1.85	11	10	1.85
1.70	9	8	1.70
1.55	6	5	1.55
1.40	4	4	1.40
1.25	3	3	1.25
1.10	2	2	1.10
1.00	1	1	1.00

Sources

Groups are affected by a multitude of factors. The diagnosis of intragroup conflict should indicate the factors that are significantly related to intragroup conflict.

Leadership Style. A leader can virtually influence all other variables affecting conflict within a group. Three examples of group conflict and their relationship to the leader, called situations A, B, and C, were provided by Maier and Verser (1982, p. 153; see Figure 7–1).

Table 7–4
Collegiate Reference Group Norms of Intragroup Cofnflict

Variables	N	M	SD	F
Organizational level				1.22
Top	11	2.63	.36	
Middle	100	2.47	.53	
Lower	131	2.37	.56	
Non-management	222	2.39	.55	
Worker	133	2.47	.61	
Education				.28
Undergraduate	502	2.40	.53	
MBA	172	2.43	.59	
Gender				4.42*
Male	402	2.45	.54	
Female	263	2.36	.57	
Total sample	676	2.36	.58	

$*p < .05$.

Figure 7–1
Three Sources of Intragroup Conflict

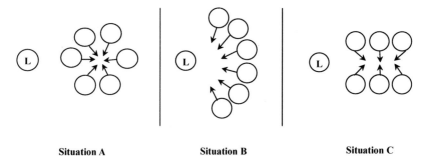

Situation A   Situation B   Situation C

Source: Maier, N. R. F., & Verser, G. C. (1982). *Psychology in industrial organizations* (5th ed.). Boston: Houghton Mifflin, p. 119. Reprinted with permission.

Situation A. This occurs when the leader treats group members differently. Group members may be in conflict with one another if the leader provides favor to one or two members.

Situation B. Intragroup conflict will increase if the group members unite against the leader. This may happen if the leader changes the task structure, schedules, or procedures, or removes some privileges, changes perceived by the members as unfair and/or unfavorable.

Situation C. This represents a split in the group. Differences in status, work interest, office space, and so on can encourage the formation of subgroups and conflict among them and the leader.

It should be emphasized that leadership style as a source of intragroup conflict has not been exclusively established through empirical studies. However, it can be hypothesized that a more directive style of leadership generates conflict, whereas a relations-oriented style provides for its reduction. Likert and Likert (1976) persuasively argue and provide some evidence that a leadership style based upon System IV can provide for a more functional management of conflict than Systems I, II, or III. Likert (1967) classified his Systems I, II, III, and IV as exploitive–authoritative, benevolent–authoritative, consultative, and participative organizations, respectively. This is consistent with Blake and Mouton's (1964, 1984) approach to conflict management, which says that there is one best style (which is characterized by the leaders' high concern for both production as well as people) to manage conflict in groups.

Chapter 4 indicated that the contingency or situational theories of leadership are consistent with the approach to conflict management presented in this book. This contingency or situational approach to conflict management is not consistent with Likert's System IV or universalistic approach to the same. Whereas the universalistic approach takes the position that there is one best approach (i.e., System IV for Likert and high concern for both production and people for Blake and Mouton) to managing conflict, the contingency approach suggests that how we effectively deal with a conflict depends on the nature of the situation.

Leadership can influence other variables, such as task structure, group composition, size, and so on, which affect the amount of intragroup conflict and the styles of handling conflict by the group members. These variables are discussed as follows.

Task Structure. This represents the extent to which the task is simple (routine) or complex (nonroutine). If a task is routine, it is likely to have clearly defined goals, methods, or procedures for doing the task and have a verifiably correct solution(s). Nonroutine tasks are not well defined and do not have verifiably correct solutions. Recent studies by Jehn (1995, 1997a, b), Jehn et al. (1999), and Pelled et al. (1999) reported positive relationship between substantive conflict and performance. This relationship was significant only for groups performing nonroutine tasks. In other words, substantive conflict is harmful for groups performing routine or standardized tasks.

As discussed by House (1971; see also Schriesheim & Denishi, 1981; Keller, 1989), in simple, routine, and structured tasks, a considerate or supportive leadership style may be more closely related to high job satisfaction and performance than a more directive leadership style. In this situation, there is a lower possibility of conflict within a group. On the other hand, in less structured tasks, subordinates appreciate more direction by their immediate supervisor. Although there is a greater possibility of conflict among group members when the task is complex or nonroutine than when the task is simple or routine, the management of such conflict can be effective if there is an appropriate match between leadership style and task and other contingency variables.

Several earlier studies reported the leadership–task–conflict interaction effects on performance. Bass (1960), Fiedler (1967), and Torrance (1954) asserted that groups under tension and stress perform better under task-oriented leaders. A review of several studies (e.g., Oaklander & Fleishman, 1964; Schriesheim & Murphy, 1976) by Katz (1977) showed that, while structuring leadership tends to be more positively related to performance under conditions of high stress, the consideration leadership tends to be positively related to performance under low stress. Katz's (1977) field and experimental studies showed "that initiating-structure was directly related to performance more significantly when high affective conflict was present. Thus, the moderating influence of affective conflict on the effectiveness of structuring leadership was upheld for individuals performing a routine task in laboratory experiment as well as for the more complex and somewhat autonomous tasks performed by the individuals in the field setting" (p. 281).

Group Composition. If a group is composed of individuals with too diverse interpersonal styles, attitudes, values, and interests, the members will have divergent perspectives toward group and organizational goals. In this situation, the members will experience undesirable interpersonal conflict and will have a difficult time in attaining synergistic solutions to the group problems. Rahim's (1979) experimental study found intragroup conflict to be significantly less in homogeneous than heterogeneous groups. However, in organizations where roles are more standardized, the association between conflict and heterogeneity may not be significant (Becker & Geer, 1960). Hall and Williams (1966) found that whereas established groups responded to conflict creatively, the ad hoc groups resolved conflict through compromise procedures.

A change in group membership can intensify conflict (Kelly, 1974, p. 565). When a new member joins the group, group stability may be disrupted. The manager of a group can affect group composition and conflict by selecting a newcomer for differing attitudes, backgrounds, and experiences. It is generally accepted that diversified or heterogeneous groups tend to perform better on many problem-solving tasks than do extremely homogeneous groups (Shaw, 1981). Recent studies by Jehn et al. (1999) and Pelled et al. (1999) show that diversity influences conflict and that conflict, in turn, influences work-group performance. Pelled et al.'s study shows that functional background diversity is positively associated with substantive conflict. Race and tenure diversity are positively associated with affective conflict, while age diversity is negatively associated with affective conflict. Jehn's study showed differential impact of social category diversity, value diversity, and informational diversity and moderating variables (task type and task interdependence) on workgroup performance. "If the type of diversity measured is social category diversity, the most positive effects will likely be on worker morale (satisfaction, intent to remain, commitment, and perceived performance). In contrast, groups that have greater diversity as measured in terms of values may suffer significant performance decrements (being less effective and efficient as well as having poorer perceived performance) and diminished worker morale (decreased satisfaction, commitment, and intent to remain in the group) " (Jehn et al., 1999, pp. 759–760).

Conflict Asymmetry. This is a neglected but important area for research on intragroup conflict and effectiveness. Existing literature assumes that team members perceive the same level of conflict in their respective groups. This approach ignores that there may be divergence in the perception of group members on intragroup conflict that may have significant influence on the performance and satisfaction of the group members.

Group conflict asymmetry refers to the extent to which members differ in their perceptions of the level of intragroup conflict. Individual conflict asymmetry refers to the perception of a member of more or less conflict than other members of a group. A study by Jehn, Rispens, and Thatcher (2010) shows that group conflict asymmetry reduces performance and creativity in groups. The study also shows that social processes and group climate mediate the relationships of individual conflict asymmetry to reported performance and satisfaction with the group (i.e., Conflict asymmetry → Social processes, Group climate → Performance, Satisfaction).

Size. The size of a group can affect group processes and conflict; as a group grows, potential for conflict increases. Several earlier studies found a positive relationship between group size and dissatisfaction and tension (Corwin, 1969; Hackman & Vidmar, 1970). A large group generally encourages the formation of subgroups each with its informal leader. Some of these subgroups may engage in conflict unless the formal leader follows a more directive and structured approach.

One study indicates that, with respect to decision quality, groups of more than five members may not be justified (Yetton & Bottger, 1983). The researchers recognize, of course, that "to meet needs other than high decision quality, organizations may employ groups significantly larger than four or five" (p. 158).

Cohesiveness and Groupthink. One of the major liabilities of a group is that one or more individuals may be forced to conform to the mode of thinking of their majority group members. Asch's (1951) study found that individuals under group pressure will change their opinions about highly objective matters. In a cohesive group, there is a greater possibility that individual members will unwillingly censor their opinions to avoid conflict and stay together on all important issues. Janis (1982) used the term "groupthink" as a "quick and easy way to refer to a mode of thinking that people engage in when they are deeply involved in a cohesive ingroup, when the members' strivings for unanimity override their motivation to realistically appraise alternative courses of action.... Groupthink refers to a deterioration of mental efficiency, reality testing, and moral judgment that results from ingroup pressures" (p. 9).

The victims of groupthink attempt to avoid being too critical of the ideas of their superiors, peers, or subordinates. The group members "adopt a soft line of criticism, even in their own thinking. At their meetings, all the members are amiable and seek complete concurrence on every important issue, with no bickering or conflict to spoil the cozy, 'we-feeling' atmosphere" (Janis, 1971, p. 43). Janis identified the following eight main symptoms of groupthink that reduce intragroup conflict:

1. *Invulnerability.* Most or all of the members of the ingroup share an *illusion* of invulnerability that provides for them some degree of reassurance about obvious dangers and leads them to become overly optimistic and willing to take extraordinary risks.
2. *Rationale.* Victims of groupthink ignore warnings; they also collectively construct rationalizations in order to discount warnings and other forms of negative feedback that, taken seriously, might lead the group members to reconsider their assumptions each time they recommit themselves to past decisions.
3. *Morality.* Victims of groupthink believe unquestionably in the inherent morality of their ingroup; this belief inclines the members to ignore the ethical or moral consequences of their decisions.
4. *Stereotypes.* Victims of groupthink hold stereotyped views of the leaders of enemy groups: they are so evil that genuine attempts at negotiating differences with them are unwarranted, or they are too weak or too stupid to deal effectively with whatever attempts the ingroup makes to defeat their purposes, no matter how risky the attempts are.
5. *Pressure.* Victims of groupthink apply direct pressure to any individual who momentarily expresses doubts about any of the group's shared illusions or who questions the validity of the arguments supporting a policy alternative favored by the majority.
6. *Self-Censorship.* Victims of groupthink avoid deviating from what appears to be group consensus; they keep silent about their misgivings and even minimize to themselves the importance of their doubts.
7. *Unanimity.* Victims of groupthink share an *illusion* of unanimity within the group concerning almost all judgments expressed by members who speak in favor of the majority view.
8. *Mindguards.* Victims of groupthink sometimes appoint themselves as mindguards to protect the leader and fellow members from adverse information

that might break the complacency they shared about the effectiveness and morality of past decisions (pp. 44, 46, 74).

Kroon, Hart, and Kreveld (1991) concluded from their experimental study that both individual and collective accountability reduced the tendency for groupthink. Particularly, under conditions of individual accountability, groups displayed less readiness to reach consensus. It also appears that anticipated accountability may counteract one of the preconditions for groupthink and greater accountability results in less risky decisions.

Whyte (1989) suggests that, in addition to pressures for uniformity of groupthink, another approach—prospect polarization—should be considered in analyzing group policy decisions that resulted in fiascoes. This approach suggests that a decision failure results from an option that is framed to appear as one in the domain of losses (i.e., certain losses at the expense of the greater losses). Such a frame elicits risk-seeking preferences. In other words, "groups whose members frame the choice as one between losses will evidence a moderately inappropriate preference for risks even more frequently and to a greater degree than would their average member" (Whyte, 1989, p. 42).

External Threats. The proposition that external conflict increases internal cohesion is an old one. Coser (1956, p. 87), in his Proposition No. 9, suggested that conflict with outgroups increases ingroup cohesion. After an exhaustive review of the theoretical formulations and empirical tests of this proposition, Stein (1976) concluded the following:

> there is a clear convergence in the literature in both the specific studies and in the various disciplines, that suggests that external conflict does increase internal cohesion under certain conditions. (p. 165)

Under external threats, group members temporarily put aside their differences and unite against the common enemy. The ingroup often develops stereotypes against the outgroup to justify the conflict and its causes. Bass (1965, pp. 333–334), Blake and Mouton (1961), and others found in their experiments that all groups (in conflict) rated themselves better than the other groups. As a result, conflicts among the members of a group are reduced significantly when the members perceive their group to be in conflict with another group (Sherif, 1958; Sherif, Harvey, White, Hood, & Sherif, 1961). In order for external conflict to reduce intragroup conflict, the following conditions must be satisfied (Stein, 1976):

1. The external conflict needs to involve some threat.
2. [The external conflict must] affect the entire group and all its members equally and indiscriminately, and involve a solution (at least there must be a useful purpose in group efforts regarding the threat).

3. The group needs to have been an ongoing one with some pre-existing cohesion or consensus, and to have a leadership that can authoritatively enforce cohesion (especially if all the members of the group do not feel the threat).
4. The group must be able to deal with the external conflict, and to provide emotional comfort and support to its members (p. 165).

External conflict may not reduce intragroup conflict if the external aggressor can tactfully split a subset of the group from the rest of the group members and create dissension and distrust leading one subgroup to blame others. In such a situation conflict within a group may be increased rather than reduced. Another factor of equal importance for intragroup conflict is the conflict aftermath, that is, whether the group wins or loses. The losing group may experience more tension and may reassess its strategies or composition. This may lead to an upset in its internal relationships, for example, change in leadership and undermining of group cohesiveness. In the winning group the amount of conflict may decrease, and the group cohesiveness may increase.

A diagnosis of intragroup conflict should particularly indicate whether there is too little, too much, or a moderate amount of conflict and whether conflict is handled by the group members effectively. A diagnosis should also indicate the functional and/or dysfunctional aspects of intragroup conflict in an organization. Based on this information, an intervention decision can be made.

Intervention

The process and structural interventions recommended for managing intergroup conflict follow.

Process. An organization development technique, such as team building, has been presented as a process intervention that can be used to manage intragroup conflict.

Team Building. This can be viewed as an extension of organization development intervention, such as sensitivity training or T–group. Team building puts emphasis on group learning rather than individual learning as in the case of T–group. Team building is a planned strategy to bring about changes in the attitudes and behavior of the members of an organizational group (or team), whether permanent or temporary, to improve the group's overall effectiveness (Dyr, 1987). A team-building exercise may be designed to enable the members to learn the styles of handling conflict and their appropriate uses. The intervention should also enable the group leader and members to become aware of the symptoms of groupthink and make appropriate changes in the group structure and process to remedy them. A team-building discussion should enable the group to attain the following:

1. To formulate new and/or revise the existing goals.
2. To formulate and/or revise tasks.
3. To allocate tasks to group members to attain the revised goals.
4. To examine the effectiveness of group processes (such as communication, conflict, leadership, motivation, etc.).

Team building, used inappropriately, may have dysfunctional consequences. For example, "the development of a team that results in high conformity may be more dysfunctional than having the existence of conflict" (Bobbitt, Breinholt, Doktor, & McNaul, 1978, p. 339). To guard against high cohesiveness and groupthink, which may result from team building intervention, the following steps, adapted from Janis (1971, p. 76), may be useful:

1. The leader may encourage each member to evaluate the group decisions critically. The leader should legitimize this practice by accepting some criticisms of his or her own behavior.
2. The leader should refrain from stating his or her preference to a problem solution when the problem is being discussed by the members.
3. The group should split into several subgroups to work on the same problem, each under a different leader. The separate solutions prepared by the subgroups should be integrated by the members of the group or the representatives of the subgroups.

A plan for the implementation of the solutions should be prepared, and several persons should be assigned the responsibilities for implementation. A tentative date(s) for the evaluation of the implementation should also be decided.

Team building is very similar to problem-solving intervention, which is discussed in connection with intervention in intergroup conflict. Designed properly, team building can help the group participants to learn the integrative or collaborative style of behavior in handling disagreements.

Structural. Unlike process intervention, such as organization development, systematic structural interventions are not available for the management of intragroup conflict. Following, however, are some structural changes that a manager can make to manage intragroup conflict.

The reduction of intragroup conflict may not be a problem. Conflict may be reduced by making a group more cohesive and homogeneous. If the manager of a group finds that there is less than adequate amount of substantive conflict within his or her group, he or she undertakes the difficult task of increasing conflict through structural changes. Following are intragroup conflict management strategies:

1. One of the potential strategies available to a manager to generate or intensify conflict is to change group membership. When a new member joins a

group, the level of conflict may be significantly affected if the newcomer is specifically selected for her or his differing beliefs, training, and experiences. The manager can reduce conflict by transferring one or more conflicting members to other units. This should not be done unless the styles for handling conflict by the members in question are clearly dysfunctional.

2. The level of conflict may also be altered by changing the group size. The potential for conflict increases as the size of the group is increased. A literature review by Gist, Locke, and Taylor (1987, p. 251) suggests that relatively small groups tend to be more efficient. Therefore, size of the group should not be increased just for the purpose of generating conflict.

3. The administrator of a group can change the level of conflict by altering difficulty and variability of the task. The amount of conflict may be reduced by redefining and restructuring tasks and reducing the interrelationships among tasks performed by different members.

4. The group leader can change the amount of conflict by altering the reward system. A reward system based on performance can generate productive competition and conflict among group members, which can increase group effectiveness. This is probably one of the effective ways of managing conflict within groups.

5. The amount of intragroup conflict can be affected by the group leader by altering the rules and procedures and appeals system.

Summary

A group was defined as consisting of two or more members who are interdependent and interact with each other and work toward the attainment of common goals. Groups can be classified as formal and informal. The formal groups can be classified as task or functional group and project group or task force. The task groups have been classified as interacting, coaching, and counteracting groups. The informal groups can be classified as interest and friendship groups.

Intragroup conflicts, such as affective and process are associated with dysfunctional outcomes. Effective conflict-management strategies can minimize the deleterious effects of these types of conflicts on group functioning. It is generally agreed that a moderate amount of substantive conflict is associated with group performance and job satisfaction of members, but some studies have reported that its effects can be negative. In order to obtain the full potential of substantive conflict on group outcomes, a moderate amount of this conflict should be attained and maintained and it should to be handled with appropriate styles. It was suggested that a greater use of the problem solving plus a lower use of the bargaining conflict-handling strategies should be effective in minimizing the negative outcomes of affective and process conflicts and enhancing the positive effects of substantive conflict.

The diagnosis of intragroup conflict involves the measurement of the amount of intragroup conflict, the styles of handling intragroup conflict, sources of conflict, and the effectiveness of the group(s). The analysis of diagnostic data should indicate the amount of intragroup conflict and the styles of handling such conflict in each group, department, unit, and so on and whether conflict deviated from the national norms; relationship between conflict and its source; and the relationship between conflict and group effectiveness and learning. There are various antecedent conditions or sources of intragroup conflict, such as leadership style, task structure, group composition, conflict asymmetry, size, cohesiveness and groupthink, and external threats. These sources of conflict may be altered to reduce or increase intragroup conflict.

Organization development techniques, such as team building, may be used to manage intragroup conflict effectively. Structural interventions designed to manage intragroup conflict include changing group composition; increasing or reducing the size of the group; transferring or exchanging group members and bringing new membership into the group; redefining and restructuring tasks; altering the reward system; and altering rules and procedures and appeals system. The next chapter discusses intergroup conflict and its management.

8

Intergroup Conflict

Intergroup conflict refers to the collective incompatibility or disagreement between two or more divisions, departments, or subsystems in connection with tasks, resources, information, and so on. Roloff (1987) has rightly indicated that, "while this form of conflict implies each member of a group is in conflict with those of another, quite often the actual dispute is carried out between representatives (e.g., department heads, or labor–management negotiators)" (p. 501).

There is a "law of intergroup conflict," which states that all groups are in partial conflict with each other (Downs, 1968). Intergroup conflict is inevitable in complex organizations. "In complex organizations having differentiated subsystems with different goals, norms, and orientations, it appeared that intergroup conflict would be an inevitable part of organizational life" (Lawrence & Lorsch, 1967a, p. 42; see also Friedkin & Simpson, 1985). Complex organizations create different subsystems with homogeneous tasks and distinct goals to increase overall organizational effectiveness. Although these subsystems develop distinct norms, orientations, and attitudes (i.e., they become internally homogeneous), they are required to work with each other for the attainment of organizational goals. This *interdependence* of the subsystems on tasks, resources, and information and the *heterogeneity* among them often are the major generators of conflict between two or more subsystems. Blake and Mouton (1984; see also Brown, 1983) classify this as *interface conflict*. They explain why this conflict is common in organizations:

> The potential for interface conflict is already present in the structure of modern organizations. Structures that combine similar work activities into functional groupings and separate them from others that are different are viewed as effective for maximizing effort and avoiding duplication. Interface conflict is likely to arise, however, when separated organizational components must reconnect and work together to achieve a goal. (Blake & Mouton, 1984, pp. 4–5)

Some of the classic examples of organizational intergroup conflict are between line and staff, manufacturing and sales, production and maintenance, headquarters and field staffs, and labor and management.

Dynamics of Intergroup Conflict

Chapter 6 presented a model of organizational conflict. This model requires further analysis for intergroup conflict, because this type of conflict displays certain unique patterns. Earlier studies by Bass (1965), Blake and Mouton (1961), Campbell (1967), and Sherif (1958) and recent literature review by Fisher (2006) present a highly consistent process of what happens when two groups engage in conflict.

It is possible to explain this process, in part, with the help of social identity theory (Tajfel, 1970). Social identity was defined by Tajfel (1981) "as that part of individuals' self concept which derives from knowledge of their membership in a social group (or groups) together with the value and emotional significance attached to that membership" (p. 255). The theory posits that individuals tend to classify themselves and others into various social categories. This is done to derive a positive social identity from their group membership and, as a result, individuals compare their group with the other group and they conclude that the ingroup is better than the outgroup. This is how members of each group enhance and protect their unique social identity and this can happen even if there is no intergroup conflict (Struch & Schwartz, 1989, pp. 364–365; see also Ashforth & Mael, 1998). Accumulated evidence from social identity theory suggests that "the mere perception of belongingness to two distinct groups—that is, social categorization per se—is sufficient to trigger intergroup discrimination favoring the in-group. In other words, the mere awareness of the presence of an out-group is sufficient to provoke intergroup competitive or discriminatory responses on the part of the in-group" (Tajfel & Turner, 1986, p. 13)

Following is a detailed discussion of the process that takes place within and between two conflicting groups in an organization. The process becomes distinct during periods of intense win–lose conflict.

Perceptual and Behavioral Changes

When intergroup conflict of win–lose orientation occurs, competition among members within each group is reduced, and the groups become more cohesive. The group members tend to conform to the group norm more, and they become loyal to the group. Although this is temporary, team conformity and loyalty increase substantially. In each group there is greater emphasis on task-oriented behaviors relative to relations-oriented behaviors (Schein, 1980).

Under external threats, the ingroup members close ranks, play down their disagreements, and become more loyal to the group so that a united front can be maintained against the outgroup. In other words, an increase in the intergroup conflict may reduce intragroup conflict (see Chapter 7). This encourages groupthink, which will affect the problem solving capability of the groups.

One of the possible consequences of win–lose intergroup conflict is that it creates significant distortions in the judgment and perceptual processes of the conflicting groups. During periods of intense intergroup conflict, judgmental and perceptual distortions become progressively greater. The achievements of one's group are seen as superior to those of the opposing group (Brewer, 1979). The members of the ingroup perceive the members of the other group as enemies, and they describe each other with negative stereotypes. The members of each group are likely to hear only those things that are consistent with their group's positions. Sometimes ingroup members dehumanize the outgroup as a way to justify intergroup aggression (Wilder, 1986).

Two types of errors occur that tend to magnify the differences between groups and escalate the conflict. The two groups fail to see the similarities in their solutions and see only the differences between their solutions. In other words, areas of agreement are seen as less than they actually are. The other kind of perceptual error relates to the belief of the ingroup members that their solutions are superior to those of the outgroup. These errors occur even though members of both groups consider the solutions carefully and feel they understand them well (see Blake, Shepard, & Mouton, 1964).

Structure Formation

Intergroup conflict may result in the emergence of autocratic leaders and the establishment of a new power structure. Very often "it is the aggressive person or the ones who express themselves clearly and well who take over. Sometimes those who like fights emerge in leadership positions. Those members who can provide the best leadership and the most skillful leadership processes often are submerged along with the questioning and sounder thinking which they would foster" (Likert & Likert, 1976, p. 61). The new leader(s) is well accepted by the group and is perceived as friendly and perceptive in the analysis of the other group's information. There is also greater pressure on the leader or representative to carry out the wishes of the ingroup when interacting with outgroup leader or representative.

The new leader may establish a power structure quickly. Emphasis on task attainment is increased together with the emergence of a greater degree of formality and structure. A structure of interaction is formulated that discourages free exchange of information. Rules and procedures are established prohibiting intergroup communication. All information is screened by group leadership before dissemination.

Decision Process

Differences among ingroup members that can lead to better decisions are no longer tolerated. Any member who questions the quality of a decision is renounced or ostracized and pressure is applied on him or her to conform. This suppression of intragroup conflict blocks the process that could lead to effective solutions.

The groups establish the means of negotiation, which are usually bargaining, ultimatums, and nonnegotiable demands. These result in further rationing of information or deliberate distortion of facts. Contacts with other group(s) become formal, rigid, and carefully defined.

Conflict Aftermath

If bargaining is exclusively utilized as a method of conflict resolution, the possibility exists that both groups will perceive themselves as partly losers after the cessation of conflict. Such a situation often occurs after a labor–management conflict is resolved. If a third party imposes a solution on the conflicting groups, there is a possibility that a victor and a vanquished will be created. The losing group may reassess and change its strategies and structure to deal with the other group. Likert and Likert (1976) described the aftermath of win–lose intergroup conflict quite succinctly:

> The winning group glorifies its leaders under whom it achieved success. The group becomes "fat and happy," coasts, and rests. There is little motivation to strive for improvement. The group members make little or no effort to analyze their performance to see how it could have been done better, nor do they look at their group processes to see how these could be improved. While they smugly glory in their success, all their weaknesses continue unchanged.
>
> The defeated group displays bitterness among members. Internal fighting and splintering occur. Cliques and factions emerge. The aggressive leaders and those who took over early in the consolidation of the group in response to the win–lose battle are rejected. There is a substantial shift in the acceptance and status of different persons. The rejected leaders may fight back and heighten the split in the group. This internal struggle may be quite intense, and the group may be so badly shattered that it is never able to recover and develop into an effective group. (Likert & Likert, 1976, pp. 63–64)

The model just discussed indicates that the outcomes of win–lose type of intergroup conflict will be dysfunctional for the organization. Morano (1976) rightly points out that "by behaving in a win/lose manner, managers may inadvertently stifled creative approaches to solving certain problems that may, in fact, be more beneficial than the one that is settled on. In this case, by winning, the manager actually loses" (p. 393). The following section discusses further the effects of intergroup conflict on individual and organizational outcomes.

Effects of Intergroup Conflict

Some of the effects of intergroup conflict were discussed in the dynamics of intergroup conflict. Walton and Dutton's (1969) literature review suggested that the consequences of intergroup conflict can be both functional and dysfunctional, depending on the attributes of conflictual, lateral relationships. Some of these relations are shown in Table 8–1.

Table 8–1 shows that whether conflict will be harmful or helpful depends on the nature of specific conflict relationships and the tasks involved. Several earlier studies provide some support to the consequences of inter-unit conflict presented by Walton and Dutton (e.g., Seiler, 1963; Dalton, 1959). However, further comparative studies are needed to check the validity of these consequences.

Julian and Perry's (1967) experimental study found that groups in competitive condition increased quality and quantity of their output more than the groups under cooperative condition. Persico's (1986) field study with the employees in four organizations showed no relationship between intergroup conflict as measured by the ROCI–I and supervisory rating of individual performance. Rahim's (1990) field study found significant positive relationship between

Table 8–1
Consequences of Interunit Conflict

Attributes of conflictful lateral relationships	Illustrative consequences
Competition in general	Motivates or debilitates
	Provides checks and balances
Concealment and distortion	Lowers quality of decisions
Channeled interunit contacts	Enhances stability in the system
Rigidity, formality in decision procedures	Enhances stability in the system
	Lowers adaptability to change
Appeals to superiors for decisions	Provides more contact for superiors
	May increase or decrease quality of decisions
Decreased rate of interunit interaction	Hinders coordination and implementation of tasks
Low trust, suspicions, hostility	Psychological strain and turnover of personnel or decrease in individual performance

Source: Walton, R. E., & Dutton, J. M. (1969). The management of interdepartmental conflict: A model and review. *Administrative Science Quarterly*, 14, p. 81. Reprinted with permission.

conflict (sum of intrapersonal, intragroup, and intergroup conflicts) as measured by the ROCI–I and job burnout of employees. This measure of conflict was also positively associated with job stress. But there was no association between conflict and supervisory rating of job performance of individual employees. In a field study with a collegiate sample of business students, intergroup conflict was also found to be negatively associated with perceptions of organizational effectiveness (i.e., productivity, adaptability, and flexibility), organizational climate, and job satisfaction (Rahim, 1983e).

It appears, then, that intergroup conflict may be associated with certain outcomes, such as job burnout, dissatisfaction, and stress, and so on, on the part of the organizational members. The effects of intergroup conflict on effectiveness have not been properly investigated. Many of the assertions made by researchers are merely judgmental. Whether the outcome of intergroup conflict is effective or ineffective depends on how the conflict was handled by the involved groups. The consequences of intergroup conflict may be quite dysfunctional if it is handled through obliging, dominating, avoiding, and compromising styles. The model of intergroup conflict just discussed shows why win–lose conflict leads to ineffective outcomes. If the group members or their representatives manage their conflict with an integrating or problem-solving style, the consequences could be quite functional (Blake & Mouton, 1984). Lawrence and Lorsch (1967a) found integrating or collaborating style of handling interdepartmental conflict positively associated with organizational effectiveness. The following section discusses how intergroup conflict can be managed effectively.

Managing Intergroup Conflict

The management of intergroup conflict involves channeling the energies, expertise, and resources of the members of conflicting groups for synergistic solutions to their common problems for the attainment of overall organizational goals. The diagnosis and intervention for managing intergroup conflict are as follows.

Diagnosis

The diagnosis of intergroup conflict can be performed by means of interviews, observation, company records, and the perceptions of the organizational members. The ROCI–I may be used to measure the amount of intergroup conflict in an organization. If it is needed to measure the amount of conflict between two specific departments, such as production and marketing, the members of production may be asked to respond to the intergroup conflict items to indicate how much conflict they think exists between their department and the marketing department.

The members of the marketing department may be asked to indicate how much conflict they think exists between their department and the production department. The items of the ROCI–II, Form C, may be appropriately altered to measure the styles used by the members in handling their intergroup conflict. For example, the item "I try to investigate an issue with my peers to find a solution acceptable to us" may be altered to, "I try to investigate an issue with the members of the marketing department to find a solution acceptable to production and marketing departments," to measure how integrating the members of the production department are in handling their conflict with the marketing department.

DuBrin (1972, pp. 213–214) has suggested a way of utilizing the judgments of the administrators to prepare a matrix to understand the location of intergroup conflict. Preparation of this matrix requires the judgment of the chief executive officer (CEO) of an organization about the conflict that exists between the head of each unit and the head of every other unit. The CEO should make proper judgments about interdepartmental conflict after discussing the problem with staff experts in small groups. In Table 8–2, conflict between each department and every other department has been rated. The head of the production department, in this case, is perceived by top management as being in frequent conflict with

Table 8–2
The Conflict Matrix

Departments	1	2	3	4	5	6	7
1. Marketing		–	0	–	–	–	–
2. Production	–		+	+	+	–	+
3. Quality control	0	+	+	0	+	+	+
4. Engineering	–	+	+		–		+
5. Finance	–	+	+	–		+	+
6. Systems	–	–	–	0	+		+
7. Personnel	–	+	+	+	+	+	
Conflict Index	5	2	1	2	2	2	1

Note: Code: + means better than average cooperation
0 means normal, average, typical cooperation
– means lack of cooperation, frequent conflict
Conflict Index: Number of other departments with which that department is in conflict.

Source: Dubrin, A. J. (1972). *The practice of managerial psychology: Concepts and methods of manager and organization development.* New York: Pergamon Press, p. 214. Reprinted with permission.

four department heads. The preparation of the matrix is an exercise by which top management becomes more conscious about intergroup conflict.

Measurement. A comprehensive diagnosis of intergroup conflict should include the measurement of the following:

1. The amount of conflict that exists between two specific groups;
2. The styles of handling conflict of the ingroup members with the outgroup members;
3. The sources of intergroup conflict and the style of handling such conflict; and
4. Organizational learning and effectiveness of the intergroup relations.

Analysis. The analysis of the preceding diagnostic data should indicate:

1. The amount of intergroup conflict and whether it deviated from the national norm(s) significantly;
2. The relationships of the amount of intergroup conflict and styles of handling such conflict to their sources; and
3. The relationships of intergroup conflicts and the styles of handling such conflict to learning and effectiveness of intergroup relations.

National Norms

The data for the preparation of national norms were collected from 1,188 executives, as described in Chapter 4. Table 8–3 shows the national percentile norms of these executives.

Table 8–4 shows the sample size (N), means (M) (reference group norms), standard deviations (SD) of intergroup conflict classified by organizational levels, functional areas, and educational categories, and the results of one-way analyses of variance (F). The results of one-way analyses of variance show that there were significant differences in the perception of intergroup conflict among the executives of the three organizational levels, functional areas, and educational categories. In particular, the relationship between organizational level and intergroup conflict shows that as the organizational level increases, the perception of intergroup conflict reduces.

Additional percentile and reference group norms computed from the collegiate samples are presented in Tables 8–5 and 8–6.

Students generally enjoy this sort of feedback. Two one-way analyses of variance show that there were significant differences in the perception of intergroup conflict between undergraduate and graduate students and between males and females. The normative data are useful for undergraduate and graduate courses on organizational behavior, organizational psychology, and conflict management where students can compare their perceptions of intergroup conflict with corresponding percentile and reference group norms.

Table 8–3
National Managerial Percentile Norms of Intergroup Conflict

Mean Scores	Percentiles	Mean Scores
5.00		5.00
4.85		4.85
4.70		4.70
4.55		4.55
4.40		4.40
4.25	99	4.25
4.10	98	4.10
3.95	96	3.95
3.80	94	3.80
3.65	93	3.65
3.50	91	3.50
3.35	87	3.35
3.20	82	3.20
3.05	78	3.05
2.90	71	2.90
2.75	65	2.75
2.60	57	2.60
2.45	49	2.45
2.30	36	2.30
2.15	32	2.15
2.00	28	2.00
1.85	12	1.85
1.70	6	1.70
1.55	4	1.55
1.40	2	1.40
1.25	1	1.25
1.10		1.10
1.00		1.00

Note: N = 1,188.

Sources

The sources of intergroup conflict are mainly structural. The diagnosis of intergroup conflict should identify these sources, which can be altered to attain and maintain a moderate amount of conflict.

Table 8-4
National Managerial Reference Group Norms of Intergroup Conflict

Variables	N	M	SD	F
Organizational level				25.94*
Top	196	2.30	.6067	
Middle	407	2.54	.6135	
Lower	547	2.69	.7111	
Functional area				3.99*
Production	216	2.66	.6904	
Marketing	27	2.49	.6594	
Finance & Accounting	36	2.37	.5391	
Personnel	24	2.50	.5774	
General management	252	2.41	.6533	
R & D	198	2.63	.6843	
Engineering	196	2.66	.6597	
Other	214	2.63	.7036	
Education				2.86*
High school	136	2.18	.5829	
2-year college	231	2.26	.6985	
Bachelor's degree	529	2.25	.6910	
Master's degree	208	2.35	.7487	
Other	57	2.21	.6814	
Total sample	1,188	2.26	.6913	

*$p < .05$.

System Differentiation. Complex organizations develop differentiated subsystems to attain overall objectives effectively. Differentiated subsystems develop distinct functions, objectives, and norms and compete with each other for resources, power, and status (Blake & Mouton, 1984; Seiler, 1963; Walton & Dutton, 1969). Lawrence and Lorsch (1967b) found that subsystems develop different types of internal structures—the formality of structure and time, goal, and interpersonal orientations—to respond to their relevant subenvironments. This heterogeneity in the structures of subsystems has important implications regarding the amount of interdepartmental conflict that may arise. Manheim's (1960) experimental study found intergroup hostility "to vary directly with the number of differences between the groups" (p. 426). Smith (1966) found interlevel conflicts to result from difficulties of communication, differences in major interests and goals, and lack of common attitudes and perceptions among members of different levels.

Table 8–5
Collegiate Percentile Norms of Intergroup Conflict

Mean Scores	Percentiles		Mean Scores
	MBA (*n* = 172)	Undergraduate (*n* = 504)	
5.00			5.00
4.85			4.85
4.70			4.70
4.55			4.55
4.40			4.40
4.25			4.25
4.10	99		4.10
3.95	98		3.95
3.80	95	99	3.80
3.65	93	96	3.65
3.50	92	95	3.50
3.35	88	93	3.35
3.20	79	91	3.20
3.05	74	88	3.05
2.90	69	83	2.90
2.75	61	76	2.75
2.60	55	68	2.60
2.45	45	59	2.45
2.30	34	46	2.30
2.15	31	40	2.15
2.00	27	35	2.00
1.85	9	15	1.85
1.70	6	8	1.70
1.55	3	4	1.55
1.40	2	3	1.40
1.25	1	1	1.25
1.10			1.10
1.00			1.00

Task Interdependence. As discussed at the beginning of this chapter, intergroup conflict in an organization results from its structural design, which requires both system differentiation as well as task interdependence. Thompson (1967) distinguished among three categories of interdependence: pooled, sequential, and reciprocal. Pooled interdependence refers to a situation where the groups are relatively independent of each other (e.g., the relatively autonomous

Table 8–6
Collegiate Reference Group Norms of Intergroup Conflict

Variables	N	M	SD	F
Organizational level				1.87
Top	11	2.50	.70	
Middle	100	2.43	.54	
Lower	131	2.45	.61	
Non-management	222	2.40	.60	
Worker	133	2.58	.65	
Education				14.50*
Undergraduate	502	2.40	.59	
MBA	172	2.61	.65	
Gender				3.52*
Male	402	2.49	.58	
Female	263	2.40	.66	
Total sample	676	2.58	.67	

*$p < .05$.

divisions of a company) but contribute to the attainment of an organization's goals. Sequential interdependence exists where the output of one unit becomes the input of another unit, as in the case of automobile assembly line activities. Under conditions of reciprocal interdependence, the outputs of one group become the input of other groups, in any direction. Sequential and reciprocal interdependencies are the major sources of intergroup conflict.

White (1961; see also Blake & Mouton, 1984) found that both the drive for departmental autonomy and interdepartmental hostility were the greatest where the interrelationship of tasks was highest. It was suggested that complex interdependencies contribute to a general sense of uncertainty, which is a major source of conflict (Crozier, 1964; March & Simon, 1958).

Dependence on Scarce Resources. Brett and Rognes (1986, p. 210) argue that while the basic causes of intergroup conflict are differentiation and interdependence, the intensity of intergroup conflict is partly a function of the subsystems' dependence on scarce resources. The subsystems of an organization often must depend on common resources, material and nonmaterial, to attain their respective goals. Friedkin and Simpson (1985) observed that "inconsistency among subunits is said to occur when not all subunit preferences can be simultaneously satisfied, given the organization's resources....Differences in subunit preferences are viewed, in turn, as a source of ongoing tension and periodic conflict among subunits, especially over the distribution of resources"

(p. 377). This is consistent with Walton and Dutton's (1969) conclusion: the greater the perceived dependence on common resources, the greater is the possibility of intergroup conflict.

Jurisdictional Ambiguity. Jurisdictions over property, authority, and responsibility between two or more subsystems are not always clearly defined; therefore, disagreements may arise between purchasing and production or between line and staff to determine the relative contribution to a solution that requires joint effort (Walton, Dutton, & Cafferty, 1969; Kochan, Huber, & Cummings, 1975). Ambiguities often lead to wasteful use of energy and effort between departments over authority, territory, and so on (Seiler, 1963).

Relationship between Line and Staff. Some researchers have argued that conflict between line and staff personnel is inherent in the line-staff organization arrangement (Sampson, 1955; Browne & Cotton, 1975). Whether this is true or not is uncertain (Belasco & Alutto, 1969); yet reports about line and staff conflicts are frequent enough to make this a probable causal factor. There are several sources of conflict between line and staff. Staff group members often resent that they are required to understand the line's need, advise them, and justify their own existence (Dalton, 1959). In other words, the success of staff depends on the acceptance of their ideas by line. But the success of line does not necessarily depend on the staff advice, which the line can have when it pleases. This asymmetrical interdependence is a major source of conflict.

A diagnosis of intergroup conflict should particularly indicate whether there is a moderate amount of this conflict, the functional and dysfunctional aspects of such conflict, and how the ingroup members handle their conflict with outgroup members. It was emphasized before that a formal diagnosis should precede any intervention strategy designed to manage conflict. But sometimes conflict may become so manifest that a formal diagnosis may not be necessary to understand it. For example, the relationship between two department or division heads may have reached such an impasse that they refuse to communicate with each other except in writing.

Intervention

Several intervention techniques, which can be broadly classified as process and structural, are presented for the management of intergroup conflict. The intervention methods presented here are quite comprehensive and are expected to affect the amount of intergroup conflict and the styles of handling such conflict.

Process

Process interventions, such as organization development, are designed to help the participants to learn mainly collaborative behavior to find the sources of conflict and to arrive at creative solutions. It should be noted that these interventions are useful when the intergroup conflict is strategic rather than frictional or minor. Two intervention strategies for managing intergroup conflict, problem solving and organizational mirroring, are presented. Problem solving is designed to help the members of two groups to learn the integrating style to handle their differences. The organizational mirroring intervention is appropriate when more than two groups are having problems in working together.

Intergroup Problem Solving. Several studies have demonstrated the importance of problem solving in managing intergroup conflict (e.g., Blake & Mouton, 1984; Blake et al., 1964; Likert & Likert, 1976; Schmidt & Tannenbaum, 1960). Blake and Mouton have discussed the following conventional approaches to the resolution of intergroup conflict, which often lead to frustration and failure:

1. Cooperation by edict
2. Negotiations and the hero–traitor dilemma
3. Leadership replacement
4. Personnel rotation
5. Structural solutions
6. Liaison persons
7. Flexible reporting relationships
8. Mediation and arbitration (pp. 10–17)

These interventions are ineffective in improving intergroup relationships in an organization on a long-term basis. These approaches to intergroup conflict resolution were ineffective in dealing with underlying dynamics of intergroup conflict and establishing a basis for continued collaboration. To deal with intergroup conflict effectively, the members or representatives of the groups should learn the problem-solving process. Problem solving involves four distinct steps (Rahim & Bonoma, 1979).

1. *Problem Formulation.* The process of problem formulation starts with the diagnosis of the nature and sources of intergroup conflict. It includes four parts.
    a.   The representatives or leaders of the two groups and/or the consultant present the diagnostic data to the intergroup members.
    b.   The participants divide into subgroups and meet separately to discuss and identify the intergroup problems that are causing unnecessary conflict.
    c.   The intergroup discusses and integrates the problems identified by the subgroups. It prepares the final list of problems.
    d.   The intergroup ranks the final list of problems.

2. *Problem Solution.* This step involves the formulation of alternative solutions to the problems identified earlier. It involves three sections.

    a.   The intergroup formulates the criteria for solutions.

    b.   The subgroups meet separately and formulate alternative solutions to problems identified in step 1(c) with reference to step 2(a).

    c.   The intergroup discusses and integrates the alternative solutions. It ranks the alternative solutions for each problem.

3. *Implementation Plan.* This step in problem solving involves the preparation of a plan for the implementation of the solutions decided earlier. Five parts are identified.

    a.   The subgroups prepare a plan for implementation (including monitoring of implementation) of the problem solutions.

    b.   The intergroup discusses and analyzes the implementation plans prepared by the subgroups. The intergroup prepares the final plan for implementation (including monitoring of implementation) of the solutions.

    c.   The intergroup identifies the problems of implementation. It prepares strategies for overcoming resistance to change.

    d.   The intergroup assigns responsibilities for implementations and monitoring implementation to specified individuals.

    e.   The intergroup prepares a schedule for follow-up.

4. *Implementation of the Plan.* This involves actual implementation of the prepared plan. It involves the following:

    a.   Responsible representatives implement the plan.

    b.   Responsible representatives monitor implementation.

5. *Implementation Review.* This is the final step in problem solving. The first session is devoted to the attainment of steps 1, 2, and 3. A second session is required to review the results of Step 4. In this,

    a.   The intergroup meets to evaluate the impact of the plan as specified in step 3(b).

    b.   The intergroup may recommend corrective actions if the results of implementation deviate from the standards.

    c.   The intergroup decides whether to recycle the problem-solving process.

It has been observed that the process of problem solving often leads to the emergence of superordinate goals (Blake et al., 1964). The characteristics of superordinate goals are such that they are attractive to the members of the conflicting groups, but the goals cannot be attained by any one group singly. Sherif (1958) has demonstrated that the introduction of a series of superordinate goals is indeed effective in reducing intergroup conflict. Hunger and Stern's (1976) experimental study suggested that "the superordinate goal retards the development of felt conflict even if the frustrating antecedent conditions remain and, although a nonachieved superordinate goal does not reduce or even retard the development of felt conflict, the resultant conflict is no worse than if no superordinate goal had been introduced" (p. 591).

Problem solving can also be used to manage intragroup conflict provided that the group is large so that two or more subgroups are engaged in conflict. Another intervention that has been used to manage intergroup conflict is the confrontation technique. Several variations of confrontation designs have been used in organizations with improved intergroup relations reported (Beckhard, 1967; Blake, Mouton, & Sloma, 1965; Golembiewski & Blumberg, 1968). Confrontation and problem solving use different designs, but they attempt to attain similar objectives—to enable the participants to learn the integrating or collaborating style to deal with intergroup problems synergistically.

Organizational Mirroring. This intervention is designed to improve the relationship among three or more groups (Fordyce & Weil, 1971). Generally, the representatives of the work-related groups participate in an intervention exercise to give quick feedback to the host group as to how it is perceived.

The host group that is experiencing conflict with the work-related groups may invite key people from these groups to attend an organizational mirror exercise. The consultant diagnoses the intergroup conflict before the exercise and prepares the results for presentation. The steps involved in the exercise are eight (Fordyce & Weil, 1971).

1. The manager of the host group explains the objectives of the meeting and the schedule for the exercise.
2. The consultant presents the findings of the conflict diagnosis performed on the participating groups.
3. The members of work-related groups form a "fishbowl" to interpret and discuss the data presented by the consultant. The host group members listen and take notes.
4. The host group members form a "fishbowl" to discuss what they learned from work-related groups. They may ask for clarification from the work-related groups.
5. Subgroups of members of host and work-related groups are formed and asked to identify the significant intergroup problems that must be solved to enhance the host group's effectiveness.
6. The subgroups report the problems identified by them. The participants discuss these problems and prepare a final list for which actions are needed.
7. Action plans and strategies for implementation are prepared for each problem by subgroups.
8. The intergroup reviews and accepts the action plans and implementation strategies and agrees on a tentative date(s) for a follow-up meeting.

This intervention strategy is particularly suitable where the solution of an interface problem requires the collaboration of several work-related groups. The intervention requires careful planning and management for which the service of an efficient consultant is required.

Structural

As previously discussed, one of the major sources of intergroup conflict is the significant interdependencies between departments, units, or groups. Structural interventions may be made to deal with these interdependencies effectively.

Analysis of Task Interdependence. This intervention involves the analysis of tasks to reduce and/or manage the task interdependencies between two groups effectively. The following steps, appropriately integrated into a problem-solving process, may achieve this objective (Rahim, 1977):

1. The representatives of the conflicting groups engage in identifying and explaining the task items that create interface problems.
2. When the list of interdependent task items is prepared, the participants engage in the process of a qualitative factor analysis of the task items. This will lead to the classification of tasks into several clusters.
3. The task clusters are assigned to the groups on the basis of congruence between the needs of the tasks and the skill, and materials and other resources possessed by the groups necessary to perform these tasks.
4. One or more of the task clusters cannot be assigned to a particular group because no one group has the expertise, resource, or authority to perform the task cluster(s). Integrative teams or committees must be set up consisting of representatives of the conflicting groups to perform these interface tasks. Lawrence and Lorsch (1967b) found that in organizations where the departments achieved a higher degree of differentiation, the use of "integrator" units or individuals facilitated the management of interdepartmental conflict.

Structural changes also may be made by the superior through authoritative command. Intergroup conflict may be increased or reduced by hiring, transferring, or exchanging group members to increase homogeneity–heterogeneity within and between groups. Stern, Sternthal, and Craig (1973) suggested that exchange of members between groups may resolve intergroup conflict by reducing ingroup–outgroup bias.

The amount of intergroup conflict may be altered by clarifying and formulating rules and procedures, which affect intergroup relationship; altering the system of communication between groups; developing an appeals system; and providing valid information when the perceptions of the ingroup about the outgroup are distorted.

Summary

Intergroup conflict is inevitable in complex organizations. Some of the classic examples of intergroup conflict in an organization are between line and staff, manufacturing and sales, production and maintenance, and headquarters and field staffs. The processes of intergroup conflict follow certain patterns that may not be found in other types of organizational conflict.

The management of intergroup conflict requires the diagnosis of, and intervention in conflict. The diagnosis should indicate whether intergroup conflict is at a moderate level, the functional and dysfunctional aspects of such conflict, and the styles of handling conflict of the ingroup with the outgroup members.

The sources of intergroup conflict are system differentiation, task interdependence, dependence on scarce resources, jurisdictional ambiguity, and the relationship between line and staff. Process interventions, such as problem solving, confrontation, and organizational mirroring, have been presented for managing conflict between groups. Structural interventions, such as the analysis of task interdependence, may be used to manage intergroup conflict. Other structural interventions involve hiring, transferring, or exchanging group members, clarifying and formulating rules procedures, developing an appeals system, altering the system of communication, and providing valid information when the perceptions of the ingroup about the outgroup are distorted. The next chapter discusses ethics and morality.

9

Ethics and Morality

Continued academic and practitioner interest in ethical behavior in organizations is evidenced by the ongoing discourse in both practitioner oriented and scholarly-oriented publications (e.g., Mulki, Jaramillo, & Locander, 2009; Pettijohn, Pettijohn, & Taylor, 2008; Premeaux, 2009). There is great deal of interest now among the public, media, and professionals on business ethics as a result of many of the recent business scandals. "One has only to scan the headlines on the financial pages of the world's top newspapers over the past several years to realize why corporate ethics—or lack thereof—has become perhaps the single most prominent and important business issues of current times and a flash point in the public's eye. The list of companies and top executives investigated for, charged with, or convicted of malfeasance of one type or another during the first years of the twenty-first century reads like a who's who of the brightest stars of the 1990s" (Hernez-Broome, Steed, & Lundberg, 2004, p. 3). The lack of ethical business conduct on the part of senior executives has seriously undermined their integrity and expectations that they can institute and enforce ethical standards in their corporations.

The issue of ethics is more than academic, as a growing body of literature indicates that unethical (and illegal) actions adversely affect measures of profitability. For example, Baucus and Baucus (1997; see also Pettijohn, Pettijohn, & Taylor, 2008) found lower financial performance to be associated with illegal firm behavior, and it persisted for many years after the conviction of the firms. According to Kotey and Meredith (1997), firms whose leaders have low regard for the values of honesty and truth are lower-performing than firms whose leaders value highly honesty and truth. These values, of course, are associated with ethical standards.

Both Kennedy and Lawton (1993) and Soutar, McNeil, and Molster (1994) review a growing literature in ethical choices, yet questions remain. How individuals make moral and ethical choices is a central issue in the study of morality and ethics in organizations. A dilemma, of course, is a condition in which no one choice is clearly superior to the others, and a moral or ethical dilemma is one in which the various alternatives to some degree violate one or more ethical standards.

Because of the complexity of the situations, decision makers confront as well as the fact that individuals must bring their own sets of values and priorities to bear on decisions, and even highly ethical individuals may differ in their judgments, so that it is sometimes difficult to identify a "right" (ethical) choice (Beauchamp, 1988; Freeman & Gilbert, 1988; Anton, 1990). Perhaps because the moral dilemma is so central to problems, scholars have been interested in the manner in which individuals reason through such problems. The process of moral reasoning has been explored in many contexts by scholars such as Kohlberg (1969, 1971) and Rest (1986). More recently, studies have focused on the differences in moral reasoning and ethics in a cross-cultural framework (Abratt, Nel, & Higgs, 1992; Husted, Dozier, McMahon, & Kattan, 1996). Some research has found an association between moral development and moral behavior (French & Albright, 1998).

One area in which moral reasoning has been less thoroughly explored is conflict management. The issue is not simply academic, for it is estimated that up to 75 percent of managers report conflict related to ethics (Soutar et al., 1994), and the inappropriate application of some conflict management techniques may either exacerbate a conflict that already exists or create one where there was not been one before. Rahim, Garrett, and Buntzman (1992) proposed that positive results for organizations are associated with ethical, rather than unethical, applications of certain styles of handling conflict. A wealth of anecdotal evidence exists to suggest that, for example, dominating and avoiding approaches to managing conflict can lead to disastrous financial results and even tragic personal loss when the dominance and avoidance are motivated by less than ethical motives. The Challenger shuttle disaster, in which engineers had concerns about the low temperature launch but did not press their concerns with senior managers, and the Dow-Corning breast implant controversy, in which managers at various levels apparently chose to avoid confronting possible problems with silicon implants, are only two such cases (Jones, George, & Hill, 1998).

Ethics and Morality Defined

Since the terms *ethics* and *morality* are used throughout this chapter, it is appropriate to clarify their meanings. Generally, the two terms can be used interchangeably. Boatright (1997; see also Beauchamp & Bowie, 1997) indicated that the "presence of two words in English language with the same meaning is due to the fact that they derive from different roots: *morality*, from the Latin word *moralitas*, and *ethics*, from the Greek word *ethikos*. There is no difference, therefore, between describing discrimination as a moral issue or an ethical issue, or between saying that discrimination is morally wrong or that it is ethically wrong" (p. 22). However, there are some differences between ethics and morality that should be discussed.

Morality generally refers to rules and standards of conduct in a society. It is specific to societies that exist in a certain time and place and is concerned with practices defining right and wrong. Ethics is often restricted to rules and norms relating to specific codes of conduct for specialized groups (e.g., code of ethics of the accounting profession).

Behavioral Perspectives for Conflict Management

Although managers are required to deal with different conflict situations almost routinely, there is little in the way of explicit guidelines to help them do their job ethically (Rahim, Garrett, & Buntzman, 1992). This chapter provides some guidelines so that organizational members can handle different conflict situations with their superiors, subordinates, and peers effectively and ethically.

The literature of organization theory makes judgments concerning usefulness, appropriateness, or functionality of various methods under different situations. From an ethical perspective, these judgments are often limited by failure to distinguish between usefulness for the individuals involved, usefulness for the organization involved, and usefulness for everyone affected, all things considered, over the long term. (In one important ethical theory, utilitarianism, the latter just is the basis of ethical judgment.) While on a very sophisticated interpretation of the facts, individual, firm, and social utilities may largely coincide, failure to distinguish between ordinary conceptions of these utilities may interfere with sound ethical judgment.

As discussed in Chapter 4, it is generally agreed by organization theorists that conflict should be managed, rather than resolved, to enhance individual, group, and system-wide effectiveness. The management of organizational conflict involves the diagnosis of, and intervention in, conflict at intrapersonal, interpersonal, intragroup, and intergroup levels. A diagnosis should indicate whether there is need for intervention and the type of intervention needed. *Intervention may be designed to (1) minimize affective and process conflicts and substantive conflict relating to routine tasks, (2) attain and maintain a moderate amount of substantive conflict relating to nonroutine tasks, and (3) enable the organizational members to learn and use the styles of handling conflict so that the individual, group, and overall organizational learning and effectiveness are enhanced.*

In the preceding summary of the literature on intervention in conflict management, more than one ambiguous judgment of appropriateness or usefulness may be considered. Some of these judgments will need to be revisited in the more explicitly ethical sections of this chapter.

Ethical Evaluation of Conflict Management

It is good to begin from an Aristotelian perspective and assume that officials of organization, acting in their capacities as officials of the organization, *make ethically correct decisions* when they decide wisely in light of the organization's proper end (PE). Decisions in situations of conflict or practical disagreement are no exception.

This starting point calls for some justification and clarification. Though a full justification would divert us from the main task, it can be said that an Aristotelian perspective is helpful because it differs from major alternatives in the following ways: (1) it realistically presupposes the socially situated nature of the moral self; (2) the Aristotelian notion of the common good (which is our model for the key notion of "proper end") combines considerations of justice and utility in a common framework without trying to reduce one to the other, and (3) Aristotle's ethical and political writings interweave descriptive analysis and normative judgment and so provide a model for this work.

To clarify the notion of an organization's PE, it can be said that a self-sufficient organization or association has a PE identical to the good life for its members, or, what comes to the same thing, the common good [Aristotle (1), I, 2; Aristotle (2), III, 6]. Aristotle regarded the city-state as such an association.

A business organization, on the other hand, is not self-sufficient; it is a fragment of the larger social whole with which it interacts. Business organizations have productive or service functions; they exist largely for the sake of fulfilling needs that arise outside themselves.

Nevertheless, as human associations, businesses have PEs analogous to the PE of self-sufficient communities. A business's PE will include the fulfillment, within the firm's activity, of the moral and intellectual capacities of those attached to it. The good of the individual member includes conducting his or her life in accord with moral excellence (i.e., in accord with justice) [Aristotle (1), I, 7; V, 1]. It cannot be just to trample on rights that other individuals really possess. Hence, violation of such rights is harmful to the rights violator. So when the good of this moral actor is part of an organization's PE, his or her violation of rights necessarily involves a disservice to that PE.

Ethics and Leadership Structure

Ideally, an organization's leadership will be composed of the members who are most ethical and most capable of wise decision making, while those deficient in justice and wisdom are excluded from the governing group. The model used here does not suppose that everyone in the best organization is a paragon of virtue; but the best organization requires that the least virtuous have the least power and/or the most supervision. Undesirable forms of disagreement, those least likely to reach satisfactory solutions, tend more to arise in organizations where this is less so.

The word "wisdom" has been used so far without explanation. By "wisdom" in this context we mean the ability to choose correctly, in light of the facts of the situations in which one acts, actions that promote an organization's PE [Aristotle (1), VI, 5–13; Aristotle (2), III, 4]. Only people of sufficiently just character possess insight into PEs. Just character, in turn, is a kind of disposition to do the right actions and feel emotions in the right way, at the right time, toward the right objects [Aristotle (1), II, 6]. It is possible to provide some criteria for rightness, beginning with the purely formal criterion of justice ("treat cases equal in the relevant sense equally, cases unequal in the relevant sense unequally, to the extent of their inequality"). Further discussion of the general principles of justice is beyond the scope of this chapter. For an introductory treatment see Velasquez (1988, Chapter 2).

Aristotle recognizes a variety of organizational patterns or "constitutions." For our purposes, the most important way in which they vary is along a continuum from fully healthy to maximally perverse. Healthy organizations operate so as to serve the organization's PE; perverse ones operate so as to serve the narrow self-interest of the ruling group. Typical organizations fall between the extremes in this range. So, it should not be surprising that all or almost all organizations of significant size have some internal conflict, which would for Aristotle signify a degree of imperfection.

Practical reasoning in an organizational context ought to begin with an organization's PE; the task is then to specify the means, working back from means close to the end (let's call them *primary means*) to the means or actions that are in the power of subordinate members of the organization to immediately do (let us call them *secondary means*). Leadership typically takes responsibility for the primary means. In the healthy constitution, the non-leaders are consulted for the information they can provide, but they do not determine the primary means to the PE.

The question of how many persons should occupy the leading ranks in an organization is an important, ethical one. Its answer is the same as the answer to the question: How many people possess the moral decency, quickness, and subtlety of judgment and sufficient education and experience to process correctly the data on which decisions on primary means are to be based? Where these leadership conditions (perhaps with some other, more material ones such as sheer personal energy) are widely shared, collegial leadership is ethically superior, for collegial leadership will most effectively promote the organization's PE. Where one person possesses these conditions in an eminent degree and others do so only to a much smaller degree, one-person leadership is ethically most appropriate, with the best person in the top position, of course.

Four Methods of Discourse

Conflict situations in human organizations are semantically meaningful and so can be considered linguistic objects. To discuss them, therefore, it may be useful to adapt Watson's (1985) classification of four basic methods for organizing linguistic subject-matter. Watson's distinctions are derived from the Aristotelian tradition, most immediately from philosopher-rhetorician McKeon (1951).

These methods are *logistic, problematic, dialectical,* and *agonistic.* As Watson describes them, agonistic and dialectic methods are "two-voiced," with dialectic tending toward a higher unity that leaves difference behind, while agonistic does not. Logistic and problematic are "single-voiced," with logistic proceeding linearly, for example, from premise to conclusion or parts to whole, while problematic involves a circling through the parts to the whole and back, until a single consistent account is reached.

Our concern is less general than Watson's, for he was attempting an account of all possible coherent "texts." Our concern here is practical method for the sake of action and, more specifically, practical method within organizations.

Logistic Method

Perhaps the most familiar form of this method in business organizations is instrumental reasoning in a well-defined field of production or service. From a goal more or less given in advance, one reasons step-by-step to the means (physical movements in the group's power) that should be adopted to reach the goal. This form of reasoning fits a hierarchical command structure and corresponds to the relationship between active ruler or ruler group and passive, ruled section in most organizations. It is compatible with subordinates being consulted for information.

Problematic Method

This can take the form of a group problem-solving process that presupposes basic agreement on ends. Conflict is not deeply entrenched, although the parties, sensitive to different relevant considerations, may begin being unsure that the primary concerns of the others are compatible with their own. As discussion proceeds, however, a more balanced and mutually acceptable picture of the best course emerges. Insofar as all parties anticipate that basic agreement potentially exists and that everyone is, in the relatively short run, able to reach it, this method is "single-voiced."

Dialectical Method

This method is "two-voiced": it involves an attempt by each of two parties in apparently basic disagreement to rationally persuade the other. Each probes the other's assumptions. Each must be willing to reflect upon the adequacy of his or her own assumptions and to change them when the evidence presented against them is weighty enough.

Agonistic Method

This is dramatically illustrated in those rhetorical debates in which there are few or no rules. Any device is permitted if it leads to victory; might-make-right; what is good is what works; and so on. Agonistic discourse includes the use of informal logical fallacies such as the appeal to force, the illegitimate appeal to authority, irrational appeals to fear, playing upon a person's emotional relations to a group, and so forth.

Akin to agonistic discourse are the "political tactics" typically used in factional struggles, such as unfairly blaming others for an unsuccessful policy or program; selectively releasing information to create a false impression to maximize the interests of one's faction; using control over scarce resources to create obligations to oneself or one's faction; flattering the already powerful to gain his or her protection; and priming a minority of a committee in order to get a quick consensus from an apparently free but actually constrained, discussion (Velasquez, 1988, pp. 390–397).

It should be noted that the regulated agonistic method (e.g., a competitive marketplace or U.S. court procedure) can sometimes be harmless or even productive of ethically positive ends. But the rules that regulate the agonistic method in such cases can hardly themselves be justified by recourse to agonistic discourse alone.

General Appropriateness of the Methods

Logistic Method, being monological, works effectively only where complete agreement as to the meaning of terms exists or can be imposed by fiat. Like deductive logic, which is a form of logistic, its usefulness lies in checking consistency and exploring consequences of a policy. But it provides little direct help for resolving or attenuating cases of serious disagreement.

Problematic Method is most appropriate for the internal discourse of the ruling group of an organization or subunit. In the case of one-person rule, the wise leader will internalize the process in his or her own practical reasoning. The process serves to make sure all the important values are consciously addressed. The problematic method allows for primary as well as secondary means to be re-described in the process of discussion or reflection.

A Circumscribed Problematic Approach among subordinates in, say, quality circles would also be appropriate in certain circumstances. The point is that what the subordinates are free to decide for themselves is circumscribed and thus does not include the primary means to the PE of the entire organization.

Dialectical Discourse has a place within the overall context of problematic. It is appropriate where the attempt to use the problematic method has revealed entrenched differences, yet the opponents respect one another, have a certain humility about their convictions, and wish to find common ground. Dialectical discourse corresponds to the cases of beneficial internal conflict noted by the behavioral studies mentioned earlier. The conflict serves as an occasion for becoming aware of prejudgments and possibly revising them in light of facts and values of which the participants are reminded in the course of discussion.

The Agonistic Method will never be a dominant method in a healthy organization. (It is justifiable only if ethically regulated, as in contests and competitions, which can be both entertaining and useful for an organization's PE.) In an imperfect organization, driven by factionalism, the ethical moral agent will strive to minimize recourse to manipulative logical fallacies and "political tactics" reflecting the unregulated agonistic method, since using them makes it less likely that factional opposition can be overcome in the future.

The only justification for forming a faction (as distinct from expressing one's differences in a non-factional way) is a justified conviction that the leaders of the organization are not devoted to the organization's PE or are incompetent to pursue it and that the leaders' mis-leadership can be productively resisted or the leaders replaced at reasonable cost with respect to the PE. In that case, one must aim to replace them with ethically superior as well as competent individuals, and one who is willing to rely heavily on manipulative "political tactics" hardly gives evidence of ethical superiority.

Though some of the "political tactics" mentioned are not always unethical, those necessarily involving deception are generally so, while those appealing to emotion rather than reason can easily become so. The reason is that a habit of truth-telling and rationality is the best basis for joint pursuit of the organization's PE. Downplaying these virtues is likely to increase the danger of permanent internal disharmony.

Practical Methods and Conflict Management Styles

The following section, summarized in Table 9–1, discusses the five styles and the situations where their uses are ethically appropriate and inappropriate. The reader should remember that to describe an action in terms of contribution to an organization's PE is already to make a judgment about its ethical appropriateness.

Integrating Style

This style corresponds largely to problematic discourse. The style is most satisfying ethically, as it treats all participants with maximum respect. (A warning, however, is in order here: the participants must not deliberate as if *non-participants* affected are undeserving of respect!)

Table 9–1
Ethically Appropriate or Inappropriate Uses of the Conflict Styles

Conflict Style	Ethically Appropriate	Ethically Inappropriate
Integrating	1. Generally appropriate.	
Obliging	1. When a subordinate is in a healthy organization.	1. When subordinates ignore own needs.
	2. When supervisor has a subordinate with better grasp of what needs to be done.	2. When superior's decisions go against the proper end of the organization.
		3. When subordinates have the needed expertise.
Dominating	1. When decisions support the organization's proper end.	1. When exploitative of others.
	2. When supervisors take into account subordinates' concerns as well as the organization.	
Avoiding	1. Temporarily, when other matters have greater moral claim.	1. When motive is to avoid morally correct but personally painful processes.
Compromising	1. Sometimes when one is a weaker party.	1. When one is right in principle
	2. When required to avoid protracted conflict.	2. When one is wrong.
		3. Compromise of an intellectual sort.

Source: Adapted from Rahim, M. A., Garrett, J. E., & Buntzman, G. F. (1992). Ethics of managing interpersonal conflict in organizations. *Journal of Business Ethics, 11,* 423–432.

But even within healthy organizations it will not be the only mode of discourse. Unless we assume that all participants will possess the preconditions of leadership mentioned earlier, there will have to be a command structure in which the primary means decided in advance by superiors will dictate the tasks of a separate group of subordinates.

There is a danger that a hierarchy in service of the organization's PE will be corrupted into exploitation and oppression, which would be contrary to the PE itself. But the latter is not a logical consequence of hierarchy as such. One can reasonably ask how we know (including how the de facto leaders of an organization know) that someone is morally decent enough to have the right to issue commands.

The question is itself complex. One can know, of course, whether a leader spends a lot of time reflecting over the various alternatives, looking at their consequences, doing research, and running what seem to be the legitimate interests of various stakeholders through his or her mind. But one does not necessarily know that the weighting given to some factors as opposed to others is not perverted by self-deception in the service of narrow self-interest or semiconscious motives such as will to power.

One way to answer this concern is for leaders to surround themselves with colleagues able to exercise independent judgment and therefore to critically comment upon the adequacy of the leaders' practical reasoning. But what can prevent the tendency of leadership teams, which, like any culture, function from day to day on the basis of unspoken, shared prejudgments, from developing a shared moral insensitivity that precludes mutual correction?

Partial insurance against such a corruption of the ostensibly virtuous are the existence of a wider dialogue and dialectic and the ever-renewed willingness of the leaders to listen and participate in them. This wider dialogue includes the discourse of the humanities and social sciences (in which the role of self-deception and semiconscious motives is discussed in a general way) and the political discourse of the wider community, in which, for example, unions, consumer groups, and environmentalists interact with business leaders.

Returning to Rahim's (1983a) typology of conflict management styles, originally developed without specific focus upon their ethical appropriateness, certain distinctions must be made when one takes such a focus.

Obliging Style

This style appears to be ethically appropriate in some situations and not in others. Being obliging most of the time is correct for persons rightly in a subordinate position in a healthy organization. Lacking the education or the firm values to qualify to set policy for the organization, the person can participate only by carrying out the policies established by others. She or he neglects her or his "own concern" only in the sense that she or he does not insert her or his own idiosyncratic values into the leadership's decision process. On the other hand, she or he may well provide her or his superiors with information about her or his own needs, say, for interesting work, for a healthy physical environment, for fair pay, and so on. It is not good or ethical for her or him to ignore these; and it is not compatible with the organization's PE that they be ignored.

The other side of the coin is that in some occasions it is wrong merely to oblige a superior who is incompetent or seriously out of touch with the organization's PE. These are circumstances in which the ethics of internal and external whistle-blowing become relevant. This is itself a complex question about which a large literature already exists (Elliston, 1985).

Sometimes conflicts arise from the fact that the all-round better people are in subordinate positions, while those over them are, in fact, less able to pursue the organization's PE. In this case, the short-term, ethically optimum response for the de facto superior may be to be obliging to the subordinate. A longer-term optimum choice is to raise the subordinate to a more equal level with oneself or even, if possible, to step down in her or his favor. (Doing the morally right thing may on occasion require sacrifice of status and income.)

Dominating Style

If this style is characterized by the dominator's high concern for self and low concern, including lack of respect, for others, then its use is unethical. Such behavior is contrary to a firm's PE, since a PE is partially defined in terms of action in accord with justice, and justice implies respect for persons.

On the other hand, something like the dominating style might be ethically defensible as an expression of firm leadership if all the following conditions are met:

1. The leaders have made essentially wise decisions in accord with the firm's PE.
2. Some subordinates do not understand this wisdom.
3. There is insufficient time to resolve the impasse using other styles.

Such a style would take into account the proper interests of subordinate members of the group, for the PE of the organization includes those interests. The superior in a healthy organization may not show as much concern for the values of the subordinate as she would with, say, the values of a fellow superior, but she or he would not ignore the needs and personal sensitivities of the subordinate either. Therefore, it is ethically appropriate to distinguish *exploitative domination* from a more tempered *respectful domination* in light of the organization's PE. There seem to be at least two forms of domination—one sometimes ethically defensible; the other not.

Obliging and dominating styles correspond to the logistic method to the extent that in the ideal situations where both styles are appropriate together, they occur at the interface between giver and receiver of instructions in a management hierarchy inspired by logistic reasoning.

Avoiding Style

This style is ethically defensible if other matters have greater moral claim to one's attention. The behavioral characterization of this style as reflecting "low concern for self and others" seems out of place here: when rightly used, the avoiding style reflects a high concern with doing the right thing, and such concern maximizes rationally justifiable respect for all involved.

Compromising Style

Compromising corresponds indirectly to the agonistic method. A factional situation is one already at least partly characterized by unregulated agonistic (i.e., unethical) behavior. If all parties were paragons of virtue and intelligence and in possession of relevant information, their demands would all correctly reflect the organization's PE and they would not conflict. But they do conflict, and at least one faction's demands do not reflect the organization's PE.

The best practical approach may be compromise. From an ethical point of view, however, compromising differs in ethical value depending on whether one is giving up the best course or not. If one's demands are wrong, and one's opponent's right, then compromise is better than bullheadedly sticking to one's guns. But if one's demands are right and one's opponent's wrong, then compromise could be wrong (e.g., a compromise might still require one to violate antitrust, consumer safety, or environmental laws).

If compromise would entail cooperating to produce serious social harm, alternatives such as quitting (a form of avoidance) or whistle-blowing should be considered. Either tactic may be justified for the sake of the organization's PE: the loss of a good employee may shock a superior into rethinking his or her conduct, and justifiable whistle-blowing, while deservedly injuring the firm's reputation, may spark its future reform or prevent similar conduct in other organizations.

When compromises in such cases do occur, they may require a twofold evaluation: If a subordinate's resources are weak, and her or his superior is corrupt and powerful, mitigating conditions should be taken into account: she or he may not be highly blameworthy (Velasquez, 1988, pp. 34–43). Nevertheless, the superior's insistence on the compromise may be wrong.

Conflicts are perhaps more likely to occur over division of material resources than over sharp divisions concerning right and wrong. Opponents may differ over which distribution of the resources best serves the organization's PE. (If they are not convinced of their own rectitude but are self-consciously making demands from a motive of greed or power-hunger, their compromising, while superior to refusing to compromise, receives quite low ethical marks.) Normally, the PE as one conceives it will be better served if one has some resources rather than none at all. Therefore, it is reasonable, at least from their own perspective, for parties who are convinced of their own rectitude not to prevent an agreed-upon distribution that will secure them some resources. To the extent that the PE is the sum of the interests of the parties, it would be served by such compromise if the alternative is continuing conflict.

Compromises of an intellectual sort are much more problematic. If a person believes that shipping toxic wastes to the Third World is wrong under all circumstances and another believes that it is frequently morally permissible, there is no way they could reach a compromise unless one or both changed their belief. If either gave up her or his belief merely because she or he valued social agreement for its own sake, ethics would condemn her or him as intellectually irresponsible. It is not wrong to change one's mind, but it is not a mark of sound moral reason to change one's mind merely to bring it into conformity with the crowd's.

Of course, opponents might agree, without necessarily violating ethical duty, to respect whatever policy is endorsed at the moment as a result of debate and accepted decision-procedure within the group. But this would not imply that either would ever have to give up the right to advocate that the policy should be reviewed and changed at a later date.

Stages of Moral Development

This section discusses a field study that is quite relevant for this chapter. The study investigated the relationship between the stages of moral development and the five styles of handling conflict with superior, subordinates, and peers as measured by the ROCI–II (Rahim, Buntzman, & White, 1999; see also Chow & Ding, 2002). The study uses Kohlberg's (1969, 1971) formulation of moral development, which is perhaps the best known of the contemporary theories and is closely followed by that of Rest (1986). Moral development concerns the manner in which individuals make judgments about right and wrong.

The theory divides individuals on the basis of their moral development into six stages, two at each of the following levels. The stages are distinct and it is not possible for an individual to regress to a lower state or "jump" to a higher stage (Kohlberg, 1971).

Level 1: Pre-conventional
    Stage 1: Obedience and punishment (How can I avoid punishment?)
    Stage 2: Self-interest (What's in it for me?)
Level 2: Conventional
    Stage 3: Interpersonal approval (The good boy/nice girl attitude)
    Stage 4: Maintaining social order (Obeying laws and social conventions)
Level 3: Post-Conventional
    Stage 5: Social contract and individual rights (Attaching more value to
          human rights and social justice than laws)
    Stage 6: Universal principles (Abstract reasoning using universal ethical
          principles)

Pre-Conventional Level

At the pre-conventional level of moral development the concepts of good and bad, right or wrong are interpreted in terms of pleasure/pain consequences or physical power. Pre-conventionals are restrained from possible wrongdoing by their fear of the consequences. They may be spurred to other action by their expectations of pleasant consequences. This stage is mainly common among children, but some adults may engage at this type of reasoning.

Conventional Level

At the conventional level of moral development, conformity and meeting social expectations and roles are important. "Good" behavior is behavior that pleases or helps others or in other words, one receives approval by being nice. For conventional individuals, decisions and actions are judged moral to the extent that they meet social standards. Their judgments focus mainly on maintaining law and order by following rules, performing one's duty, and showing respect for authority.

Post-Conventional Level

At the post-conventional level, also known as principled level, individuals begin to account for differences in values, beliefs, and opinions of other people. In contrast to "conventionals," who revere social norms and laws, "post-conventionals" question and oppose norms and laws that seem to violate universal principles such as distributive justice and respect for life. Abstractions such as morality, utilitarianism, reciprocity, and justice constitute the ethical framework of individuals at the post-conventional level. Actions are judged according to the extent to which they are consistent with lofty ideals.

The Study

The study described here involved the administration of two well-known instruments approximately two weeks apart in an attempt to control for common method variance. First was Rest's (1986) Defining Issues Test or DIT (to assess the three levels of moral development), followed by the Rahim Organizational Conflict Inventory–II (ROCI–II), Forms A, B, and C. The DIT has excellent psychometric properties including high validity and reliabilities in the .80s. The DIT scores have shown expected relationships with measures of cognitive variables and behaviors.

Participants in the study were 443 employed undergraduate business administration majors enrolled in junior- and senior-level management courses at a southern university. The study found the following results:

1. The post-conventional level of moral development is associated with the use of integrating style of handling interpersonal conflict.
2. The conventional level of moral development is associated with the use of compromising style of handling interpersonal conflict.

3. The pre-conventional level of moral development is associated with the use of dominating and avoiding styles of handling interpersonal conflict.
4. The obliging style of handling conflict was not associated with any of the three levels of moral development.

Implications of the Study

The findings have important implications for understanding and managing conflict in organizations inasmuch as moral development and use of the styles of handling conflict are significantly associated. Since conflict in organizations is inevitable, it is critical that it be handled as effectively as possible. The integrating style is widely considered to be the generally most effective approach to conflict management and, according to this study, is associated with higher levels of moral development. For that reason alone, the results of this study should be of interest to professional managers and theoreticians alike. Should we try to select persons at higher stages of moral development or provide moral training those already in our organizations in the hope that the integrating style will be more frequently used?

With subordinates especially, who have less position power than their bosses, and with all of the concern today about accommodating the needs of a diverse workforce, avoiding sexual harassment, and finding optimal solutions to organizational problems through teamwork, it would seem very important to minimize the use of dominating and avoiding approaches to conflict management. To the extent that persons at lower stages of moral development are prone to use the dominating style and that some of them are in positions of power over others, employees and managers in organizations have every reason to be concerned about the types of moral reasoning used at work.

Since there is some research to indicate that (1) moral judgment may be developed through educational interventions (Penn & Collier, 1985; Rest & Thomas, 1986) and that (2) behaviors are at least modestly correlated with moral judgment (French & Albright, 1998; Rest & Thomas, 1986), interventions to develop the moral judgment in individuals with lower moral development may be warranted. Training in conflict management techniques that emphasize the usefulness of the integrating style as compared with other styles could even help individuals at the higher stages of moral development to use this style more frequently. Since the integrating style is a win–win approach, outcomes should be more satisfactory for both the organization and individuals after such training (Graham, 1998). Trevino and Victor (1992) suggest that the establishment of strong role norms and appropriate reward systems can help to influence appropriate in-role behavior.

Conclusions

Until now, academic interest in the ethics of conflict management in organizations has been conspicuously absent. Perhaps we have taken for granted that the use of conflict management techniques in organizations is basically ethical.

Unfortunately, experience shows that conflict management techniques may be used for unethical purposes.

A determination of whether conflict management styles are ethical or unethical is a complex matter, depending on several factors, including the motives of those who employ them, the situation, and the extent to which the proper ends of the organization are served. Evaluation of these factors is difficult at best. First is the problem of reconciling the often-conflicting claims of the various stakeholders who may wish for different benefits from the organization. How are we to set priorities? Second is the problem that we may not know, except with the passage of time, whether the proper ends of the organization really have been served by a decision. What appears to be a harm in the short run may turn out to be a good in the long run or, conversely, what appears to be a boon in the short run may turn out to be a harm in the long run.

We are aware of no simple, concise, and unambiguous means to ensure the ethical use of conflict in organizations. Early in this chapter, however, we wrote that a wise leader will behave ethically, and to do so the wise leader will be open to new information and be willing to change her or his mind. By the same token, subordinates and other stakeholders have an ethical duty to speak out against the decisions of supervisors when the consequences of these decisions are likely to be serious. With this principle in mind, it is proposed that the organization that would conduct its conflicts ethically should institutionalize the positions of employee advocate and customer and supplier advocates as well as environmental and stockholder advocates. Only if these advocates not only can be heard but must be heard by decision makers in organizations may we dare hope for an improved record of ethically managed organizational conflict.

Summary

Although managers spend over 20 percent of their time in conflict management, organization theorists have provided very few guidelines to help them do their job ethically. This chapter attempts to provide some guidelines so that organizational members can use the styles of handling interpersonal conflict, such as integrating, obliging, dominating, avoiding, and compromising with their superiors, subordinates, and peers ethically and effectively. It has been argued in this chapter that, in general, each style of handling interpersonal conflict is appropriate if it is used to attain an organization's proper end.

The study on moral development reviewed earlier showed that the three levels of moral development are associated with four styles of handling conflict: integrating, dominating, avoiding, and compromising. The highest level is associated with the use of the integrating style, the moderate level is associated with the compromising style, and the lowest level is associated with dominating and avoiding styles. Implications of this study are that people who are high on moral development should be recruited for an organization and its existing employees who are low on moral development may be trained to improve their stages of moral development.

10

The Measurement of Conflict

Two instruments have been designed by the author for measuring the amount of conflict at individual, group, and intergroup levels and the five styles of handling interpersonal conflict. The *Rahim Organizational Conflict Inventory–I* (ROCI–I) is designed to measure three independent dimensions of organizational conflict: intrapersonal, intragroup, and intergroup. The ROCI–I uses self-reports to measure intrapersonal conflict and perceptions of organizational members to measure the amount of intragroup and intergroup conflicts with 7, 8, and 6 statements, respectively. An organizational member responds to each statement on a five-point Likert scale. A higher score represents greater amount of one type of conflict. The ROCI–I can be administered in just six minutes, yet the subscales have adequate reliability and validity (Rahim, 1983b, 1983c).

The *Rahim Organizational Conflict Inventory–II* (ROCI–II) is designed to measure five independent dimensions of the styles of handling *interpersonal* conflict with superior, subordinates, and peers: integrating, obliging, dominating, avoiding, and compromising. The instrument uses self-reports for measuring the styles of handling interpersonal conflict of an organizational member with his or her supervisor(s) (Form A), subordinates (Form B), and peers (Form C) (Rahim, 1983d). The five styles of handling conflict are measured by 7, 6, 5, 6, and 4 statements, respectively. An organizational member responds to each statement on a five-point Likert scale. A higher score represents greater use of a conflict style. The ROCI–II is brief and can be administered in eight minutes, yet the subscales have adequate reliability and validity (Rahim, 1983d).

Scores from the ROCI–II can be utilized to construct the integrative and distributive dimensions as follows (Psenicka & Rahim, 1989):

Integrative Dimension (ID) = Integrating Style – Avoiding Style
Distributive Dimension (DD) = Dominating Style – Obliging Style

Since the ROCI–II measures the five styles with a 5-point scale, the scale for ID and DD dimensions ranges between + 4 and – 4. A positive value for the ID indicates a party's perception of the extent to which the concerns of both parties are satisfied. A negative value indicates a party's perception of the extent to which the satisfaction of concerns of both the parties are reduced. Whereas a score of + 4 represents maximum satisfaction of concerns received by both parties, a − 4 score represents no satisfaction of concerns received by both parties as a result of the resolution of their conflict.

A value in the DD indicates a party's perception of the *ratio* of satisfaction of concerns received by self and the other party. A value of + 4 indicates maximum satisfaction of concerns received by self and no satisfaction of concerns received by the other party. A value of − 4 indicates no satisfaction of concerns received by self and maximum satisfaction of concerns received by the other party.

After reviewing the literature in connection with the development and use of the ROCI–II, Weider-Hatfield (1988) concluded that "although the conflict literature has historically embraced the 'five-style' paradigm, recent evidence indicates that individuals might select among three, not five, distinct conflict styles" (p. 364). Hocker and Wilmot (1991) concluded after a literature review that "conflict styles cluster similarly to conflict tactics—into three types: (1) avoidance, (2) competitive (distributive) and (3) collaborative (integrative)" (p. 119). Others have classified conflict styles into two or four types. The following is a summary of the taxonomies of conflict styles proposed by different scholars:

1. 2–Styles: Cooperation and competition (Deutsch, 1949, 1990; Tjosvold, 1990)
2. 3–Styles: Nonconfrontation, solution-orientation, and control (Putnam & Wilson, 1982).
3. 4–Styles: Yielding, problem solving, inaction, and contending (Pruitt, 1983).
4. 5–Styles: Integrating, obliging, dominating, avoiding, and compromising (Follett, 1926/1940; Blake & Mouton, 1964; Rahim & Bonoma, 1979; Thomas, 1976).

This chapter discusses evidence of construct, convergent, and discriminant validities of the subscales of the ROCI–I as measures of the three types of conflict. Evidence of these validities is for subscales of the ROCI–II as measures of five styles of handling conflict are also discussed. This was done, in part, by comparing 2–, 3–, and 4–factor models with the 5–factor model of conflict styles.

Development of the ROCI–I

Four convenience samples were used to generate and select suitable items for the measurement of the three types of organizational conflict; a large national sample to construct three factorially independent and reliable subscales of conflict; two large convenience samples to check convergent and discriminant validities; and a convenience sample to test the retest reliability of the sub-scales and to check whether the subscales were free from social desirability or response distortion bias.

Exploratory Factor Analysis

The ROCI–I was designed on the basis of repeated feedback from respondents and faculty and an iterative process of factor analyses of various sets of items. Much attention was devoted to the study of published instruments on conflict. Initially an instrument was prepared with thirty-nine items, seventeen of which were adapted from Rahim's (1979, 1980) organizational conflict instrument. The first step in the development and testing of the instrument involved the completion of the questionnaire by MBA and undergraduate students ($N = 60$). After the sub-jects filled out the questionnaire, an item-by-item discussion was initiated by the instructor. Critiques of the instrument were also received from four management professors. The items that were reported to be difficult, ambiguous, or inconsistent were either dropped or revised. A new item was added to compensate for the elimination of an item. The order of items was randomized. Special attempts were made to make the items free from social desirability response bias.

Four successive factor analyses were performed to select items for the instrument (Ns: students = 95, 189, 351; managers = 1,188). After each of the first three factor analyses, the items that loaded .40 and/or loaded on an uninterpretable factor were rephrased. About 92 items were considered for inclusion in the instrument.

The 21 items for the final instrument were selected on the basis of a factor analysis of ratings of the 24 items from the national sample of 1,188 managers (Rahim, 1983b). In this and the previous analyses the initial factors were derived through principal factors solution, and the terminal solution was derived through varimax rotation. The analysis extracted four factors. The items were selected on the basis of criteria: factor loading $\geq$.40, eigenvalue ≥ 1.00, and the scree test. Based on these criteria, the first three factors with 21 items were selected.

The compositions of items of the three factors supported the *a priori* grouping of items. Factors I, II, and III, which supported the three independent dimensions of organizational conflict, were named as Intrapersonal, Intragroup, and Intergroup conflicts, respectively. The indices of the three types of conflict were constructed by averaging the responses to the selected items within each factor. This resulted in the creation of three continuous subscales.

Reliability Coefficients

Table 10–1 shows the means, standard deviations, intercorrelations, and test-retest (with one-week interval) and internal consistency reliabilities of the three types of conflict (Rahim, 1983e).

Table 10–1
Means, Standard Deviations, and Intercorrelations of the ROCI–I Subscales and Their Retest and Internal Consistency Reliabilities

Conflict Subscale	Mean		SD		IP		IG		NG		Retest Reliability ($n = 91$)	Cronbach Reliability		Kristoff's Reliability	
	M	S	M	S	M	S	M	S	M	S		M	S	M	S
Intrapersonal (IP)	2.26	2.78	.69	.78	1.00	1.00	.29	.31	.35	.20	.85	.83	.88	.82	.83
Intragroup (IG)	2.36	2.41	.69	.78			1.00	1.00	.40	.37	.74	.81	.78	.81	.78
Intergroup (NG)	2.58	2.46	.68	.62					1.00	1.00	.77	.80	.79	.80	.78

Note: M = Managers ($N = 1,188$), S = Students ($N = 676$), IP = Intrapersonal conflict, IG = Intragroup conflict, NG = Intergroup conflict; Kristoff's reliability refers to Kristoff's unbiased estimate of reliability

The retest reliability coefficients (ranging between .74 and .85), internal consistency reliability coefficients as assessed by Cronbach α (ranging between .79 and .88), and Kristoff's unbiased estimate of reliability (ranging between .78 and .83) are satisfactory (Nunnally, 1978).

Social Desirability Response Set

Faking of questionnaire responses or social desirability response bias has been a major concern among social scientists. An attempt was made to check if the three subscales were free from social desirability or response distortion bias. Table 10–2 shows Pearson's correlations between the three conflict subscales and impression management (Paulhus, 1984), social desirability (Crowne & Marlowe, 1960), and lie (Eysenck & Eysenck, 1968) scales, which were computed with data from a collegiate sample. The impression management, social desirability, and lie scales range between 1–7, 0–33, and 0–9, respectively. A higher score in a scale represents greater response distortion bias.

The correlations ranged between –.04 and –.18, and four of the nine correlations were marginal but significant. These correlations indicate that the conflict subscales are relatively free from social desirability responding or response distortion bias.

Confirmatory Factor Analysis

One of the central issues in organizational research is the assessment of the construct validity of measures (Bagozzi, Yi, & Phillips, 1991). Researchers have often used classical statistical methods, such as exploratory factor analysis (Harman, 1967; Kerlinger, 1986), and heuristics, such as Campbell and Fiske's (1959) multitrait-multimethod (MTMM) matrix, to assess construct validity.

Table 10–2
Scales, Sample Size, Means, and Standard Deviations of Impression Management, Social Desirability, and Lie Scales and Their Correlations with ROCI–I Subscales

Scales	N	M	SD	ROCI–I Subscales		
				IP	IG	NG
Impression Management	627	4.42	.71	–.11*	–.18*	–.16*
Social Desirability	475	16.26	8.26	–.05	–.04	–.15*
Lie	248	2.86	.04	–.10	–.09	.08

Note: IP = Intrapersonal conflict, IG = Intragroup conflict, NG = Intragroup conflict
* $p < .05$. (two—tailed)

Unfortunately, these methods have serious deficiencies because "they make naive assumptions as to the meaning of concepts, provide limited information as to measurement and method error, and examine only primitive aspects of construct validity" (Bagozzi & Phillips, 1982, p. 459). It has been recently confirmed that confirmatory factor analysis (CFA) is a more powerful method for investigating the construct validity of a measure than the MTMM matrix (Schmitt & Stults, 1986). CFA provides an indication of overall fit and precise criteria for assessing convergent and discriminant validity.

Anderson and Gerbing (1988) correctly recommended that one should go from exploratory (classical) to confirmatory (contemporary) analysis in an ordered progression. In the present research, we used CFA to investigate the convergent and discriminant validities of the inventory.

CFA of the 21 final items of the ROCI–I was performed in the national sample of 1,188 managers (Rahim & Psenicka, 1995) with LISREL 7 computer package (Jöreskog & Sorbörm, 1988). In the measurement model, each of the 21 items was allowed to load on only its associated factor (which was identified *a priori*), and the factors (representing the Intrapersonal, Intragroup, and Intergroup subscales) were allowed to correlate. The covariance matrix for the 21 items was used for performing the analysis, and parameter estimates were made under the maximum-likelihood method. Table 10–3 shows the item numbers and their corresponding standardized loadings based on correlation matrix, and t–ratios.

Chi-square tests for the 3–factor model were significant, suggesting an unsatisfactory fit. However, χ^2 is dependent on sample size such that a large sample is likely to produce a significant χ^2 even when there is a reasonably good fit to the data (Bentler & Bonett, 1980). In addition, models with many variables and degrees of freedom will almost always have significant χ^2s.

LISREL provides three other measures of fit—the goodness-of-fit index (GFI), the adjusted goodness-of-fit index (AGFI), and root mean square residual (RMSR)—that are less affected by sample size. These measures generally range between 0 and 1, with higher values for the GFI and AGFI and lower values for the RSMR indicating a better fit. The GFI, AGFI, and RSMR for the 3–factor model generally indicate a good fit to the data which were .92, .90, and .05, respectively.

Chi-square, GFI, and AGFI are absolute, or stand-alone, measures of fit in that they directly assess how well the model accounts for observed covariance (Gerbing & Anderson, 1993). I also applied another measure, the relative noncentrality index (RNI), that assesses the fit of a proposed model relative to that of a null model. Evidence indicates that RNI is independent of sample size (Bentler, 1990), and Gerbing and Anderson (1993) recommended RNI as one of the best available measures of fit for structural equation models. Researchers have suggested .90 as a minimum value for satisfactory fit when using RNI and similar indices (e.g., Bentler & Bonnett, 1980). Applying this criterion, the 3–factor model had a satisfactory fit (RNI = .89).

Table 10–3
Factor Loadings and t–Ratios for the ROCI–I

| | Factors: Conflict Types | | | |
Item No.	IP	IG	NG	t–ratio
3	.53			22.88
6	.59			21.77
7	.73			25.53
11	.60			24.60
15	.63			20.73
17	.56			20.00
21	.74			22.52
2		.62		25.36
4		.54		20.45
10		.43		14.40
12		.72		25.72
14		.44		21.71
16		.59		19.64
18		.33		17.84
20		.47		20.01
1			.41	16.86
5			.73	22.94
8			.66	26.18
9			.70	23.89
13			.53	24.96
19			.57	18.69

Note: $N = 1,188$. t–ratio for each factor loading was significant at .001. IP = Intrapersonal conflict, IG = Intragroup conflict, NG = Intergroup conflict. Items of the ROCI–I can be found in Rahim (1983b).

Respondents were divided into top ($n = 196$), middle ($n = 407$), and lower management ($n = 547$) (missing $= 38$), and a factor analysis was computed for each group. The goodness-of-fit indices (GFI, AGFI, and RNI) for the top, middle, and lower management groups were .83, .79, .83; .88, .86, .82; and .91, .89, .90, respectively. These indices generally indicate a moderate fit of the model to the data.

Convergent Validity. This was assessed by examining whether each item had a statistically significant factor loading on its specified factor. All factor loadings were significant ($p < .001$), with t–ratios ranging between 14.40 and 26.18 (see Table 10–3). These results support the convergent validity of the subscales.

Discriminant Validity. This was assessed with two tests. First, the correlation between each pair of factors was constrained to 1.0, and the χ^2 for the constrained model was compared with the χ^2 for the unconstrained model (the test was performed on one pair of factors at a time). A significantly lower χ^2 for the unconstrained model indicates that the factors are not perfectly correlated, which supports the discriminant validity of the subscales. For all nine pairs of factors, the χ^2 of the proposed model was significantly ($p < .001$) less than the χ^2 for the constrained model. A complementary test of discriminant validity is to assess whether the confidence interval (two standard errors) around the correlation estimate between two factors includes 1.0. For each pair of factors, the confidence interval did not contain 1.0, providing further support for the discriminant validity of the three subscales of the ROCI–I.

Confirmatory Factor Analyses in Two Additional Samples

Confirmatory factor analyses were also computed in two convenience samples to obtain support for the preceding results. These analyses were conducted with data collected in the U.S. from a collegiate sample of 1,047 (Sample 1) employed business administration students from two universities and a sample of 1,254 (Sample 2) organizational members from a number of industries. Standardized factor loadings based on the correlation matrix ranged between .59–.80 and .49–.71 in Samples 1 and 2, respectively. The t–ratios for these loadings ranged between 16.90–27.80 and 17.30–26.40, respectively (each t–ratio $p < .001$).

Table 10–4 shows indices that were used to assess the extent to which the proposed 3-factor model fitted the data in the two samples. For comparative purposes, fit indices are also presented for a null model (i.e., no relationships between the observed variables) and a 1–factor model.

Table 10–4
Goodness-of-Fit Indices for the ROCI–I in Two Samples

Sample and Model	N	χ^2	df	GFI	AGFI	RNI
Sample 1	1047					
Null Model		7941.50	210	.40	.34	
One-Factor Model		3710.61	189	.65	.57	.54
Three-Factor Model		819.90	186	.93	.91	.92
Sample 2	1254					
Null Model		7333.68	210	.45	.40	
One-Factor Model		3163.37	189	.72	.66	.58
Three-Factor Model		1099.71	186	.91	.86	.87

Note: GFI = Goodness-of-Fit Index, AGFI = Adjusted Goodness-of-Fit Index, RNI = Relative Noncentrality Index

$p < .001$ for all χ^2 values.

Chi-square tests for the 3–factor model were significant, suggesting an unsatisfactory fit. However, the GFIs and AGFIs for the 3-factor model generally indicate a good fit to the data, which were .93 and .91 and .91 and .86 for samples 1 and 2, respectively.

As discussed before, Chi-square, GFI, and AGFI are absolute, or stand-alone, measures of fit in that they directly assess how well the model accounts for observed covariance. We also applied another measure, the RNI, which shows that the 3–factor model had a satisfactory fit only in Sample 1 (RNI = .92) and a moderate fit in Sample 2 (RNI = .87).

On whole, these results suggest that the proposed 3-factor model has satisfactory fit. Bagozzi and Heatherton (1994, p. 43) noted that it is not uncommon to have unsatisfactory fit when measurement models have more than four or five items per factor and sample sizes are large; in these cases, poor fit may relate to the high levels of random error found in typical items and the many parameters that must be estimated.

Factor Invariance

Two analyses were conducted with LISREL to examine the invariance of the 3-factor model for the ROCI–I across different groups. The first multigroup analysis was performed with Samples 1 and 2. The second analysis tested the invariance of the 3–factor model across top, middle, lower, and non-management organizational levels.

For each multigroup analysis, a covariance matrix for the twenty-one items was computed for each group. Then the following models were estimated with LISREL and compared sequentially on the basis of fit (Jöreskog, 1971): (1) Model 1, the pattern of factor loadings was held invariant across groups, (2) Model 2, the pattern of factor loadings and the factor loadings were held invariant across groups, (3) Model 3, the pattern of factor loadings, the factor loadings, and the errors were held invariant across groups, and (4) Model 4, the pattern of factor loadings, the factor loadings, the errors, and the variances/covariances were held invariant across groups. For each model, the covariance matrices for all groups were analyzed simultaneously, with one loading for each factor fixed at 1.0 so that the factors were on a common scale.

When estimating an invariance model, LISREL provides a GFI for each group, as well as a χ^2 measure of the overall fit of the model for all groups. In addition, an RNI was computed for each invariance model based on a null model in which there are no relationships between the variables and the variances of the variables were not held equal across groups.

Invariance across Samples. Table 10–5 shows the results of the multigroup analysis across the two samples of the ROCI–I. Although the χ^2 of each model was significant, the other indices provide evidence that all four models had a

Table 10–5
Invariance Analysis for the ROCI–I across Samples

Model and Sample	GFI	χ^2	df	RNI
Model 1				
Equal factor pattern		2100.19	372	.98
Sample 1 ($N = 1047$)	.89			
Sample 2 ($N = 1254$)	.93			
Model 2[a]				
Equal factor pattern and loadings		3253.25	390	.96
Sample 1	.89			
Sample 2	.84			
Model 3[b]				
Equal factor pattern, loadings, and errors		3413.89	411	.96
Sample 1	.88			
Sample 2	.83			
Model 4[c]				
Equal factor pattern, loadings, errors, and variances/ covariances		5527.74	417	.93
Sample 1	.85			
Sample 2	.83			

Note: [a] Model 2 — Model 1: $\chi^2 (36) = 1425$ ($p < .001$), $RNI_d = .02$
[b] Model 3 — Model 2: $\chi^2 (42) = 1547$ ($p < .001$), $RNI_d = .00$
[c] Model 4 — Model 3: $\chi^2 (12) = 2553$ ($p < .001$), $RNI_d = .03$

good fit from a practical standpoint: the RNI for each model was .93 or greater, and each GFI was .83 or greater.

As a test of the hypothesis that the factor loadings are equal across the two samples of the ROCI–I, the χ^2 of Model 2 was compared with the χ^2 of Model 1. The difference in χ^2 was significant, meaning that the hypothesis of equal factor loadings can be rejected on a statistical basis. Furthermore, the difference between the RNI of Model 2 and Model 1 was small ($RNI_d = .02$), indicating that the models had virtually an identical fit from a practical standpoint. The difference in χ^2 between Model 3 and Model 2 was significant, meaning that the hypothesis of equal errors across forms must be rejected on a statistical basis. However, the RNI of Model 2 was no different from that of Model 3 ($RNI_d = 0$) and suggests that the equality of errors can be accepted from a practical standpoint. The hypothesis of equal variances/covariances across forms must also be rejected from a statistical standpoint, as the χ^2 of Model 4 was significantly different from that of Model 3. Again, however, the difference in RNI between the models ($RNI_d = .03$) is small, providing practical support for the equality of variances/covariances. On the whole, the results provide support for the invariance of the 3-factor model of the ROCI–I across samples 1 and 2 with respect to factor pattern and factor loadings and reasonable support for invariance with respect to errors and variances/covariances.

Invariance across Levels. Respondents in samples 1 and 2 who reported their organizational level were then divided into top management, middle management, lower management, and non-management, and an analysis was conducted to assess the invariance of the 3-factor model of the ROCI–I across these four groups. Results for this analysis are presented in Table 10–6. Notwithstanding the significant χ^2 for each model, each RNI was .96 or greater, and each GFI was .66 or greater, suggesting that all four models had a moderate fit from a practical standpoint.

The difference in χ^2 between Model 2 and Model 1 was significant, indicating that the hypothesis of equal factor loadings across organizational levels can be rejected on a statistical basis. However, the RNI of Model 2 was no different from that of Model 1 ($RNI_d = 0$), providing practical support for the equality of factor loadings. The hypothesis of equal errors across organizational levels must be rejected statistically, as the difference in χ^2 between Model 3 and Model 2 was significant. However, there was no difference in RNI between the models ($RNI_d = 0$), suggesting that the equality of errors can be accepted from a practical standpoint. Because the χ^2 of Model 4 was significantly different from that of Model 3, the hypothesis of equal variances/covariances across organizational levels must also be rejected on a statistical basis. Nevertheless, the small difference in RNI between the models ($RNI_d = .01$) provides practical support for the equality of variances/covariances. On the whole, the results provide support for the invariance of the 3-factor model of the ROCI–I across organizational levels with respect to factor pattern and factor loadings and reasonable support for invariance with respect to errors and variances/covariances.

Data from the two samples were used to investigate the construct validity of the ROCI–I subscales and their invariance across groups. Results from the confirmatory factor analysis provided evidence of both the convergent and discriminant validities of the subscales. Evidence of these validities together with the evidence reported in other field and experimental studies (Rahim, 1993e; Johnson, 1989; Persico, 1986) provide support for the construct validity of the instrument. Results also provided general support for factor invariance across the two samples and across top, middle, lower, and nonmanagement organizational levels.

Development of the ROCI–II

Seven nonrandom samples were used to generate and select suitable items for the ROCI–II. From a national sample, five factorially independent and reliable

Table 10–6
Invariance Analysis for the ROCI–I across Levels

Model and Level	GFI	χ^2	df	RNI
Model 1				
Equal factor pattern		2793.43	744	.97
Level 1	.68			
Level 2	.89			
Level 3	.90			
Level 4	.88			
Model 2[a]				
Equal factor pattern and loadings		2875.13	798	.97
Level 1	.68			
Level 2	.89			
Level 3	.90			
Level 4	.88			
Model 3[b]				
Equal factor pattern, loadings, and errors		3185.29	861	.97
Level 1	.66			
Level 2	.88			
Level 3	.88			
Level 4	.86			
Model 4[c]				
Eaual factor pattern, loadings, errors, and variances/covariances		3650.53	879	.96
Level 1	.66			
Level 2	.87			
Level 3	.88			
Level 4	.83			

Note: [a] Model 2 — Model 1: $\chi^2 (18) = 82$ $(p < .06)$ $RNI_d = .00$
[b] Model 3 — Model 2: $\chi^2 (27) = 310$ $(p < .06)$, $RNI_d = .00$
[c] Model 4 — Model 3: $\chi^2 (18) = 465$ $(p < .06)$ $RNI_d = .01$

subscales for handling interpersonal conflict were constructed. Five nonrandom samples were used to test the convergent and discriminant validities of the instrument. Also used were two convenience samples to test the subscales' retest reliabilities and to check whether the subscales were free from social desirability and response distortion bias.

Exploratory Factor Analysis

This instrument was designed based on repeated feedback from respondents and faculty and an iterative process of factor analyses of various sets of items. Considerable attention was devoted to the study of published instruments on conflict-handling modes. Initially, an instrument was designed and filled out by MBA and undergraduate students ($N = 60$) and managers ($N = 38$). After the subjects filled out the questionnaire, an item-by-item discussion was initiated by the instructor. Critiques of the instrument were also received from four management professors. The items that were reported to be difficult, ambiguous, or inconsistent were either dropped or revised. A new item was added to compensate for the elimination of an item. Special attempts were made to make the items free from social desirability bias.

Six successive factor analyses were performed to select items for the instrument (Ns: Students = 184, 351, 133; teachers and principals = 380; hospital management personnel = 185; managers = 1,219). After each of the first five factor analyses, the items that loaded .40 and/or loaded on an uninterpretable factor were rephrased. About 105 items were considered for inclusion in the instrument.

The 28 items for the final instrument were selected on the basis of a factor analysis of ratings of 35 items from the national sample of 1,219 managers (Rahim, 1983a). In this analysis, the initial factors were derived through principal factors solution and the terminal solution was reached through varimax rotation. The analysis extracted eight factors. The selection of an item was based upon the criteria: factor loading $\geq$ .40, eigenvalue $\geq$ 1.00, and the scree test. Based on these criteria, the first five factors with twenty-eight items were selected. The compositions of items of five factors supported the *a priori* grouping of items. Ting-Toomey et al. (1991) reported similar factor analytic properties of the inventory from their study in five cultures.

Factors I through V, which supported the five independent dimensions of conflict styles, were named as integrating, avoiding, dominating, obliging, and compromising styles, respectively. The indices of the five styles were constructed by averaging the responses to the selected items within each factor. This resulted in the creation of five continuous subscales.

Reliability Coefficients

Table 10–7 (A & B) shows the means, standard deviations, intercorrelations, and retest reliabilities of the subscales of ROCI–II, computed with data collected from a collegiate sample at one-week intervals, ranged between .60 and .83 (Rahim, 1983a). The internal consistency reliability coefficient for each subscale, as assessed with Cronbach α and Kristoff's unbiased estimate of reliability, ranged between .72 and .80 and between .65 and .80, respectively.

Table 10–7(a)
Means, Standard Deviations, and Intercorrelations of the Five Subscales of the ROCI–II

Subscales of Conflict Styles	Mean		SD		OB		DO		AV		CO	
	M	S	M	S	M	S	M	S	M	S	M	S
Integrating (IN)	4.22	4.02	.41	.40	.14	.12	−.04	.17	−.08	−.23	.24	.41
Obliging (OB)	3.37	3.50	.55	.55	1.00	1.00	.11	−.02	.33	.29	.26	.09
Dominating (DO)	3.13	3.35	.68	.68			1.00	1.00	.00	−.10	.07	.11
Avoiding (AV)	2.80	3.09	.73	.73					1.00	1.00	.16	−.06
Compromising (CO)	3.48	3.71	.67	.67							1.00	1.00

Note: M = Managers ($N = 1,219$), S = Students ($N = 712$). Statistics for the collegiate sample is based on the 1,444 ROCI–II Forms (A, B, and C) completed by 712 students.

Table 10–7(b)
Means, Standard Deviations, and Intercorrelations of the Five Subscales of the
ROCI–II

Subscales of Conflict Styles	Retest Reliability (n = 119)	Cronbach		Kristoff's Reliability	
		M	S	M	S
Integrating	.83	.7	80	.76	80
Obliging	.82	.72	75	.72	75
Dominating	.77	.72	76	.72	76
Avoiding	.80	.76	78	.76	78
Compromising	.60	.73	65	.73	65

Note: M = Managers (N =1,219), S = Students (N = 712). Statistics for the collegiate sample is based on the 1,444 ROCI–II Forms (A, B, and C) completed by 712 students. Kristroff's reliability refers to Kristoff's unbiased estimate of reliability.

These retest and internal consistency reliability coefficients compare quite favorably with those of existing instruments. Thomas and Kilmann (1978, p. 1141) reported that the ranges of the test-retest reliabilities for the existing instruments on conflict styles were .14–.57 for Blake and Mouton (1964); .41–.66 for Hall (1969); .33–.63 for Lawrence and Lorsch (1967); and .61–.68 for Thomas and Kilmann (1974). They also reported that the ranges of Cronbach α for the Hall, Lawrence-Lorsch, and Thomas-Kilmann instruments were .39–.73, .37–.59, and .43–.71, respectively. The α for the Blake-Mouton instrument could not be computed because it contained only one item for measuring each conflict mode.

Social Desirability Response Set

Table 10–8 shows Pearson's correlations between the five subscales of conflict styles for each of the three forms and impression management, social desirability, and lie scales, which were computed with data from the collegiate sample.

The correlations ranged between .00 and .25, and 4 of the 45 correlations were marginal but significant. These correlations indicate that the subscales for conflict styles are relatively free from social desirability responding or response distortion bias.

The psychometric properties of the ROCI–II, reported earlier, were based on classical analytical methods, such as exploratory factor analysis. Rahim and Magner (1994, 1995) used confirmatory factor analysis to test the construct validity of the five subscales of the ROCI–II. As discussed at the beginning of

Table 10–8

Scales, Sample Size, Impression Management, Social Desirability,
and Lie Scales and Their Correlations with the ROCI–II Subscales

Scales	N	M	SD	IN	OB	DO	AV	CO
Impression Management								
Form A	176	4.50	.75	.11	.00	−.04	.04	.02
Form B	157	4.48	.74	.14	−.03	−.20	−.04	.05
Form C	175	4.50	.75	−.00	−.09	−.11	.04	−.06
Social Desirability								
Form A	454	15.94	5.80	.19*	−.01	−.06	−.01	−.09*
Form B	113	15.98	5.97	.16	−.09	−.05	.14	−.07
Form C	202	15.25	5.70	.16*	−.03	−.16*	.08	−.03
Lie								
Form A	135	2.87	1.90	.10	−.07	.03	−.06	−.06
Form B	33	3.61	3.80	.11	.04	.06	−.22	.25
Form C	112	2.65	1.42	.12	.04	−.21*	−.01	−.01

Note: IN = Integrating style, OB = Obliging style, DO = Dominating style, AV = Avoiding style, CO = Compromising style.
* $p < .05$. (two-tailed)

the chapter, this is a powerful method of investigating the construct validity of a scale.

MTMM Matrix

A recent laboratory study assessed the convergent and discriminant validity of the ROCI–II and Thomas and Kilmann (1974) MODE instruments with the MTMM matrix (Ben-Yoav & Banai, 1992). Results indicated moderate convergent and discriminant validity across the data collected on the two instruments. The ROCI–II data suggested greater convergence between self and peer ratings on dominating and avoiding subscales, but not the integrating, obliging, and compromising subscales. As a result of the limitations of the Campbell and Fiske (1959) procedure, discussed earlier, these conclusions are questionable.

Confirmatory Factor Analysis

Confirmatory factor analysis of the twenty-eight final items was performed with LISREL 7 (Jöreskog & Sörborm, 1989). The analysis was done with the national sample of 1,219 managers (Rahim & Magner, 1994). Each of the twenty-eight items was allowed to load on only its associated factor (which was identified *a priori*), and the factors (representing the five styles) were allowed to correlate. The covariance matrix for the twenty-eight items was analyzed for performing the analysis and parameter estimates were made under a maximum likelihood method. Table 10–9 shows factor loadings and *t*–ratios for the items.

Table 10–9
Factor Loadings and t–Ratios for the ROCI–II

Item No.	IN	OB	DO	AV	CO	*t*–ratio
			Factors: Styles			
1	.52					17.00
4	.55					18.28
5	.56					18.63
12	.64					21.89
22	.59					19.96
23	.52					17.30
28	.60					20.22
2		.52				17.01
10		.72				25.06
11		.63				21.49
13		.47				15.21
19		.37				11.71
24		.56				18.60
8			.67			22.21
9			.69			22.89
18			.53			17.21
21			.37			11.61
25			.65			21.76
3				.48		15.85
6				.49		16.17
16				.73		25.91
17				.67		23.59
26				.61		21.05
27				.52		17.25
7					.64	21.24
14					.77	25.98
15					.56	18.26
20					.59	19.64

Note: N = 1,219. t–ratio for each factor loading is significant .001. IN = Integrating style, OB = Obliging style, DO = Dominating styles, AV = Avoiding style, CO = Compromising style. Items of the ROCI–II can be found in Rahim (1983d).

Several statistics were used to assess the extent to which the model fitted the data. χ^2/df (4.12), goodness-of-fit index (.92), adjusted goodness-of-fit index (.90), root mean square residual (.06), and relative noncentrality index (.93) all indicate a good fit of the model to the data.

Convergent Validity. This was assessed by examining whether each item had a statistically significant factor loading on its specified factor. All factor loadings were significant ($p < .001$), with t–ratios ranging between 11.61 and 25.98. These results support the convergent validity of the subscales.

Discriminant Validity. This was assessed with two tests. First, the correlation between each pair of factors was constrained to 1.0, and the χ^2 for the constrained model compared with the χ^2 for the unconstrained model (the test was performed on one pair of factors at a time). A significantly lower χ^2 for the unconstrained model indicates that the factors are not perfectly correlated, which supports the discriminant validity of the subscales. For all the pairs of factors, the χ^2 of the proposed model was significantly ($p < .001$) less than the χ^2 for the constrained model. A complementary test of discriminant validity is to assess whether the confidence interval (two standard errors) around the correlation estimate between two factors includes 1.0.

CFA was also computed in five samples to obtain further support for the 5–factor model. These samples were as follows (Rahim & Magner, 1995):

Sample 1. Data collected from the MBA and undergraduate students who had full-time work experience and were registered in the author's management courses during 1983–93. The students filled out 1,112 ROCI–II forms (Form A, $n = 484$; Form B, $n = 305$; Form C, $n = 323$).

Sample 2. Data on Form A were collected from a national sample of 550 public administrators who were randomly selected from the Dunhill Hugo Lists of over a million administrators.

Sample 3. Data for this sample came from 214 university administrators in Ohio (Neff, 1986).

Sample 4. Data for this sample came from 250 managers and employees in three banks in Bangladesh.

Sample 5. Data from this national sample came from 578 managers and employees. For this sample, the items of the ROCI–II, Form A, were modified to require the respondents to predict the conflict-handling styles of his or her superior.

These diverse samples of organizational members provide an excellent basis for testing the psychometric properties of the ROCI–II.

Confirmatory Factor Analysis in Five Additional Samples

As discussed before, Bagozzi and Heatherton (1994, p. 43) noted that it is not uncommon to have unsatisfactory fit when measurement models have more than four or five items per factor and when sample sizes are large; in these cases, poor fit may relate to the high levels of random error found in typical items and the many parameters that must be estimated. To address this problem, they proposed a method in which subsets of items within factors are summed to create aggregate variables. This approach was adopted, forming two subsets of items for each factor. Bagozzi and Heatherton suggested that two aggregate variables per factor is appropriate when the number of measured items per factor is in the range found in the present study (4–7 items per factor).

Table 10–10 reports fit indices for the proposed 5–factor model based on a maximum likelihood LISREL analysis of the covariance matrix for the 10 aggregate variables in Samples 1–5. Fit indices for a null model (i.e., no relationships between the aggregate variables) and a 1–factor model are again presented for comparative purposes. Although the χ^2s for the 5-factor model were generally significant, Sample 1–Form B and Sample 1–Form C had nonsignificant values on this measure. The GFIs and AGFIs for the 5–factor model were generally high, ranging from .93–.98 and .85–.96, respectively. The RNIs for the 5–factor model exceeded the .90 criterion for satisfactory fit in each sample (range = .91–.99). This analysis indicates that the 5–factor model has a satisfactory fit from a practical standpoint.

Table 10–11 shows the measures of goodness-of-fit for the null and 1–5 factor models of conflict styles in Sample 1 (Form A). The groupings of the 10 items for the 2– and 3–factor models were created as follows. The items of the integrating, obliging, and compromising; and dominating and avoiding subscales of the ROCI–II were used to create the cooperative and competitive subscales of the 2–factor model (Deutsch, 1990), respectively. The items of the dominating; obliging and avoiding; and integrating and compromising subscales were used to create the confrontation, nonconfrontation, and solution-orientation subscales of the 3–factor model (Putnam & Wilson, 1982), respectively. For the 4–factor model (Pruitt, 1983), the items constituting the integrating and compromising styles in the 5–factor model were grouped together, while the remaining three factors were comprised the same items as in the 5–factor model.

The GFIs, AGFIs, and RNIs ranged between .68 and 97, .61 and .93, and .40 and .94, respectively. Each of the goodness-of-fit indices suggests that the 5–factor model has a better fit with the data than the 2 through 4–factor models. Therefore, the 2 through 4–factor models were not explored any further.

Factor Invariance

Three analyses were conducted with LISREL to examine the invariance of the 5–factor model for the ROCI–II across different groups. The first multi-group analysis was performed in Sample 1 to test the invariance of the model across forms A, B, and C; samples 2–5 were excluded from this analysis because they provided data on Form A only. The second and third multi-group analyses

Table 10–10
Goodness-of-Fit Indices for the ROCI–II in Five Samples

Sample and Model	χ^2	df	GFI	AGFI	RNI
Sample 1 (Form A):					
Null model	964***	45	.68	.61	—
1–factor model	584***	35	.80	.68	.40
5–factor model	84***	25	.97	.93	.94
Sample 1 (Form B):					
Null model	775***	45	.64	.56	—
1–factor model	447***	35	.78	.65	.44
5–factor model	29	25	.98	.96	.99
Sample 1 (Form C):					
Null model	964***	45	.61	.52	—
1–factor model	563***	35	.75	.61	.43
5–factor model	34	25	.98	.96	.99
Sample 2:					
Null model	1,928***	45	.57	.47	—
1–factor model	1,216***	35	.68	.50	.37
5–factor model	77***	25	.97	.94	.97
Sample 3:					
Null model	653***	45	.61	.52	—
1–factor model	412***	35	.72	.56	.38
5–factor model	77***	25	.93	.85	.91
Sample 4:					
Null model	541***	45	.65	.58	—
1–factor model	260***	35	.81	.71	.55
5–factor model	50**	25	.96	.92	.95
Sample 5:					
Null model	3,723***	45	.34	.20	—
1–factor model	903***	35	.76	.63	.76
5–factor model	161***	25	.95	.88	.96

Note: GFI = Goodness-of-Fit Index, AGFI = Adjusted Goodness-of-Fit Index, RNI = Relative Noncentrality Index. Ns: Sample 1 (Form A = 484, Form B = 305, Form C = 323), Sample 2 = 550, Sample 3 = 214, Sample 4 = 250, Sample 5 = 578.
** $p < .01$. *** $p < .001$.

were performed with samples 1–5 and involved data on Form A. These latter two analyses tested the invariance of the 5–factor model across top, middle, lower, and non-management organizational levels and across samples 1–5, respectively.

For each multigroup analysis, a covariance matrix for the ten aggregate variables was computed for each group. Then the following models were estimated

Table 10–11
Goodness-of-Fit Indices for One–, Two–, Three–, Four–,
and Five–Factor Models (Sample 1, Form A)

Model	χ^2	df	GFI	AGFI	RNI
Null model	964***	45	.68	.61	—
1–factor model	584***	35	.80	.68	.40
2–factor model	403***	34	.85	.76	.60
3–factor model	266***	32	.90	.82	.75
4–factor model	148***	29	.94	.89	.87
5–factor model	84***	25	.97	.93	.94

Note: GFI = Goodness-of-Fit Index, AGFI = Adjusted Goodness-of-Fit Index, RNI = Relative Noncentrality Index
*** $p < .001$.

with LISREL and compared sequentially on the basis of fit (Jöreskog, 1971): (1) Model 1, the pattern of factor loadings was held invariant across groups; (2) Model 2, the pattern of factor loadings and the factor loadings were held invariant across groups; (3) Model 3, the pattern of factor loadings, the factor loadings, and the errors were held invariant across groups; and (4) Model 4, the pattern of factor loadings, the factor loadings, the errors, and the variances/covariances were held invariant across groups. For each model, the covariance matrices for all groups were analyzed simultaneously, with one loading for each factor fixed at 1.0 so that the factors were on a common scale.

When estimating an invariance model, LISREL provides a GFI for each group, as well as a χ^2 measure of the overall fit of the model for all groups. In addition, an RNI was computed for each invariance model based on a null model in which there are no relationships between the aggregate variables, and the variances of the aggregate variables are not held equal across groups.

Invariance for Forms. Table 10–12 shows the results of the multigroup analysis across the forms of the ROCI–II. Although the χ^2 of each model was significant, the other indices provide evidence that all four models had a good fit from a practical standpoint: the RNI for each model was .91 or greater, and each GFI was .93 or greater.

As a test of the hypothesis that the factor loadings are equal across forms of the ROCI–II, the χ^2 of Model 2 was compared with the χ^2 of Model 1. The difference in χ^2 was nonsignificant, meaning that the hypothesis of equal factor loadings cannot be rejected on a statistical basis. Furthermore, the RNI of Model 2 was no different from that of Model 1 ($RNI_d = 0$), indicating the models

Table 10–12
Invariance Analysis across Forms of the ROCI–II

Model and Group	GFI	χ^2	df	RNI
Model 1				
Equal factor pattern		147***	75	.97
Form A	.97			
Form B	.98			
Form C	.98			
Model 2[a]				
Equal factor pattern				
and loadings		159***	85	.97
Form A	.97			
Form B	.98			
Form C	.98			
Model 3[b]				
Equal factor pattern,				
loadings, and errors		279***	105	.93
Form A	.94			
Form B	.97			
Form C	.95			
Model 4[c]				
Equal factor pattern,				
loadings, errors, and				
variances/covariances		362***	135	.91
Form A	.93			
Form B	.96			
Form C	.93			

Note: GFI = Godness-of-Fit Index, RNI = Relative Noncentrality Index. Ns: Form A = 484, Form B = 305, Form C = 323.
[a]Model 2 — Model 1: $\chi^2(10) = 12$ ($p > .25$), $RNI_d = .00$
[b]Model 3 — Model 2: $\chi^2(20) = 120$ ($p < .001$), $RNI_d = .04$
[c]Model 4 — Model 3: $\chi^2(30) = 83$ ($p < .001$), $RNI_d = .02$
***$p < .001$.

had virtually an identical fit from a practical standpoint. The difference in χ^2 between Model 3 and Model 2 was significant, meaning that the hypothesis of equal errors across forms must be rejected on a statistical basis. However, the difference in RNI between the models ($RNI_d = .04$) seems relatively small and suggests that the equality of errors can be accepted from a practical standpoint. The hypothesis of equal variances/covariances across forms must also be rejected from a statistical standpoint, as the χ^2 of Model 4 was significantly different from that of Model 3. Again, however, the difference in RNI between the models (RNI_d = .02) is small, providing practical support for the equality of variances/covariances. On the whole, we believe the results provide strong support for the invariance of the 5–factor model of the ROCI–II across forms A, B, and C with respect to factor pattern and factor loadings, and reasonable support for invariance with respect to errors and variances/covariances.

Invariance across Levels. Respondents in samples 1–5 who reported their organizational level were then divided into top management, middle management, lower management, and non-management and an analysis was conducted to assess the invariance of the 5–factor model of the ROCI–II across these four groups. Results for this analysis are presented in Table 10–13. Notwithstanding the significant χ^2 for each model, each RNI was .95 or greater and each GFI was .88 or greater, suggesting that all four models had a satisfactory fit from a practical standpoint.

The difference in χ^2 between Model 2 and Model 1 was nonsignificant, indicating that the hypothesis of equal factor loadings across organizational levels cannot be rejected on a statistical basis. However, the RNI of Model 2 was no different from that of Model 1 (RNI_d = 01) providing support for the equality of factor loadings. The hypothesis of equal errors across organizational levels must be rejected statistically, as the difference in χ^2 between Model 3 and Model 2 was significant. Again, however, there was no difference in RNI between the models (RNI_d = 0), suggesting that the equality of errors can be accepted from a practical standpoint. Because the χ^2 of Model 4 was significantly different from that of Model 3, the hypothesis of equal variances/covariances across organizational levels must also be rejected on a statistical basis. Nevertheless, the small difference in RNI between the models (RNI_d = .01) provides practical support for the equality of variances/covariances. The results provide strong support for the invariance of the 5–factor model of the ROCI–II across organizational levels with respect to factor pattern and factor loadings and reasonable support for invariance with respect to errors and variances/covariances.

Invariance across Samples. The last multi-group analysis assessed the invariance of the 5–factor model of the ROCI–II across samples 1–5. Results for this analysis are presented in Table 10–14. Although each model had a significant χ^2, Model 1 and Model 2 displayed satisfactory fit from a practical standpoint, as their RNIs were .95 or greater, and their GFIs were .93 or greater. Model 3 had an RNI of .90, indicating adequate fit along that criterion; however, the GFI for Sample 4 in Model 3 was only .83 (GFIs for the other four samples ranged from .90 to .94). Model 4 had an unsatisfactory fit, with an RNI of .78 and GFIs ranging from .77 to .89.

Table 10–13
Invariance Analysis for the ROCI–II across
Organizational Levels

Model and Group	GFI	χ^2	df	RNI
Model 1				
Equal factor pattern		345***	100	.97
Top-level	.94			
Middle-level	.96			
Lower-level	.97			
Non-management	.95			
Model 2[a]				
Equal factor pattern				
and loadings		365***	115	.96
Top-level	.93			
Middle-level	.96			
Lower-level	.97			
Non-management	.95			
Model 3[b]				
Equal factor pattern,				
loadings, and errors		435***	145	.96
Top-level	.91			
Middle-level	.96			
Lower-level	.97			
Non-management	.94			
Model 4[c]				
Equal factor pattern,				
loadings, errors, and				
variances/covariances		529***	190	.95
Top-level	.88			
Middle-level	.95			
Lower-level	.95			
Non-management	.94			

Note: GFI = Goodness-of-Fit Index, RNI = Relative Noncentrality Index. Form A of ROCI–II. Ns: top-level = 162, middle-level = 556, lower-level = 515, non-management = 439.

[a]Model 2 — Model 1: $\chi^2(15) = 20$ (p > .15), $RNI_d = .01$.

[b]Model 3 — Model 2: $\chi^2(30) = 70$ (p < .001), $RNI_d = .00$.

[c]Model 4 — Model 3: $\chi^2(45) = 94$ (p < .001), $RNI_d = .01$.

*** $p < .001$.

Table 10–14
Invariance Analysis for the ROCI–II across Five Samples

Model	GFI	χ^2	df	RNI
Model 1				
Equal factor pattern		449***	125	.96
Sample 1	.97			
Sample 2	.97			
Sample 3	.93			
Sample 4	.96			
Sample 5	.95			
Model 2[a]				
Equal factor pattern				
and loadings		496***	145	.95
Sample 1	.96			
Sample 2	.96			
Sample 3	.93			
Sample 4	.96			
Sample 5	.94			
Model 3[b]				
Equal factor pattern,				
loadings, and errors		923***	185	.90
Sample 1	.94			
Sample 2	.94			
Sample 3	.90			
Sample 4	.83			
Sample 5	.93			
Model 4[c]				
Equal factor pattern,				
loadings, errors, and				
variances/covariances		1,930***	245	.78
Sample 1	.88			
Sample 2	.89			
Sample 3	.85			
Sample 4	.80			
Sample 5	.77			

Note: GFI = Goodness-of-Git Index, RNI = Relative Noncentrality Index. Form A of ROCI–II. Ns: Sample 1 = 484, Sample 2 = 550, Sample 3 = 214, Sample 4 = 250, Sample 5 = 578.
[a]Model 2 — Model 1: $\chi^2(20) = 47$ ($p < .001$), $RNI_d = .01$.
[b]Model 3 — Model 2: $\chi^2(40) = 427$ ($p < .001$), $RNI_d = .05$.
[c]Model 4 — Model 3: $\chi^2(60) = 1,007$ ($p < .001$), $RNI_d = .12$.
*** $p < .001$.

The difference in χ^2 between Model 2 and Model 1 was significant, indicating that the hypothesis of equal factor loadings across the samples must be rejected on a statistical basis. Nevertheless, the small difference in RNI between the models ($RNI_d = .01$) provides practical support for the equality of factor loadings. The difference in χ^2 between Model 3 and Model 2 was also significant, indicating that the hypothesis of equal errors across the samples must be rejected. Although the difference in RNI between Model 3 and Model 2 ($RNI_d = .05$) seems relatively small, the decrease in GFI for Sample 4 ($.96 - .83 = .13$) suggests that the errors in that sample may differ from those of the other four samples. The difference in χ^2 between Model 4 and Model 3 was significant, leading to rejection of the hypothesis of equal variances/covariances across the samples. The large difference in RNI between the models ($RNI_d = .12$) provides further evidence against accepting the equality of variances/covariances.

The analysis was carried further and reported in Table 10–14. As reported earlier, the factor loadings were not invariant across the five samples, but the χ^2 difference test indicates that one or more loadings between two or more samples differ. Additional analysis was done to explore whether invariance of loadings might result for four of the samples, or at least three. An invariance test was performed on samples 1–4. These samples contained data from actors, but Sample 5 had data from observers. The χ^2 of Model 2 was compared with the χ^2 of Model 1. The difference in χ^2 was nonsignificant [$\chi^2_d (15) = 21$, $p > .10$], meaning that the hypothesis of equal factor loadings cannot be rejected on a statistical basis. Furthermore, the RNI of Model 2 was no different from that of Model 1 ($RNI_d = 0$), indicating the models had virtually an identical fit from a practical standpoint. This provides stronger evidence of factor invariance for the inventory. We believe that the results provide reasonable support for the equality of factor loadings across Samples 1–4, marginal support for the equality of errors, and no support for the equality of variances/covariances.

The objective of the confirmatory factor analysis was to investigate the construct validity of the five ROCI–II subscales and their factor invariance across groups. Results from the confirmatory factor analysis provided evidence of both the convergent and discriminant validities of the subscales in diverse samples. Evidence of these validities together with the evidence reported in other field and experimental studies (Lee, 1990; Levy, 1989; Psenicka & Rahim, 1989; Ting-Toomey et al., 1991; Wardlaw, 1988) provide support for the construct validity of the instrument. Results also provided moderate support for factor invariance across the three forms (which measure how an organizational member handles his or her conflict with superior, subordinates, and peers); across top, middle, lower, and non-management organizational levels; and across four of the five diverse samples.

Uses of the Inventories

Organizational Diagnosis

The ROCI–I and ROCI–II should be used for the assessment of organizational conflict at the individual, group, and intergroup levels and the five styles of handling interpersonal conflict. Generally, the ROCI–I and ROCI–II should be completed by all or a representative number of members in an organization. After the questionnaires are filled out, the data should be coded, and the indices of the three types of conflict for various units, groups, departments, divisions, and so on and five styles of handling interpersonal conflict with superior, subordinates, and peers should be prepared.

These indices should be compared with their corresponding national norms. The percentile and reference group norms of the three types of conflict and the five styles of handling interpersonal conflict, prepared from the two national samples of 1,188 and 1,219 executives, respectively, and a collegiate sample of 712 management students are reported in chapters 6 through 9. Intervention may be needed when the indices of ROCI–I and ROCI–II are significantly different from the national norms. It should be indicated that intervention is generally needed to help the organizational members learn the appropriate use of the conflict styles depending on situations. The national norms do not indicate how organizational members handle their conflict to deal with different situations. Norms can, of course, indicate whether an organizational member is making too little, just average, or too much use of one or more styles of handling interpersonal conflict.

The items of ROCI–I can be altered to measure conflict within a specific group, such as quality control (e.g., Item No. 2 can be altered as, "There is harmony within quality control group"), or between two specific groups, such as marketing and production (e.g., Item No. 1 can be altered as, "There is agreement between marketing and production groups"). The items of ROCI–II can be altered to measure how a person handles his or her conflict with his or her group members (e.g., Item No. 2 can be altered as, "I generally try to satisfy the needs of my group members") and the members of another specific group.

The items of ROCI–II can also be altered to measure the perceptions of an organizational member regarding how his or her supervisor handles conflict with him or her. It has been found that when a person (observer) is asked to predict his or her superior's (actor) styles, the factor structure of the conflict styles is substantially altered. Exploratory factor analysis of these data from observers on styles loads on three instead of five, factors. The styles, such as integrating, obliging, and compromising, are lumped into one factor. Probably this results from the observer's perception that these styles of handling conflict by the superior are desirable for the observer. In other words, a subordinate would like to have more of these styles from his or her superior.

Management Training

The ROCI–I and ROCI–II may be used to measure the change in the amount of conflict and the styles of handling conflict of the participants in general management training programs or programs specifically designed for the management of organizational conflict. The inventories may be completed by the subjects before and after a training program so that changes in the amount of conflict experienced by the subjects and their styles of handling conflict may be assessed. The ROCI–II can also be used for training in handling interpersonal conflict in social contexts.

Teaching

The inventories have been found to be useful for explaining the measurement of the amount of organizational conflict and the styles of handling interpersonal conflict in organizational behavior, organization development, organizational communication, and industrial psychology courses. The students especially enjoy the interpretation of the intrapersonal conflict subscale of ROCI–I and the five subscales of ROCI–II. The interpretation of the scores does not generate anxiety among the subjects.

Research

The Inventories can be used in field and experimental studies for examining the relations between the subscales of conflict and conflict styles and various behavioral and structural variables in organizations. The inventories have been used in investigating the relationships of the subscales of conflict and conflict styles to personality, organizational climate, effectiveness, job burnout, job satisfaction, referent role, gender, organizational level, functional area, education, and so on (Keenan, 1984; Lee, 1990; Neff, 1986; Rahim, 1980, 1983e, 1985, 1990; Persico, 1986; Posner, 1986; Wardlaw, 1988).[1] The ROCI–II has also been used in investigating the relationships of conflict styles to social factors, such as culture and face maintenance, bargaining outcome, love styles and attachment styles, rhetorical sensitivity, and so on (Levy, 1989; Psenicka & Rahim, 1989; Ting-Toomey et al., 1991; Young, 1984). Further studies can be made to examine the effects of various behavioral and structural factors in organizations on the variables measured by the scales of the ROCI–I and ROCI–II and the effects of these scales on job performance, productivity, motivation, and so on.

Summary

Two instruments were designed by the author for the measurement of organizational conflict. The ROCI–I—a twenty-one-item instrument—was designed to measure the amount of intrapersonal, intragroup, and intergroup conflicts in an organization. The items of the instrument were selected based on repeated feedback from respondents and faculty and an iterative process of exploratory factor analyses with four nonrandom sample and a national sample. The subscales of the instrument have satisfactory retest and internal consistency reliability coefficients, and they are relatively free from social desirability response bias.

Confirmatory factor analysis of the twenty-one items of the instrument was computed in the national sample, which provided evidence of convergent and discriminant validities of the scale. Further evidence of convergent and discriminant validities of the three 3–factor model and their factor invariance across organizational levels and samples was obtained in two nonrandom samples. Evidence of these validities together with the evidence reported in other field and experimental studies provide support for the construct validity of the instrument.

ROCI–II—a twenty-eight-item instrument—was designed to measure the five styles of handling interpersonal conflict: integrating, obliging, dominating, avoiding, and compromising with superior, subordinates, and peers. The items of the instrument were selected based on repeated feedback from respondents and faculty and an iterative process of exploratory factor analyses with seven nonrandom samples and a national sample. The subscales of the instrument have satisfactory retest and internal consistency reliability coefficients, and they are relatively free from social desirability response bias.

Confirmatory factor analysis of the twenty-eight items of the instrument was computed in the national sample, which provided evidence of convergent and discriminant validities of the scale. Further evidence of convergent and discriminant validities of the five styles and their factor invariance across the three forms, organizational levels, and four samples were obtained in seven nonrandom samples. Evidence of these validities together with the evidence reported in other field and experimental studies provides support for the construct validity of the instrument.

These instruments can be used in organizational diagnosis, management training, teaching, and research. Future studies should investigate the relationships of process and structure in organizations on conflict and conflict styles as measured by the ROCI–I and ROCI–II and the effects of these latter variables on individual and organizational outcomes, such as job performance, productivity, motivation, and so on.

The next chapter presents epilogue for the book.

Note

1. A list of published and unpublished studies which used the ROCI–I and ROCI–II can be found in the website of the Center for Advanced Studies in Management (icam1990.com/2010/default.aspx?alias=icam1990.com/2010/casm).

11

Epilogue

The study of organization theory and organizational behavior cannot be complete without an analysis of conflict and its management. The classical organization theorists did not comprehend the role that conflict can play in an organization. They assumed conflict to be detrimental to an organization. As a result, they attempted to design organizations to minimize conflict. The human relations movement in the 1930s also emphasized the need to enhance harmony and minimize conflict among organizational members. Whereas the classical organization theorists attempted to reduce conflict by altering the structural design of an organization, the human relationists attempted to reduce it by strengthening its social system. This notion of organizational conflict dominated management thinking during the first half of the twentieth century.

In recent years, a somewhat different set of background assumptions about conflict have come to be endorsed. Organizational conflict is now considered inevitable and even a positive indicator of effective management of an organization. It is generally agreed that conflict may be both functional and dysfunctional for an organization. It is functional to the extent to which it results in better solutions to problems or effective attainment of individual, subsystem, or organizational objectives that otherwise would not have been possible. Evidence from recent studies generally indicates that substantive conflict may be functional, but affective and process conflicts may be dysfunctional for an organization. In general, either too much affective or process conflicts, or too little, or too much substantive conflict may be dysfunctional for an organization. The relationship between substantive conflict and organizational effectiveness approximates an inverted-U function. Whereas too little substantive conflict may lead to stagnation, too much of this conflict may lead to confusion and organizational disintegration. A moderate amount of substantive conflict, managed effectively with problem-solving strategy, is essential for attaining and maintaining an optimum level of individual, group, and organizational effectiveness.

There is no generally accepted definition of social or organizational conflict. Organizational conflict can be defined as an interactive process manifested in disagreement, incompatibility, or dissension within or between social entities (i.e., individual, group, and organization). For conflict to take place, it has to exceed the threshold level, that is, the disagreements or incompatibilities must be serious enough before the parties are drawn to conflict. There are differences in the threshold of conflict awareness or tolerance among individuals or groups. Competition can be distinguished from conflict. It was suggested that competition may be viewed as a subset of conflict.

Organizational conflict may be classified on the basis of its sources or antecedent conditions. Accordingly, it was classified as substantive conflict, affective conflict, substantive-affective conflict, process conflict, goal conflict, conflict of interest, conflict of values, structural or institutionalized conflict, realistic versus nonrealistic conflict, retributive conflict, misattributed conflict, and displaced conflict. Conflict can also be classified as intraorganizational and interorganizational. The former may be classified on the basis of organizational level at which it may originate, such as individual, interpersonal, group, and intergroup. The classification of conflict based on organizational levels suggests that the analysis at a level can be appropriate depending on the nature of the problem(s).

Interpersonal conflict may be handled with various styles of behavior. These are integrating, obliging, dominating, avoiding, and compromising styles. Greater insights into the five styles of handling interpersonal conflict may be obtained by organizing them according to the integrative and distributive dimensions. The former dimension (integrative–avoiding) represents a party's perception of the extent (high–low) of satisfaction of concerns received by both self and the other party. The latter dimension (dominating–obliging) represents a party's perception of the ratio of the satisfaction of concerns received by self and the other party.

A Design for Managing Conflict

Organizational conflict must not necessarily be reduced, eliminated, or avoided but managed to reduce its dysfunctional outcomes and enhance its functional outcomes. The management of organizational conflict involves, in general, minimizing affective and process conflicts, minimizing substantive conflict for routine or structured tasks, maintaining a moderate amount of substantive conflict for nonroutine or unstructured tasks at various levels, and enabling the organizational members to learn the five styles of handling interpersonal conflict for handling different conflict situations effectively. In other words, a moderate amount of substantive conflict in unstructured tasks, handled in a proper fashion, may be functional for an organization.

The management of organizational conflict involves the diagnosis of, and intervention in, conflict. A comprehensive diagnosis involves the measurement of the amount of conflict and the styles of handling interpersonal conflict; the sources of conflict; and individual, group, or organizational effectiveness. The data for the diagnosis should be collected through questionnaires, interviews, and observation. The analysis of diagnostic data should indicate whether conflict at various levels and the styles of handling interpersonal conflict deviated from their corresponding national norms significantly; whether the styles of handling interpersonal conflict are used to deal with different situations effectively; and the relationships of the amount of conflict and conflict styles to their sources and effectiveness.

Intervention is needed when there is too little or too much substantive conflict for unstructured tasks, or too much substantive conflict for structured tasks, or too much affective and process conflicts exists at any level and when the organizational members have difficulty in selecting and using the five styles of handling conflict to deal with different situations effectively. The analysis of diagnostic data should be studied carefully before designing an intervention strategy. In particular, the sources of conflict that correlate significantly with conflict should be selected for change to generate or reduce conflict or to change the styles of handling interpersonal conflict. The two types of intervention are process and structural.

Management scholars and practitioners have particularly neglected the diagnosis of a problem before intervention. The methodology for a comprehensive diagnosis of organizational conflict was presented in chapters 4 through 8. Every organization, of course, may not need to conduct the comprehensive diagnosis presented in this book. But some diagnosis is needed to improve the effectiveness of an intervention.

The national norms of the three types of conflict and the five styles of handling interpersonal conflict have been prepared to help the managers or organizational consultants decide whether an organization has too little, too much, or a moderate amount of conflict and whether the organizational members are making too little, too much, or a moderate use of the styles of handling interpersonal conflict. It should be noted that the norms are the averages based on the responses of managers from different types of firms. Therefore, they provide some crude indicators of what may be an acceptable level of conflict.

The norms of the styles of handling conflict cannot provide any indication as to whether a style has been appropriately used to deal with a particular situation. In-depth interviews with the organizational members are needed to determine whether they are selecting and using the styles to deal properly with different situations.

Table 11–1 shows the taxonomy for the management of organizational conflict at the individual, interpersonal, group, and intergroup levels discussed throughout the book. Following is a discussion of this taxonomy.

Intrapersonal Conflict

Intrapersonal conflict occurs when a person must perform a task that does not match his or her expertise, interests, goals, and values. Such conflict also occurs

Table 11–1

A Taxonomy for the Management of Organizational Conflict

Intrapersonal Conflict

Diagnosis

Measurement

  a. Amount of intrapersonal conflict
  b. Sources of intrapersonal conflict
  c. Effectiveness of the individual members of an organization

Analysis

  a. Amount of intrapersonal conflict in various organizational levels, units, departments, or divisions and whether they deviated from the national norms significantly
  b. Relationship between intrapersonal conflict and its sources
  c. Relationship between intrapersonal conflict and individual effectiveness

Intervention

  1. Technique of role analysis
  2. Job design

Results

  a. Low amount of conflict
  b. Greater individual effectiveness

Interpersonal Conflict

Diagnosis

Measurement

  a. Styles of handling interpersonal conflict used by the organizational members to deal with different situations
  b. Factors that affect the styles of handling conflict
  c. Effectiveness of the individual members of an organization

Analysis

  a. Styles of handling interpersonal conflict used by members of various units, departments, and divisions and whether they deviated from the national norms significantly
  b. Whether organizational members are using appropriate styles to deal with different situations effectively
  c. Relationships of styles to situations and individual effectiveness

Intervention

  1. Transactional analysis
  2. Provision for appeal to authority
  3. Provision for corporate ombudsman

Results

  a. Appropriate selection and use of the five styles of handling interpersonal conflict to deal with different situations
  b. Improved communication
  c. Greater individual effectiveness

Table 11–1 (continued)

Intragroup Conflict

Diagnosis

Measurement
  - a. Amount of intragroup conflict and the styles of handling such conflict
  - b. Factors that affect intragroup conflict and the styles of handling such conflict
  - c. Effectiveness of groups

Analysis
  - a. Amount of intragroup conflict and the styles of handling such conflict in different groups, departments, units, etc. and whether the amount of conflict deviated from the national norms
  - b. Relationships of intragroup conflict and the styles of handling such conflict to their sources
  - c. Relationships of the amount of intragroup conflict and the styles of handling such conflict to group effectiveness

Intervention
  1. Team building
  2. Structural changes

Results
  - a. Moderate amount of substantive conflict
  - b. Improved intragroup relationship
  - c. Greater group effectiveness

Intergroup Conflict

Diagnosis

Measurement
  - a. Amount of conflict between two specific groups
  - b. Styles of handling conflict of the ingroup with the outgroup members
  - c. Sources of intergroup conflict
  - d. Effectiveness of intergroup relations

Analysis
  - a. Amount of conflict between two specific groups and whether it deviated from the national norm
  - b. Styles of handling conflict of the ingroup with outgroup members
  - c. Relationships of intergroup conflict and the styles of handling such conflict to the effectiveness of intergroup relations

Intervention
  1. Intergroup problem solving
  2. Organizational mirroring
  3. Analysis of task interdependence
  4. Structural changes

Results
  - a. Moderate amount of conflict
  - b. Greater synergy in intergroup decisions
  - c. Improved communication between groups
  - d. Better relationship between groups

when the role a person expects to perform and the role that is demanded of him or her by the organization are incongruent. Intrapersonal conflict may lead to job dissatisfaction, tension, absenteeism, and organizational withdrawal. Existing literature did not indicate any functional outcome of intrapersonal conflict. Therefore, an attempt may be made to minimize intrapersonal conflict.

The management of intrapersonal conflict involves matching the individual goals and role expectations with the needs of the task and role demand so that the organizational and individual goals can be attained. The management of this conflict involves the diagnosis of, and intervention in, such conflict.

The diagnosis of this type of conflict involves the measurement of the amount of intrapersonal conflict, the sources of such conflict, and individual learning and effectiveness. The sources of intrapersonal conflict are misassignment and goal incongruence, inappropriate demand on capacity, organization structure, supervisory style, position, and personality. These sources may be altered to reduce or generate intrapersonal conflict.

The analysis of diagnostic data should indicate the amount of intrapersonal conflict existing at various organizational levels, units, departments, and divisions and whether they deviated from the national norms significantly; the relationship between conflict and its sources; and the relationship between intrapersonal conflict and individual learning and effectiveness. At the very least, a diagnosis should indicate whether there is a low, moderate, or high amount of intrapersonal conflict in various levels or units of an organization. A diagnosis should indicate whether there is a need for intervention and the type of intervention needed.

The techniques of role analysis and job design are two processes and structural interventions, respectively, which can be used to manage intrapersonal conflict. Role analysis may be used to analyze and differentiate individual, group, and intergroup roles and to enable organizational members to deal with tasks and role interdependencies more systematically. Job design is a structural intervention for changing several dimensions of a job for increasing motivation and job performance and reducing dysfunctional intrapersonal conflict.

Interpersonal Conflict

Interpersonal conflict refers to disagreements or incompatibilities between an individual and his or her superior(s), subordinates, and peers. Chapter 6 presented a model of organizational conflict, especially interpersonal, intragroup, and intergroup conflicts. The model begins with the sources of conflict, such as behavioral, structural, and demographic factors. These factors affect the amount of conflict and the styles of handling conflict. The model shows how the behavior and attitudes of the parties are affected during conflict and the consequences of such change on the relationship between parties. If the conflict intensifies, it may lead to structure formation; for example, the parties may decide to communicate only through writing. As a result of the win–lose conflict, the parties may decide to use a new decision process that is bargaining rather than problem solving. The aftermath of conflict may be a feeling of victory or defeat, which will affect future conflict resolution methods used by the parties. This model should enable an organizational practitioner to understand the dynamics of conflict and to design appropriate intervention methods to deal with conflict effectively. This shows that the management of interpersonal conflict is much more complex than the Prisoner's Dilemma, which is a well-known strategy in game theory.

Negotiation skills are essential for managing interpersonal conflict. The four essentials of principled negotiation are to separate the people from the problem; focus on interests, not positions; invent options for mutual gains; and insist on using objective criteria. Negotiation scholars generally remember the BATNA (best alternative to a negotiated agreement) principle, which is an alternative that negotiators can turn to if current negotiations fail and an agreement cannot be reached. Principled negotiation is different from the positional or "hard" bargaining where the negotiator wants to win at all costs and also from the "soft" bargaining that may result in undue concessions to the opponent.

There are five styles of handling interpersonal conflict: integrating, obliging, dominating, avoiding, and compromising. The literature indicated that the use of a problem-solving or integrating style increases job satisfaction, organizational commitment, and performance. Existing studies neglected to investigate the appropriateness of the five styles depending on situations. It has been suggested that each of these styles is appropriate depending on the situation. Chapter 4 discussed the conflict-handling styles and the situations where they are appropriate or inappropriate. In general, integrating, and to some extent, compromising styles are appropriate for handling conflicts involving complex problems, and obliging, dominating, and avoiding styles are appropriate for dealing with day-to-day or minor problems. The management of interpersonal conflict involves enabling the organizational participants to learn the five styles of handling conflict situations with superior(s), subordinates, and peers effectively.

The diagnosis of interpersonal conflict involves the measurement of the styles of handling interpersonal conflict used by organizational members to deal with different situations, the factors that affect the styles of handling conflict, and the effectiveness of the individual members of an organization. The factors that affect the styles of handling interpersonal conflict are personality, bases of supervisory power, organizational culture, and referent role. Gender does not have any effect on conflict styles.

The analysis of data should indicate whether the styles of handling conflict used by the members of various units, departments, or divisions deviated from their corresponding national norms significantly or whether the styles are appropriately used to deal with different situations. The analysis should also indicate which factors affect the styles of handling conflict and the relationships of styles to organizational learning and effectiveness.

Intervention is particularly needed if the organizational members have difficulty in selecting and using the five styles of handling interpersonal conflict to deal with different situations effectively. Several intervention methods have been presented for the effective management of interpersonal conflict. Transactional analysis training is a process intervention. It is designed to improve communication among the members of an organization to enhance integrating style and, to some extent, the compromising style, and, to reduce obliging, dominating, and avoiding styles.

Structural intervention techniques, such as provision for appeal to authority and corporate ombudsman, are designed to help the organizational members to deal with routine interpersonal conflict. Structural interventions are not designed to alter the styles of handling conflict of organizational members but to enable them to resolve certain minor conflicts quickly.

Intragroup Conflict

This refers to disagreements, incompatibilities, or disputes among the members of a group or its subgroups. Organization theorists generally agree that lack of conflict or cooperation enhances positive relationships among group members, but the group members may not be able to attain a higher level of performance. Several studies indicate that competitive groups perform better than cooperative ones. The management of intragroup conflict involves effectively channeling the energies, expertise, and resources of a group in conflict toward the formulation and/or attainment of group goals.

A comprehensive diagnosis of intragroup conflict involves the measurement of the amount of intragroup conflict and styles of handling such conflict, the factors that affect intragroup conflict and the styles of handling such conflict, and the effectiveness of groups. The factors that affect intragroup conflict are leadership style, task structure, group composition, conflict asymmetry, size, cohesiveness and groupthink, and external threats.

The analysis of diagnostic data should indicate the amount of intragroup conflict and the styles of handling such conflict in different groups, departments, units, and so on and whether the amount of intragroup conflict deviated from the national norms significantly; and the relationships of intragroup conflict and the styles of handling such conflict to the sources of conflict, learning, and effectiveness of groups.

At the minimum, the diagnosis of intragroup conflict should indicate whether there is too little, too much, or a moderate amount of conflict and whether conflict is handled by the group members effectively. The process intervention available for the management of intragroup conflict is team building. It is designed to enable a group to analyze and redefine its goals, tasks, task assignment, and group processes. A team-building intervention can be used to manage intragroup conflict effectively.

Several structural interventions are available to deal with intragroup conflict. Conflict may be reduced by making a group more cohesive and homogeneous. A manager can intensify intragroup conflict by altering the composition of group members. The amount of conflict may also be altered by changing the group size, task structure, reward system, rules and procedures, and appeals system.

Intergroup Conflict

Intergroup conflict refers to disagreements, incompatibilities, or dissension that occurs between the members and/or representatives of two or more groups so that the groups have difficulties in attaining their common goals. The effects of intergroup conflict can be both functional and dysfunctional, depending on the nature of conflict relationships and the tasks involved. The management of conflict between two or more groups involves channeling the energies, expertise, and resources of the conflicting groups for synergistic solutions to their common problems or attainment of overall organizational goals.

The diagnosis of intergroup conflict requires the measurement of the amount of conflict between two specific groups, the styles of handling conflict of the ingroup members with outgroup members, the sources of intergroup conflict, and the effectiveness of intergroup relations. The sources of intergroup conflict are system differentiation, task interdependence, dependence on scarce resources, jurisdictional ambiguity, and relationship between line and staff.

The analysis of diagnostic data should indicate whether the amount of intergroup conflict deviated from the national norms significantly, whether the intergroup conflict is handled effectively, and the relationships of the amount of intergroup conflict and the styles of handling such conflict to the sources of intergroup conflict and the effectiveness of intergroup relations. A diagnosis, at a minimum, should indicate whether there is a moderate amount of intergroup conflict and whether the ingroup members are handling their conflict with outgroup members effectively.

The process intervention strategies, such as problem solving and organizational mirroring, have been presented for managing intergroup conflict. Problem solving is designed to help the members of two groups learn the integrating style to deal with their incompatibilities. The organizational mirroring intervention is appropriate when more than two groups are having problems in working together.

Intergroup conflict often results from interdependence between groups. The analysis of task interdependence is a structural intervention designed to handle the interdependent tasks more effectively. Other structural changes to reduce or generate intergroup conflict are hiring, transferring, or exchanging group members, clarifying and formulating rules and procedures, developing an appeals system, and providing valid information when the perceptions of ingroup about outgroup are distorted.

Ethics of Managing Conflict

Managers are required to deal with different conflict situations almost routinely. Unfortunately, few guidelines exist to help them do their job ethically. Academic interest in the ethics of conflict management in organizations has so far been conspicuously absent. Perhaps we have taken for granted that the use of conflict management techniques in organizations is basically ethical. Unfortunately, experience shows that conflict management techniques may be used for unethical purposes.

Chapter 9 provides a brief outline of the ethical use of the styles of handling interpersonal conflict in organizations. It has been argued that, in general, each style of handling interpersonal conflict is appropriate if it is used to attain an organization's proper objectives. This discussion is based on the work by Rahim, Garrett, and Buntzman (1992).

There are no simple, precise, and unambiguous means to ensure the ethical use of conflict in organizations. Whether the use of a style(s) to deal with a conflict is ethical or unethical is situationally determined. The use of a style is appropriate if it contributes to the common goal of the organization. An attempt was made to provide some guidelines so that organizational members can handle different conflict situations with their superiors, subordinates, and peers ethically and effectively. There is no inconsistency between managing conflict ethically and enhancing the learning and effectiveness of an organization.

Two points about the "common goal" should be noted. First, the common goal cannot be promoted without promoting the good of all or at least a significant number of the members of the community. Secondly, we ought to understand the individual human good as containing an important ethical component. A person's individual good includes conducting his or her life in accordance with moral excellence.

Measurement of Conflict

Two instruments were developed to measure organizational conflict. The Rahim Organizational Conflict Inventory–I (ROCI–I) was designed to measure the amount of intrapersonal, intragroup, and intergroup conflicts. The Rahim Organizational Conflict Inventory–II (ROCI–II) was designed to measure the styles of handling interpersonal conflict with superior(s) (Form A), subordinates (Form B), and peers (Form C). Some of the items and instructions of this inventory may be altered to measure how a person handles his or her intragroup and intergroup conflicts.

The two instruments were constructed on the basis of several pilot studies and two separate national studies. The results of the data analysis suggest that the scales have adequate internal consistency and retest reliabilities and construct, criterion, convergent, and discriminant validities.

The national norms of conflict, reported in chapters 5 through 8, were prepared on the basis of data from the two national samples collected with the ROCI–I and ROCI–II. The two instruments were primarily developed for the diagnosis of the amount of the three types of conflict and the five styles of handling interpersonal conflict with superiors, subordinates, and peers. The inventories can be used for the diagnosis of organizational conflict, basic research, and teaching.

Appendix A
Cases

In this section, four cases are presented. The names of individuals and companies in the first three cases were disguised at the request of the company officials.

The cases can be used to enable the participants in a management workshop to learn how to deal with conflict situations in an organization. In particular, the participants should be encouraged to work on the following aspects of a case:

1. Recognition of the major and minor problems of a company or one or more of its subsystems.
2. Detailed analyses of these problems.
3. Recommendations for alternative courses of action.

The cases should not be used to demonstrate the superiority of one course of action over another. They should be used to help the participants to develop their problem-solving skills.

Case 1
Allen Manufacturing Corporation

Allen Manufacturing was founded in 1966 by Frank Allen, who personally managed the company until his death in 1972. He was succeeded by his sons Steve, who became the president of the corporation, and Walter, who assumed the position of general manager.

The company manufactures exothermic products for use in steel production, such as fiber mold liners, superimposed consumable hot tops, and exothermic sideboards. The manufacturing plant consists of mixing operations, where raw materials are blended in electric powered ribbon mixers, and molding operations, where the mixture is placed into dies and formed as per mold design of the customer. Following the molding operation, the product is transported to the curing area by means of a gasoline-powered forklift and placed into the furnace for a period of 4 to 6 hours at 400 degrees Fahrenheit. The product is cooled and transported to the packing area to be packed and shipped.

Production Department

The production department is under the supervision of David Blake, production superintendent. He joined the company in 1964 as a laborer and, subsequently, worked his way through the ranks.

David Blake's assistant is John Donovan, who was hired in 1970 as an assistant quality control manager. He was appointed as David's assistant in 1972 because of his abilities in administrative procedures. Currently, John handles all the administrative duties, while David supervises production.

The third in command in production is Donald Nelson, who is the general foreman. His job is to schedule production on a day-to-day basis and to follow it through.

Maintenance Department

The maintenance department is headed by James Seibert, maintenance superintendent. James has been with the company since its inception and is a close personal friend of David Blake. It is James's duty to order replacement parts and perform necessary repairs of company equipment.

James's assistant, Joe Kelly, directly assigns and supervises the maintenance duties. The maintenance department usually receives assignments for maintenance by means of work orders written by one of the production foremen and approved by John Donovan.

Incident 1. Don Nelson approached Jim Seibert with, "Our furnaces are in desperate need of repair. They are inconsistent. The ware is constantly being overbaked in certain sections and not baked enough in others."

Jim Seibert's reply was, "We are constantly repairing the furnaces, but with the parts and equipment available we are not able to repair them to your satisfaction. I have been told that funds are not available for the purchase of these parts."

Incident 2. Don Nelson again approached Jim Seibert, "How are we expected to meet our orders if we cannot get our ware to the furnace? Two of our forklifts are out-of-order; and the remaining two, which are in use, are unsafe to operate."

Jim Seibert replied, "You can't expect miracles from my men. They are underpaid and overworked as it is. You will have to get by with the two lifts you are now operating until we get the opportunity to repair the ones in the shop."

When Don Nelson passed this information to his supervisor, David Blake, he was told, "I feel that under the circumstances maintenance is doing the best they can. Just give them time."

Dissatisfied with David Blake's answer, Don Nelson decided to take the situation into his own hands and to write a memo to Walter Allen.

To: Walter Allen

From: Donald Nelson

Subject: Unsatisfactory condition of equipment

I feel a problem has arisen in the plant that you should be aware of. We are finding great difficulty in meeting our orders. Our furnaces are not working properly and our forklifts are in deplorable condition. Every time I approach Jim Seibert on the subject I get a poor excuse instead of action.

Upon receipt of the memo, Walter Allen called a meeting with David Blake, John Donovan, Jim Seibert, Don Nelson, and Joe Kelly. All participants at the meeting were free to discuss their respective problems. The results of this meeting were as follows:

1. Jim Seibert was given more freedom in purchasing parts and equipment.
2. It was suggested that Don Nelson submit his orders and complaints to maintenance in the form of written work orders, so that his views would not be put off or overlooked.
3. Through the work order process, David Blake and John Donovan would be made aware of the problems that Don Nelson was experiencing.

Case 2
New Employee at the Credit Union

The credit union is a fast growing financial institution that is serving the banking needs of educators and other members of the seventeen counties surrounding the local university. The credit union, unlike other banking institutions, is completely owned by its members; therefore, the members have a large degree of control over its operations. The office personnel of the credit union consists of the following: a president, a vice president in charge of loans, an accountant, a marketing director, two credit officers (part-time student employees), a head teller, five regular tellers, an accounts clerk, and a receptionist. The receptionist is also in charge of handling the insurance coverage that the credit union offers to its members through a local insurance firm. She makes the insurance payments for each member through the electronic funds transfer system.

The credit union strives to maintain a personal approach in dealing with its members. It prides itself on the friendly atmosphere of the office and the high quality of interpersonal relationships among the staff members. The personality of each employee reflects the commitment to "individual attention and personal caring for each member." The board of directors ensures that the ambience of the office is maintained. By visiting the office frequently, keeps the employees alert and ensures that they will treat the members with the respect that each member has become accustomed to expect. The board, which is made up of five elected members, meets monthly to discuss the progress of the credit union and any needs that should be addressed. The board has complete control over the actions of the president and any other employees or persons acting on behalf of the credit union.

Before a person is hired, a "team spirit" is stressed to the prospective employee so that the applicant understands the "organization culture" that exists in the credit union. A new employee is allowed to meet the other employees and is encouraged to interact with them by asking questions and engaging in conversation. During an interview with a new employee, it is emphasized that employees work together as a team and that each employee can depend on other team members for support and assistance. Prospective employees are made to understand that they don't just perform their assigned tasks with several different employees; it is a team effort with trust and friendship as the foundation upon which is built the strong working relationship.

Hiring a New Employee

In October 1984 Joan Woodward applied for the position of receptionist at the credit union, which she had been referred to by a close friend. She had moved to the Richmond area from a large city in upstate New York. Her husband had been transferred to this area by his company. Joan and her husband had not been in Richmond, and they did not know any one in the area. Joan applied to the credit union so that she would have something to do with her spare time. This was Joan's first job. She was fifty-three and did not have any previous employment experience or any higher educational qualification for a professional job. After the interview, Joan was hired. The president, who was in charge of all the hiring and firing, felt that Joan could learn the process required to perform the insurance billings and could answer any questions that the members might have after she was trained. Joan began working in late October and seemed to understand and enjoy her work.

Breach of Confidence. Joan had developed a normal working relationship with everyone in the office. She had even become a close friend of Kim, the director of marketing, winning her confidence and trust. One day in late February, the two persons discussed something very personal to Kim. This conversation concerned the private life of Kim and had nothing to do with the credit union or its operations. Kim did not expect this conversation to be repeated. She definitely did not expect it to be spread around the office as "office gossip." However, Joan told several people in the office of Kim's problem. Everyone realized that Kim did not want Joan to repeat the contents of the conversation; therefore, everyone began to defend Kim from the gossip. The conflict became so intense that the president was forced to call a meeting of the entire office staff so that they could clear up the misunderstanding.

During the staff meeting, Kim assaulted Joan verbally for violating their trust. Joan reacted by claiming that she was not under the impression that their conversation was "top secret" and she had no idea that it would cause such a scandal. Because Joan was the newest employee, it was plain to see that everyone had sided with Kim and that no matter what Joan said, she was going to be found guilty of "office gossip."

After the staff meeting, Joan, who felt as if she had just been scolded by everyone, returned to her desk and resumed working. She later went to the president's office to discuss the events of the staff meeting in private. When she returned from the office, she was even more upset than before. The president had told her that she had damaged the personal intraoffice relationship and had established an environment of distrust among the employees. Joan took the remainder of the afternoon off and left the office without speaking to anyone.

Dealing with a Member. About a week after the staff meeting, Joan went to work as she had done every morning since the scolding. She walked into the office, put away her purse and coat, booted up the computer and switchboard, and took her seat at her desk without speaking to anyone in the office. She had not talked with anyone in the office except to give them messages or ask them a work-related question. On this particular day, a member with a discrepancy in his insurance policy had called to clear the matter for his own personal records. The member could not understand a part of the policy that Joan had arranged for him. After trying to explain the policy to him, Joan became upset with him and slammed the receiver down on the phone base. This caused a scene in the office because Joan's desk was located in the front of the office. Joan had not only been extremely rude to a member but she had also caused a very disrupting scene in the office.

The member to whom Joan had been rude called back and wanted to speak to the president. Joan told him that the president was not in and that she did not know when the president would return. It was later discovered that he had left a message for the president that Joan did not relay to her. Joan also knew that the president would be back at the office at 11:00 A.M. and that the president was scheduled to be gone for the next three days. Joan continued to give the irate member no cooperation until he hung up without satisfaction.

That afternoon one of the tellers told the president of the earlier scene that Joan had caused and commented on how Joan had been acting toward everyone lately. The president immediately called Joan to her office. Joan sat down and began listening to the president. Midway through the conversation Joan interrupted the president and began explaining her views concerning the other office personnel. She claimed that no one had ever liked her and that she could never please anyone, including the president of the board. The president pointed out to Joan that no one had ever complained about her work or her relationship with the other office personnel until the past week.

The president then addressed the manner in which Joan had dealt with the member earlier that day. She referred to the policy that the member is always right and that the employee is there to serve the needs of the member without question. Joan agreed, and she apologized for her rude behavior. She then returned to her desk; however, she spoke to no one the rest of the day. Joan left that afternoon as usual without a nice word to anyone.

Improper Work Procedures. Three weeks later Joan came to office as usual without saying a word to anyone. She began working on her insurance account immediately because it was due that day. In order for the statement to be posted by the computer on that day, Joan had to be finished by 11:30 A.M. But at 11:00 she still could not balance the debits and credits of her account. This posed a serious problem because of the time factor. Joan had not asked for anyone to help her; instead, she had worked over the same papers for days. At 11:20, Joan decided to change a few of the entries to balance the accounts and sent the work to the data processing agency for compiling. Joan knew that this was not going to be tolerated and that she would be caught when the accountant reviewed the information.

The next day the processing agency called to inquire about the discrepancies in the data. After talking with the accountant, they talked with the president concerning this matter. That afternoon there was a meeting of the president, the vice president, the accountant, and Joan. The president told Joan about the error and asked if she knew anything about the problem. The president then showed Joan the evidence that proved that Joan had "adjusted" the figures to cover the difference that had existed.

Knowing she had been caught, Joan said that she knew everyone in the office was against her. She said that she made the changes so she could get the work to the processors on time and that she was going to correct the errors as soon as she could find the problem. This defense was completely unacceptable to the officers. Joan had violated the policy of the credit union and tried to hide her mistakes by changing the figures to balance the account.

Joan took the next several days off to give the officers time to forget about her mistakes. She had decided after discussing the situation with the president that it would be best if she took the time off. When Joan returned to work she met again with the president. However, at this meeting Joan turned in her resignation. This surprised the president because she knew Joan was not satisfied with the job but she had no idea that Joan would quit. The president later agreed that this was probably the best solution for all involved.

Case 3
Minnis Service

Minnis Service is a television, appliance, and gas engine repair service that is owned and operated by Minnis retail chain. Minnis Service is an autonomous unit whose manager reports directly to a regional office. The organizational structure of Minnis Service is shown in Figure A–1.

It is the policy of Minnis Retail Chain to provide emergency service to the customers. When a customer calls for service on a "warm" refrigerator, and there is the danger of losing food, the service call is assigned to the closest appliance technician. Since the calls are not anticipated, the technicians often work overtime. If a technician is called from home for emergency service, he is guaranteed four hours of pay.

All associates are asked on their employment application if they will be willing to work outside "normal working hours." Normal working hours are 8:00 A.M. to 4:30 P.M. All associates are allowed two fifteen-minute breaks and a thirty-minute lunch per day. They have been instructed to take the mid-morning, mid-afternoon, and lunch breaks by 1:00 PM at the latest. Therefore, lunch covers the thirty-minute break required by labor laws for workers who work in excess of five hours per day.

Emergency Service Call

About three months ago, an emergency refrigeration call was received at 2:30 PM on a Thursday. At 2:45 P.M. a message was left with service so that Harry—an appliance service technician—could respond to the emergency call. This day he had six calls to run and by 2:45 P.M. he had completed five and was headed for his last service call. At 3:45 P.M. Harry had not phoned in. A call to the customer's home revealed that Harry had left the place by 3:30 P.M. The manager and the head technician drove by Harry's home and found his service vehicle in his driveway at 3:55 P.M.

Next morning Harry was called into the manager's office, where the head technician was also present. The manager and the head technician confronted

Figure A–1
Organization Structure of Minnis Service

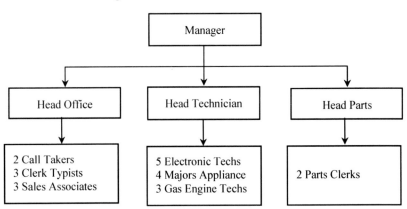

Harry with "facts." Harry's dispatch claimed that the customer was "Not Home." He said that only a young girl was in the house, so he did not go in. This was acceptable to the manager and the head technician because it agreed with the company policy. Harry was asked if he understood a long-standing company policy that required a technician to call the office upon completion of his assigned tasks and prior to returning to the office or going home. Harry said he had no reason not to call before going home.

The following Monday, Harry wanted to speak to the manager and the head technician. He said that he had been upset all weekend. He said that he had done an excellent job over his five years of employment. He resented being "followed" and accused the head technician of favoritism toward another service technician. He concluded by saying that he had worked through lunch; therefore his eight hours were completed by 4:00 P.M. The manager reminded Harry that he must have taken lunch by 1:00 P.M. according to labor laws and company bulletins and that he went home prior to 4:00 P.M.

Harry claimed that a morale problem was developing among the techs and that regular meetings were needed to stop misunderstandings between the management and techs. The manager and the head technician agreed with Harry's suggestion and told him that there would be a meeting on Friday. They also told Harry that they were reasserting the "call-in policy" in an interhouse bulletin to all technicians.

The manager and Harry's coworkers think that Harry is a competent technician and maintains a high level of productivity. Harry was a known hothead during his five years with the company. The manager decided not to take any action against Harry.

The manager and the head technician discussed Harry's comments and ulterior motives. They thought that Harry was attempting to make this incident look like a conflict between the management and technicians. However, no other technicians had previously complained about poor morale or misunderstanding.

Harry's "Not at Home" customer had called the service unit and wanted to know when her "part" would be received. She stated that her neighbor went in her house with her daughter and the service technician. She further stated that the technician had gone down to the cellar, returned shortly, and said that he would have to order a part. He then left. The call was reassigned to Harry a day later, and he repaired it with a part from his truck.

At the meeting on Friday, the "call in" letter was distributed and explained. The technicians were told that the manager would like to discuss any problems in group meetings or in private, if preferred. Harry tried to make some comments on this, but the other technicians were not willing to engage in any disagreement. The management decided to ignore the situation and hoped that Harry would be satisfied.

Friday Meeting

Two months later, at a Friday meeting of the technicians, Harry had a hot exchange with another appliance technician. This was the technician whom Harry had accused the head technician of favoring. The words between them got very personal. Both technicians blamed each other for technical incompetence and claimed the advantages of their own service area. At this point, another technician, Dick, joined Harry in attacking the other technician and quoted Harry's phraseology. The communication was allowed to run its course until the "favored" technician decided to leave, and Harry was asked by the manager to tone down his voice. One of the appliance technicians observed that they worked as four independents, which caused many of their problems. One of the electronics technicians stated that there was nothing wrong with the unit; "we just have two guys here who hate each other's guts!"

The meeting was brought to a conclusion when the manager said he would review the daily schedules of the appliance technicians for favoritism in assignments. He also promised to talk to each appliance technician individually over the next week. Information gained from the meetings with individual technicians indicated no concrete evidence of favoritism in assignments. Only Harry and Dick were related to these personnel problems. By this time, Dick apologized for verbally attacking his coworker.

Another Incident

About three weeks later, the head office associate told the manager that she was questioned at the local store by the appliance and television department manager about the "technical morale problem" at the service unit. The manager of this department is John Dickson, who happens to be Harry's neighbor and golf partner. About two weeks after this, the previous service manager (now assigned to another state) disclosed that John Dickson had called and questioned him on the "decline of service" at service unit. During this period, a manager of another store told the manager (Minnis Service) that John was "gunning for him" and intended to review the service operation. This was definitely beyond any authority that John had, explicit or implicit.

The manager called Harry into his office and explained his disappointment. The manager told Harry that he should keep the service affairs within the unit and that the unit should solve its own problems. The manager also observed that the involvement of the store in the internal affairs of service could undermine store-service relations, which could not be tolerated.

It was reported that Harry and John were attempting to get the service unit associates and store technicians involved in the dispute. During the period of conflict, Harry has consistently adhered to company rules and procedures.

Case 4
The Hormel Strike at Austin, Minnesota

The George A. Hormel Company was founded in 1891 in Austin, Minnesota. Its main business was the slaughtering of hogs and processing the meat into finished products such as packaged luncheon meats. Its most famous products were canned meats such as Spam and Dinty Moore Stew. However, by the early 1980s Hormel had expanded into other food products and seemed poised to becoming a major player in the consumer food products industry through such products as ready-to-serve frozen breakfast sausage.

Hormel grew steadily through this strategy of expanding into related product markets while still heeding the admonition to "stick to one's knitting." By 1984 it had become one of the largest and most profitable pork processors in the U.S. with $1.4 billion in sales and over $29 million in profits ("Digest of Earnings," 1984). As shown in Table A–1, Hormel had steady profits throughout the late 1970s and early 1980s (its return on equity averaged around 13 percent). Many of these profits were put back into the company. Between 1979 and 1983 the company spent $225 million in capital improvements, modernizing or replacing all of its production facilities—including a new facility at Austin.

As Hormel grew, the corporation's profitability became intertwined with the fate of the community of Austin. The corporation and its philanthropic foundation, the Hormel Foundation (which owned over 40 percent of Hormel's stock) were established in a way that ensured that control of these organizations would always remain with residents of Austin. This provision made the company an unattractive takeover target and helped foster the oft-quoted view that "Hormel equals Austin, and Austin equals Hormel." By the early 1980s Hormel had become a significant economic power in the community, providing approximately one out of four paychecks totaling $400,000 a week in the town of approximately 23,000 ("Hormel willing," 1985).

Note: Kuhle, B., Knox, K., & Ross, W. B. (1992). The Hormel Strike at Austin, Minnesota. *International Journal of Conflict Management, 3*, 45–68. © Center for Advanced Studies in Management. Reprinted with permission.

Table A–1
Seventeen-Year Financial Summary: George A. Hormel & Co.
and Subsidiaries (in thousands of dollars)

Year	(A) Operations			
	Net Sales	Net Earnings ("Profits")	Net Earnings as % of Sales	Wage Costs
1970[1]	695,768	9,933	1.43%	116,921
1971	686,487	16,664	2.43%	127,775
1972	719,755	7,788	1.08%	129,277
1973	825,671	7,403	.90%	129,419
1974	943,163	17,369	1.84%	151,052
1975	995,539	13,366	1.34%	167,049
1976[1]	1,094,832	14,717	1.34%	179,588
1977	1,106,274	21,951	1.98%	191,719
1978	1,244,865	20,039	1.61%	200,631
1979	1,414,016	30,612	2.16%	232,644
1980	1,321,966	32,758	2.48%	254,303
1981[1]	1,433,966	27,283	1.90%	270,522
1982	1,426,596	28,051	1.97%	269,964
1983	1,417,705	27,897	1.97%	250,724
1984	1,454,527	29,492	2.03%	241,210
1985	1,502,235	38,618	2.57%	233,512
1986	1,960,237	39,079	1.99%	222,535

Source: George A. Hormel & Co. and *Hormel Profitability*
Report, 1990
Note: 1 = Based on a 53–week period

Table A.1 (continued)
Seventeen-Year Financial Summary: George A. Hormel & Co.
and Subsidiaries (in thousands of dollars)

		(B) Financial Position			
Year	Working Capital	Properties (Net)	Total Assets	Long-term Debt *less* Current Maturities	Stockholders' Equity
1970[1]	37,818	45,683	129,416	NR	83,081
1971	43,646	51,841	153,144	NR	96,175
1972	39,275	60,178	149,468	NR	101,187
1973	34,256	67,481	179,950	NR	104,654
1974	48,659	74,392	193,696	NR	117,932
1975	64,350	85,398	224,488	NR	126,879
1976[1]	63,957	97,465	228,585	NR	136,792
1977	79,253	99,921	258,283	NR	153,363
1978	89,298	103,992	275,442	NR	166,870
1979	97,656	119,213	319,779	NR	190,373
1980	69,843	160,825	355,853	28,495	208,296
1981[1]	59,440	228,813	425,065	65,834	226,741
1982	69,527	276,684	488,859	88,264	245,570
1983	95,403	270,103	512,559	82,164	263,861
1984	106,332	263,929	525,322	56,695	283,362
1985	152,985	264,679	560,939	64,334	311,605
1986	196,199	255,159	584,744	63,262	339,925

Note: NR = Not reported, 1 = Based on a 53–week period

Collective Bargaining History

1933–1954

Historically, Hormel enjoyed good relations with labor. True, the meatpackers had a long strike in 1933 to get Hormel to agree to their first union contract, but since then labor agreements had always been negotiated without either side's resorting to a strike or lockout.

Jay Hormel, company president from 1929 to 1954, was sympathetic to workers' concerns. He embraced a philosophy that labor should share in both the profitability and stability of the company. To implement this philosophy, the following features characterized Hormel's labor agreements:

Table A–1 (continued)
Seventeen-Year Financial Summary: George A. Hormel & Co.
and Subsidiaries (in thousands of dollars)

	(C) Per Share of Common Stock		
	Net		Stockholders'
Year	Earnings	Dividends	Investment
1970[1]	2.09	.70	17.45
1971	3.50	.75	20.20
1972	1.63	.78	21.04
1973	1.54	.81	21.77
1974	3.62	.84	24.55
1975	2.78	.92	26.42
1976[1]	3.06	1.00	28.48
1977	4.57	1.12	31.93
1978	4.17	1.36	34.74
1979	6.37	1.48	39.63
1980	.85	.21	5.42
1981[1]	.71	.23	5.90
1982	.73	.24	6.39
1983	.73	.25	6.87
1984	.77	.26	7.37
1985	1.00	.27	8.11
1986	1.02	.28	8.85

1. A Guaranteed Annual Wage. The meatpacking business was seasonal, with frequent layoffs; workers typically were paid by the hour. Therefore, this feature was innovative because workers were guaranteed a regular paycheck. Any extra hours worked were paid in the form of a Christmas bonus. The bonus also reflected the profitability of the company; Hormel believed that the workers should share the profits.

2. A "No-Layoffs" Policy. Regular, full-time workers could not be laid off without a fifty-two-week advance notice. This gave the workers job security.

3. Worker Autonomy. Workers had a group incentive program. As long as work groups met production targets, managers gave the workers freedom to determine their own work methods. Once any group's target was met, the workers could continue to work, earning a bonus of as much as 100 percent of their base pay. Alternatively, individual workers could take a break or even quit for the day. Thus, it was not uncommon for individual workers to take breaks while their coworkers continued working.

These features fostered a cooperative labor-management atmosphere. This cooperation was crystallized in 1940, when Hormel and local union leaders negotiated a permanent "working agreement," making Hormel one of the few U.S. industries with a permanent labor contract. After 1940, union and management negotiators did not negotiate full contracts, merely memoranda of understanding modifying the permanent working agreement. Often, specific contract features were oral, based on the goodwill of both parties. These features were not universal; Hormel negotiated conventional union contracts at their plants in other cities. However, because the Austin plant accounted for approximately 75 percent of their production, the Austin contract was thought to reflect Hormel's philosophy and commitment to the community.

The consequence of these features led to low turnover among Austin's Hormel workers; many expressed a great deal of loyalty to, and pride in, their company. Their wages also gave them relatively high socioeconomic status within the community with many owning their own homes as well as luxury items such as boats (Hage & Klauda, 1989).

1954–1982

Jay Hormel served as president of Hormel until 1954; his successors continued his policies with only minor changes. Hormel was not the largest meatpacker in the industry and was usually content to follow prevailing wage and benefits trends (since World War II, Hormel workers' wages had never declined).

In 1956 Oscar Mayer & Co., a rival meatpacker, and the union representing meatpackers negotiated a contract containing a novel provision: an escalator clause. The escalator clause provided that workers would automatically receive higher wages if inflation raised the cost of living as measured by the Consumer Price Index. Because pattern bargaining prevailed in the meatpacking industry, escalator clauses soon became common features of collective bargaining agreements—including Hormel's. The wage increases resulting from this clause seemed reasonable in the 1960s, but in the 1970s labor costs skyrocketed due to the high inflation rate.

The 1960s and 1970s brought about changes within the union. Local P–9 had always had an independent streak since its founding in 1933. The union affiliated with the United Packinghouse Workers of America (UPWA) of the Congress of Industrial Organizations (CIO) in 1943. The CIO had always been considered more militant than its rival, the American Federation of Labor (AFL). However, the AFL and CIO merged in 1955, and in 1968 the UPWA also merged with its AFL counterpart, the Amalgamated Meat Cutters and Butcher Workmen of North America. In 1979 these member unions were absorbed by the United Food and Commercial Workers union (UFCW) with over one million members. Thus, Local P–9, with 1,700 members, went from being a large and influential local within the UPWA to a small local within these larger bodies.

The 1960s and 1970s also brought significant changes to the meatpacking industry. Iowa Beef Processors (IBP) began expanding aggressively. This nonunion company had a reputation for holding production costs low by paying low wages. IBP's cost-leadership strategy apparently figured heavily in leading the major meatpackers to get out of the beef slaughtering business. Instead, the major unionized firms concentrated on pork slaughtering operations and on buying other meat (e.g., beef) from nonunion slaughterhouses. Like other plants, the Austin plant converted to pork slaughtering. Unfortunately for the workers at Hormel, by 1979 nonunion companies were also making significant inroads into pork slaughtering and processing operations. Nonunion companies' labor costs were typically only half those of unionized companies. In 1983 these were $5.00–$7.00 per hour compared to $10.69 earned by Austin workers (Hage & Klauda, 1989).

Partly in response to dramatic wage increases in the face of nonunion competition, Hormel managers decided to build a new, 1-million-square-foot meatpacking plant. In 1975, Hormel managers announced that the multistory building that the company had used for over eighty years was hopelessly antiquated and that, if Hormel was to remain competitive, they must build a new facility. During the subsequent months, Hormel entered into negotiations with P–9 over the matter, as a part of contract negotiations. In early 1978, Hormel officials announced that the company was considering constructing its new plant in a community other than Austin. Workers were uncertain whether management was betraying their loyalty or whether this was merely a "bluff." Bargaining for a new contract continued.

On June 27, 1978, Local P–9 and Hormel reached an agreement that anticipated working conditions in the new facility. In return for locating the plant in

Austin, Hormel obtained significant concessions. First, because the old plant operated at only 80 percent of the industry average, the union agreed to allow the new plant to operate at higher production levels. Second, plant managers had more authority to determine work rules, to keep production high. This also had the effect of reducing worker autonomy.

A third provision was particularly difficult for some union members to accept. The old plant operated under an incentive system that was a part of the workers' guaranteed annual wage program. This system provided workers with bonuses when they exceeded their specified production targets. Hormel officials claimed that these targets had not been high enough, but because of union opposition, managers could not change the targets; consequently, the incentive system at the old facility overpaid workers. Further, the old production targets would be irrelevant at the new facility with modern equipment. Therefore, Hormel officials insisted that the union leaders agree to abolish the incentive system for the jobs to remain in Austin. However, union negotiators expressed concern that workers would reject the proposal; after all, they were already being asked to work harder in the new facility. Was Hormel now proposing that the employees work harder for less pay?

In order to reduce worker resistance to the elimination of the incentive system, a complicated plan was devised. Workers first deferred upcoming cost-of-living raises; instead, Hormel managers put the cost-of-living funds in an escrow account. These moneys were then used to supplement earning declines that resulted from eliminating the incentive system. The escrow account ensured that workers' wages would not fall below what they had been when they transferred into the new facility (new hires would not receive anything from this fund). Thus, workers who transferred would be working at higher production levels in the new plant. However, their earnings would remain at the same levels they had been under the old system. Hormel managers could justify the plan because they were getting higher productivity from the workers for the same rate of pay.

Later, Local P–9 leaders argued that the workers had loaned the money to Hormel to help the company build the new plant. They viewed the escrow account as a loan to Hormel because the workers had delayed taking scheduled cost-of-living raises that they would have otherwise received (Mills, 1986). Further, the union negotiators understood the plan to mean that there would be no reduction in pay rates until the expiration of the 1985 contract. Unfortunately, the agreement did not explicitly state this—a fact that was to haunt the union later (Green, 1990).

A fourth concession that the union made was not to insist that all of the workers at the old facility be guaranteed jobs at the new facility. Later, union officials complained that Hormel had laid off experienced workers only to turn around and hire new employees to work at the new plant. To many in the union, this violated their trust in management. It also had a tangible consequence: every new worker hired meant one less employee that Hormel had to pay from the escrow account (Green, 1990).

The union also agreed not to strike until three years after the new Austin plant went into full operation. The plant became operational on August 9, 1982. In return for the union's no-strike pledge, Hormel agreed to pay the same wage as the unionized industry leaders. This included a "me-too" clause. The "me-too" clause covered wages and other benefits (holidays, vacations, rest periods, meal periods, premium pay, health and welfare benefits, and pension plan). The clause specified that if the wages or benefits were to change at three or more of the five major pork meatpacking companies, then (1) the union would identify the three companies' provisions that it most preferred, and (2) Hormel would pay the average wage or benefit offered by those three companies. The five major meatpackers used in the clause were John Morrell & Co., Oscar Mayer & Co., Wilson Foods, Swift & Co., and Swift Independent Packing Co.

1983

The 1978 contract appeared to be the model for the industry; both sides were farsighted enough to anticipate working conditions in the new plant and to negotiate a new contract before production actually began. However, neither side anticipated dramatic changes in the meatpacking industry and, once the contract was in place, both parties found it difficult to adjust to those changes. First, in the early 1980s consumer demand for red meat—especially pork—dropped significantly, resulting in layoffs at several meatpackers. Second, nonunion operators gained a significant share of the market. It was difficult for unionized meatpackers to compete with these lower-paying operators. A few examples illustrate this:

1. Workers at Wilson Foods staged a three-week strike but finally had to accept a 25 percent wage cut. It proved "too little, too late"; by 1984, Wilson had filed for reorganization under federal bankruptcy law.
2. Rath Packing Co. also filed for bankruptcy. The irony of this bankruptcy was that Rath was owned by the workers.
3. ConAgra bought Armour Foods from Greyhound and closed thirteen Armour plants, later to reopen twelve of them as nonunion plants (paying approximately $6.00 per hour).

In summary, between 1972 and 1981, 238 out of 717 meatpackers had gone out of business. Firms that remained usually paid lower wages (Krejci, 1986).

In September 1983 Hormel asked the union to negotiate a wage reduction. Company officials notified the union that if they were unwilling to negotiate a lower wage level in the middle of the existing contract, then the company would seek to lower wages through the "me-too" clause.

The company's announcement became a prominent issue in subsequent local union officer elections. Many union members were outraged. They observed that workers had deferred cost-of-living adjustment increases and had granted numerous work rule concessions to keep the Hormel plant in Austin. Hormel also earned healthy profits (see Table A–1). To some workers, rolling back wages seemed more than a bit opportunistic on the part of management. It just didn't make sense for the workers to take pay cuts. They had already given up too much.

The campaign pitted incumbent local vice president John Anker against Jim Guyette, a former member of the executive board. Guyette was a young man, but he already had a reputation of refusing to compromise on matters of principle. His campaign had three themes: First, he ran on a platform of "no concessions." Second, Guyette disputed Hormel's interpretation of the "me-too" clause. He argued that the clause was designed only to raise wages—not lower them. When the "me-too" clause was discussed in 1978 and 1982, inflation was high, and the negotiations centered on using this clause to raise wages. Nothing was said about using the clause to lower wages. Besides, hadn't Hormel promised the workers that their wages would remain the same when they moved from the old plant into the new one? To Guyette, the use of the "me-too" clause to cut wages was both legally and ethically wrong. Finally, Guyette was suspicious of UFCW leaders; they were too willing to grant wage concessions, and they did not ensure that the contract clearly specified "no reduction in [pay] rates" language (Green, 1990, p. 57). Jim Guyette defeated John Anker by a vote of 351 to 312. He vowed to fight Hormel's interpretation of the "me-too" clause in grievance arbitration (Hage & Klauda, 1989).

1984

1984 brought bad news for Austin workers. By 1984, three of Hormel's unionized competitors had won contract settlements with hourly wages of between $8.00 and $8.25 per hour, while Hormel continued to pay $10.69 per hour, as shown in Table A–2. Reviewing these conditions, Richard L. Knowlton, Hormel board chairman, observed that Hormel had operated at a disadvantage despite the new Austin plant, "Recognizing the extremely competitive environment in which our company operates, it is impossible to offset these major wage and benefit differentials through improved technology alone" ("Hormel Shows," 1984).

In February, arbitrator George Fleischli ruled that the "me-too" contract provision applied to a downward pattern of wages as well as an upward pattern. He supported the company's right to lower wages but ruled that no wage cuts could be made until after all five of the national meatpackers had settled on a new wage rate. The final settlement occurred in October, when workers at Madison, Wisconsin, and Davenport, Iowa, reached an impasse with Oscar Mayer.

Table A–2
1984 UFCW–Meatpacking Industry Base Wage Comparisons
(in dollars per hour)

	Company							
	Hormel (Austin)	Other Hormel	Wilson Foods	Morrell & Co.	Swift & Co.	Armour-ConAgra	SIPCO	Oscar Mayer
Wage	$8.25	$9.00	$8.00	$8.25	$8.75	$6.00–$7.00	$8.25	$8.25–$9.25

Source: Krejci (1986)

Consequently, Oscar Mayer implemented a wage of $8.25 per hour. Guyette questioned whether the Oscar Mayer wage could be used in Hormel's "me-too" calculation, since the wage was not a figure jointly agreed upon by labor and management; Guyette resolved to arbitrate this question (Krejci, 1986).

At about this same time (September 1984), Hormel negotiated an agreement with all the Hormel plants, calling for wage cuts to $8.75 per hour. Workers at all the plants, including Austin, rejected the proposed contract. However, the other workers had the right to strike, whereas, under the 1978 agreement, Austin workers did not. So it was not surprising that on October 15 Hormel concluded a second agreement with the other locals, putting their wages at $9.00 per hour as of September 1, 1984, and $10.00 per hour as of September 1, 1985. The second agreement was ratified by the rank-and-file union members (Hage & Klauda, 1989).

In late September Guyette withdrew Local P–9 from these second company-wide negotiations. This move surprised many observers and effectively allowed Hormel to implement the arbitrator's ruling. Hormel immediately established a retroactive wage cut, lowering the Austin workers' wages to $8.25 per hour.

Guyette had some other ideas for taking on Hormel. That fall, Guyette hired Ray Rogers, a labor consultant from Corporate Campaign, Inc., of New York. His area of expertise was in waging a "corporate campaign" of political, economic, and social pressure against a company in order to make it difficult and expensive for the company to continue in its desired course of action. Rogers had built a reputation for winning in such confrontations with management. He was best known for having devised and directed a strategy that led to a major union victory at J. P. Stevens & Co.'s textile plants in the south in 1980. Rogers's tactics included calls for product boycotts, criticism of banks that loaned to Stevens, and embarrassment of various corporate officers who also served on Stevens' board of directors. After several years of such pressure, the company broke a seventeen-year stalemate and signed a union contract. Consequently, Rogers's services were in demand (Charlier, 1985).

Rogers devised a three-phase plan for Local P–9. The first phase of the plan was an informational campaign designed to solicit support from other unions and Austin community groups. This would be followed by an extended protest against the First Bank System and Hormel. Rogers believed that because First Bank had numerous ties to Hormel, the board of directors of the bank could influence the company to restore the wage cuts. Workers would also protest at Hormel's annual stockholders' meeting. If these two strategies failed, Guyette would call a strike effective August 1985, when the current contract expired (Brown, 1984).

Rogers effectively created an atmosphere of excitement among union members. He forced local businesses to choose between Hormel and Local P–9. He involved the wives and children of P–9 workers in the protest. Rogers also stressed the importance of the P–9 cause to the future of the labor movement. For example, at one rally, he inspired union members by telling them, "You can't allow the company to lay the ground rules. You can create a moment in history so people can turn to Austin, Minnesota, and say, 'That's where they turned back the onslaught against the labor movement'" (Serrin, 1984).

On December 26, Arbitrator Fleischli ruled that the $8.25 wage implemented by Hormel was appropriate and should continue. However, he instructed Local P–9 and Hormel officials to negotiate other economic provisions, including vacations, holidays, health and pension benefits, sick leave, and new employee hire rates. If the two sides could not agree within seven days, these issues would also be arbitrated. Indeed, the parties were unable to agree on any of these provisions, and the matters were remanded to arbitration (Andersen, 1984; "Guyette Sees," 1984; "Arbitrator Will Make," 1985).

1985

For the first time in history, Hormel decided to hold its annual shareholder's meeting in a city other than Austin. The January meeting was moved to Atlanta to avoid picketing by Local P–9 members. This decision proved to be a mixed blessing for Rogers and Guyette. On the one hand, it made disruption of the meeting more difficult—although a bus filled with union members who had bought shares of stock traveled to Atlanta so P–9ers could confront Hormel's leadership. On the other hand, it gave the union an enormous propaganda tool: The company was obviously "running away" from its problems (e.g., "Hormel Moves Annual," 1984).

Meanwhile, the rift between the Local P–9 leadership and UFCW officers was widening. UFCW packinghouse director and international vice president Lewie Anderson and UFCW international president William Wynn both urged Local P–9 voluntarily to negotiate the same wage and benefits package paid by the other Hormel plants. They also called for ending the corporate campaign and were reportedly unhappy that P–9 was soliciting funds from other, sympathetic unions (Mills, 1986).

Several other meetings were held between UFCW and P–9 officials that year; none resulted in a consensus. To the UFCW, Local P–9 was "picking the wrong target at the wrong time" and clinging to unrealistic wage demands (Krejci, 1986). To Local P–9 leaders, the UFCW leaders were out of touch with the needs of the meatpackers and unwilling to take the risks to restore wage cuts.

The dispute between P–9 and the UFCW became a running feud. P–9 pursued disciplinary charges against Anderson, charging that the international's vice president misrepresented the previous contract's wage and cost-of-living clauses to the P–9 rank-and-file members (Andersen, 1985b). Much of February and March 1985 was spent discussing whether Anderson could address a meeting of Local P–9 members (e.g., Andersen, 1985a). Guyette refused to allow such a meeting unless Ray Rogers was present to defend his corporate campaign strategy. UFCW vice president Anderson refused to address the workers if Rogers was present—Rogers was not a union member. The relationship between Local P–9 and the parent union continued to deteriorate.

In March Arbitrator Fleischli ruled on the benefits package for P–9 workers, imposing substantial cuts in fringe benefits. However, he also set the basic wage at $8.75 per hour and directed that it be increased to $9.25 on July 20, 1985 (Krejci, 1986; Andersen, 1985c).

A fourth arbitration hearing was held by Mark Kahn to determine exactly when the 1978 labor agreement expired. He ruled that the contract did not expire until August ("Hormel Union Can't," 1985). In a fifth arbitration hearing, arbitrator Fleischli ruled that the exact date of expiration was August 9, 1985. Such rulings squelched Guyette's plans for a strike in April. Instead, Rogers and Guyette intensified their campaign against the First Bank System, hoping to influence Hormel by pressuring its major creditor. Wives and nonworking union members traveled to surrounding communities and to Minneapolis to distribute leaflets at union halls and in front of branches of First Bank (Andersen, 1985d).

First Bank was a logical target for Rogers. Several officers of Hormel, including Richard Knowlton, Hormel's chairman and president, were on the First Bank System's board of directors. Similarly, a few First Bank officers, including De Walt Ankeny, First Bank President, were members of Hormel's board of directors. P–9 wanted to pressure the bank by asking depositors to write letters complaining to First Bank's leadership. In turn, it was hoped that First Bank would pressure Hormel to withdraw its demands for concessions. P–9 leaders were careful to avoid the word "boycott" and claimed that such measures were legitimate informational activities.

In May, Hormel announced its intention to terminate the contract when it expired in August. Negotiations for the new contract began in June and continued throughout the summer with the help of a mediator from the Federal Mediation and Conciliation Service (FMCS). For Hormel, the primary issue of negotiations was wages. For P–9, several other issues were also important. Among them:

1. Hormel had laid off a number of experienced workers when the new plant opened. Several months later, as the new plant expanded its capacity, new, inexperienced workers were hired. The union charged that this was an attempt to avoid paying the higher wages that experienced workers commanded.
2. Related to the first issue, the union charged that the new workers were poorly trained. This led to a higher injury rate than at other plants. Hormel disputed these charges (Andersen, 1985e).
3. The work pace was faster at the new plant. The union charged that this faster pace increased the number of accidents and disabilities such as carpal tunnel syndrome (Green, 1990).
4. The new factory had new work rules. Guyette charged that many of these work rules were dangerous and dehumanizing, claiming that workers had to raise their hands to go to the rest room (Green, 1990). Hormel responded that such claims were exaggerated; with regard to the bathroom breaks, company officials responded that on an assembly line, every worker must be at his or her station, and if a worker leaves for a break, a replacement must fill in (Hage & Klauda, 1989; Andersen, 1985e).

On August 9, 1985, the existing contract between P–9 and Hormel expired. Local P–9's leaders agreed to put Hormel's last offer before the rank-and-file members for a vote but urged them to reject the proposal. The final contract offer would have put the base wage at $9.25 per hour for the remainder of August and would have increased that amount to $10.00 per hour on September 1st. Local P–9 members rejected the offer by a vote of 1,261 to 96 ("Local P–9 Will Strike," 1985; Krejci, 1986).

On August 17, the strike began. Although the plant was closed, Hormel announced that it was unilaterally implementing its last offer—the offer rejected by the union. Meanwhile, negotiations continued at irregular intervals throughout the fall, with no real progress. The company and union positions were miles apart. For example, Hormel was offering $10.00 an hour, while P–9 was seeking an $11.25 wage. Guyette was also asking for work rule changes; finally, he wanted the guaranteed annual wage system and the old seniority system restored. His concerns about safety also remained. For its part, Hormel had already implemented its final offer. It was required to bargain in good faith, yet it could not unilaterally implement its last offer if it changed its bargaining position (Hage & Klauda, 1989).

In October, the National Labor Relations Board ruled in favor of a company complaint against P–9 that the union was conducting an illegal secondary boycott against First Bank. P–9 was barred from protesting or passing out handbills at First Bank branches.

In December the federal mediator proposed a compromise settlement. The proposal called for a base wage of $10.00 per hour but called for an end to Hormel's two-tier wage system. It replaced the Austin plant's current seniority system (which was based on the work group and had taken years to hammer out) with a confusing departmental seniority provision that had been negotiated at Hormel's Ottumwa, Iowa, plant (Green, 1990). The plan also reduced the probationary period for new employees, guaranteed a six-month advance notice of a plant closing, and limited the use of temporary workers. An ergonomics expert would study safety complaints and make recommendations. Finally, it provided for expedited grievance arbitration of outstanding union grievances (Hage & Klauda, 1989).

P–9 leaders were not impressed. They felt that the mediator's proposal was really a face-saving way for Hormel to make a new proposal. After all, many of the union concerns were not directly mentioned. For example, it did not restore the guaranteed annual wage. Nor did it obligate Hormel to abide by the ergonomics expert's safety recommendations. Why hadn't the union had more input into the proposal? As P–9er Ron Rollins recalled, "The mediators' proposal was always misunderstood. It was never the objective finding of a mediator that 'this is how the dispute should be settled.' Rather...[t]he proposal represented the farthest the company could be pushed. The mediators were as powerless as we were" (Green, 1990, p. 117).

Although P–9 leaders were ready to reject the proposed contract, the national UFCW leaders were not. William Wynn, the international president, ordered a secret ballot election, and, in the letter that accompanied the ballot, Joe Hanson, regional UFCW director, endorsed the proposal: "Voting to accept this proposal is...the best hope that Local P–9 members will have to end the strike with dignity and some hope for a better tomorrow" (Hage & Klauda, 1989, p. 243). However, in the UFCW-conducted election, workers voted down the mediator's proposal by a vote of 775 to 540.

1986

In January, Hormel announced that the Austin plant would reopen. In an attempt to avert the confrontation that could result from this action, Minnesota Governor Rudy Perpich proposed that a fact-finder be used to determine how, if at all, the mediator's proposal could be made more acceptable to both sides. Hormel agreed to this plan; Local P–9 offered to work with the fact-finder only as a way to reopen negotiations—the mediator's proposal was no longer under consideration. The plant reopened on January 13th. In the first week after reopening, nearly 2,000 people applied for jobs. Further, fifty P–9 members crossed the picket lines and returned to work. A dissident group within P–9, calling itself the P–10ers, openly called for settling quickly the dispute before all 1,500 union jobs were given to replacements.

Rogers and Guyette were still willing to talk with Hormel—there were several meetings during the month of January. However, they also kept the pressure up. P–9 members intensified their pickets at the Austin plant and used their cars to create traffic jams so replacements could not get to the plant. In late January, P–9 members traveled to Hormel's other plants to set up pickets, hoping to turn away Hormel's other workers. However, the UFCW told various local officials that their contracts did not allow workers at any plant to honor Austin's picket lines. P–9 members also picketed other producers and meatpackers who supplied Hormel or to whom Hormel had contracted work during the strike. According to some analysts, it was actually cheaper for Hormel to contract out work than it was to operate the Austin plant (Hage & Klauda, 1989).

These pressure tactics had mixed success. P–9 members effectively kept the Austin plant shut. However, the roving pickets were less successful. At Ottuma, Iowa, which had difficulty negotiating a labor contract in 1984, most workers were willing to honor the picket line. But they paid for it. Over 500 Ottumwa workers who honored P–9's picket line were fired. At other plants, relatively few workers honored the picket line (Green, 1990).

Such actions intensified the conflict between Local P–9 and the international UFCW leaders. President William Wynn called P–9's strategy "suicidal." He wrote, "Never in my experience as a union representative has a better group of members been so poorly served by inexperienced, inflexible local union representatives" (Krejci, 1986). Wynn felt that Rogers had "anointed himself the Ayatollah of Austin and is making hostages of our members at other Hormel plants" (Mills, 1986; Krejci, 1986). At Wynn's urging, the AFL–CIO refused to endorse P–9's call for a national boycott of Hormel products. For their part, many P–9 members believed that the UFCW leaders were more interested in their own careers than in the meatpackers in the plant. As one P–9er stated, "Both the company and the international are lying to us" (Green, 1990, p. 121).

On January 20, Minnesota governor Perpich ordered National Guard troops to keep access to the Austin plant open. First 500, then 300 more troops were sent. After a week, they were sent to the local armory, to be used only in emergencies. With rare exceptions, the National Guard troops were successful at keeping access open to the plant. A court-ordered injunction subsequently limited picketing to six P–9 strikers. On February 10, production at the Austin plant resumed; troops were removed in late February.

But Rogers and Guyette weren't beaten yet. On March 10, approximately 200 strikers gathered at Hormel's corporate offices. They padlocked the doors and mailed the keys to Governor Perpich. The action garnered P–9 much publicity but did Hormel little real harm; by 2:00 P.M. that afternoon, the offices were again open for business.

Shortly after this act of civil disobedience, P–9 members voted 345 to 305 for Local P–9 negotiators to soften their bargaining stand against Hormel and to resolve their disagreements with the UFCW. By this time, approximately 600 replacement workers had been hired and over 450 striking P–9 members had returned to work. This provided the opening that the UFCW leaders needed. They had authorized the strike, yet they clearly had not supported Guyette's bargaining position. Further, if Hormel continued to hire nonunion replacement workers, they worried that no strikers would be rehired and that the replacement workers would decertify the union. The latest P–9 vote provided a glimmer of hope for resolving the dilemma. UFCW president William Wynn, seizing upon the vote, ordered an end to the strike and directed all strikers to return to work. He announced that an agreement would be negotiated, using the mediator's proposal as a basis.

Local P–9 members responded to this directive with defiance. They voted on March 16, 1986, to continue their strike and product boycott (on March 20, several hundred workers blocked the plant). Further, on March 21 a meeting between P–9 representatives and UFCW leaders ended abruptly after a P–9 member was discovered secretly taping the meeting. On March 25 the UFCW announced that it was placing Local P–9 in trusteeship for defying the UFCW directive to end the strike. Trusteeship effectively gives the national union control over a renegade local and is viewed as a measure of last resort. A hearing was scheduled for mid-April.

Meanwhile, on Friday, April 11, over 300 strikers clashed with police, spraying them with homemade mace. The police responded with tear gas. Guyette and Rogers were arrested, but freed on bond. The next day, P–9 held a "Shut Down Hormel Day" rally. Over 3,000 demonstrators from throughout the country marched against Hormel, and nearly 5,000 attended a rally. On April 13, the Reverend Jessie Jackson visited Austin, meeting with company and union officials and addressing over 1000 P–9 supporters.

On April 14 a UFCW officer from Houston, Texas, held hearings in Minneapolis. Regional director Joe Hansen portrayed the issue legally: P–9 had defied a direct order from the UFCW to end the strike. Guyette portrayed the issue as one of a difference in philosophy: the international UFCW was seeking to suppress the local's right to pursue its goals. On Wednesday, May 7, the UFCW Executive Committee convened to read the hearing officer's ruling. His ruling gave the UFCW permission to place P–9 in trusteeship. That day, the Executive Committee voted unanimously to impose the trusteeship. P–9 filed a lawsuit to block the action, but the judge ordered P–9 to recognize UFCW authority.

The other Hormel contracts expired that fall and the UFCW worked to bring Austin's contract in line with the other Hormel plants. Negotiators bargained throughout the summer, using the other Hormel contracts as well as the mediator's proposal as the bases for negotiations. One sticking point continued to be wages; Hormel was simply not willing to be the first in the industry to pay wages above $10.00 an hour. When Oscar Mayer agreed to pay $10.70 an hour by 1989, the UFCW knew they could get the same from Hormel. In addition to $10.70 per hour in 1988, the UFCW also obtained an end to the two-tier wage system and negotiated a system of expedited arbitration for outstanding worker grievances. In return, the UFCW agreed to allow Hormel to discontinue the escrow account for workers who had transferred from the old plant in 1982. The 700+ workers who had lost their jobs to replacement workers would receive priority status in rehiring for the following two years (Baenen, 1986; Hage & Klauda, 1989; Rubenstein, 1990). Strikers and replacements were eligible to vote on the proposed contract. On September 13, 1986, P–9 members ratified the contract 1,060 to 440. The ordeal was over.

The next section (Appendix B) presents nine execises that can be used for training administrators and managers in various organizations.

Appendix B
Exercises

In this section, nine exercises are described that are designed for intervention in intrapersonal, interpersonal, intragroup, and intergroup organizational conflicts. These exercises have been designed for interventions in conflicts in ongoing organizations. They may be used in the classroom provided that appropriate changes in some instructions and time allocations to different steps are made.

The time allocated to different steps is based on estimates of the approximate time needed to perform each step. The allocation of time for each step may be changed depending on the nature of conflict involved, number of participants in an exercise, and time available for an exercise. Each exercise was tested in classrooms with undergraduate and MBA students and in workshops with managers. Therefore, changes in the design of the exercises should be avoided unless there are definite reasons for doing so.

The participants in the exercise should fill out the Rahim Organizational Conflict Inventory–I and II (ROCI–I and II) and prepare indices for different types of conflict and the styles of handling interpersonal conflict with superiors, subordinates, and peers.[1] The participants will require the help of the training staff in completing the inventories and preparing the indices.

The participants should read the eight chapters of this book after the Inventories are completed but before beginning the exercises. The trainees may be assigned additional reading materials if the staff so desires. Appropriate movies may also be used to highlight some of the issues involved in a conflict and intervention strategies in managing conflict.

Exercise 1
Contract Building

Objectives

1. To help the participants know each other.
2. To assess the initial expectations, needs, and resources of the participants.

3. To provide a match between the expectations of the staff and those of participants in the conflict management workshops that are to follow.

Premeeting Preparation

None

Requirements

1. Group size: Between 10 and 35.
2. Time required: 1 hour 15 minutes.
3. Materials: Felt pens, masking tape, writing tablets, magic markers, and newsprint pads.
4. Physical arrangements: A large room with open space.

Procedure

Step 1 (5 minutes)
1. The staff discusses the objectives of the exercise.
2. The staff presents the schedule for the exercise.
3. The staff entertains questions from the participants.

Step 2 (5 minutes)
The staff asks the participants to write down the following information on a sheet of paper from the writing tablet:
1. Name.
2. Expectations from the workshops.
3. Expertise, skills, or resources.

The participants may suggest additional items of information to be included in the list. The staff should also write down the preceding information on a sheet of paper.

Step 3 (35 minutes or less)
The participants and staff move around the room to examine and discuss each other's list.

Step 4 (15 minutes)
The staff invites comments from the participants regarding the following:
1. Is there any agreement among the participants as to what they expect from the workshops on conflict management that are to follow?
2. Are there any skills among the participants that can be used in the conflict management workshops?
3. Are there any concerns among the participants regarding the conflict workshops?

Step 5 (10 minutes)

1. The staff summarizes the expectations and concerns of the participants on newsprint pads.

2. The staff discusses whether and to what extent it is possible to satisfy the expectations of the participants.

Step 6 (5 minutes)

The staff asks the participants to make comments on this exercise.

Exercise 2
Technique of Role Analysis

Objectives

1. To diagnose intrapersonal conflict.

2. To clarify the role of the focal role occupant.

3. To clarify the expectations of the focal role occupant from his or her group members.

4. To clarify the obligations of the focal role occupant to other members of his or her group.

Premeeting Preparation

1. Complete the ROCI–I, to be supplied by the staff, and compute the index of your intrapersonal conflict with the help of the staff.

2. Read Chapters 1, 2, 3, 4, and 5 of this book. Additional readings may be assigned by the staff.

Requirements

1. Group size: Between 5 and 15.

2. Time required: 1 hour, 52 minutes for each group member.

3. Materials: Felt pens, magic markers, writing tablets, masking tape, and newsprint pads.

4. Physical arrangements: A room with chairs that can be easily rearranged.

Procedure

Step 1 (5 minutes)

1. The leader of the participating group or staff explains the objectives of the exercise.

2. The group leader and/or the staff entertains questions from the participants.

Step 2 (15 minutes)

1. The staff presents the results of the analysis of data collected on the ROCI–I. Additional data that the staff may have collected by interviewing the group members should also be presented.

2. The staff and participants discuss the results and draw inferences.

3. The staff presents the schedule for the exercise.

Step 3 (5 minutes)

The focal role occupant initiates discussion regarding his or her role and how it matches with the goals of the group.

Step 4 (30 minutes)

1. The focal role occupant lists the activities that he or she feels occupy his or her role on the newsprints.

2. The group members discuss these activities so that new items are added and ambiguous or contradictory items dropped.

Step 5 (30 minutes)

1. The focal role occupant lists his or her expectations from his or her group members.

2. The group members discuss these expectations to revise and clarify the list and accept their obligations.

Step 6 (20 minutes)

1. Each group member presents his or her list of expectations from the focal role occupant.

2. This list is discussed and revised until it is agreed upon by the group.

Step 7 (2 minutes)

1. The staff asks the focal role occupant to write down the role profile, consisting of the following:

   a. Prescribed and discretionary activities of the focal role occupant.

   b. Expectations of the focal role occupant from other roles in the group.

   c. Obligation of this focal role to other roles in the group.

2. A copy of this role profile is distributed to each participant before the next meeting.

Step 8 (5 minutes)

The staff asks the participants to make comments on the exercise and the new behavior they learned from it.

Steps 3 through 7 are repeated for each of the remaining members of the group.

Exercise 3
Job Design

Objectives

1. To diagnose intrapersonal conflict.
2. To prepare a list of changes that are needed to redesign a specific job.

Premeeting Preparation

1. The organizational members whose jobs are to be redesigned respond to the ROCI–I, supplied by the staff, and construct the index of intrapersonal conflict, with the help of the staff.
2. Read chapters 1, 2, 3, and 4 of this book. Additional readings may be assigned by the staff. The above two steps are not needed if the participants have already done these for Exercise 2.

Requirements

1. Group size: Between 5 and 25.
2. Time required: 1 hour, 45 minutes.
3. Materials: Felt pens, magic markers, writing tablets, masking tape, and newsprint pads.
4. Physical arrangements: A large room with chairs that can be easily rearranged.

Procedure

Step 1 (5 minutes)
1. The group leader or staff discusses the objectives of the meeting.
2. The group leader or staff announces the job which has to be redesigned.
3. The staff presents the schedule for the exercise.
4. The staff entertains questions from the participants.

Step 2 (15 minutes)
1. The staff presents the results of the analysis of data collected on the ROCI–I. Additional data that the staff may have collected by interviewing the group members should also be presented.
2. The staff and participants discuss the results and draw inferences.

Exclude these two steps if these were done for Exercise 2.

Step 3 (30 minutes)

1. Break into subgroups of 5 or 6 and elect your respective leaders to discuss how the job, assigned to you, in Step 1 can be redesigned.

2. Brainstorm a list of changes that are needed to redesign the job. In preparing the list, consider how the job can be redesigned to increase its skill variety, task identity, task significance, autonomy, and feedback, as explained in Chapter 4.

3. List the changes recommended by your subgroup on newsprint pads.

Step 4 (30 minutes)

A fishbowl exercise may be arranged for this purpose.

1. Post the newsprint listings of changes recommended by subgroups on the walls.

2. The subgroup leaders present the list of changes, recommended by their subgroups, to the group.

3. The group discusses the changes and prepares the final list of changes that are to be made in the redesigned job. The list is appropriately screened for ambiguous and redundant items.

Step 5 (10 minutes)

1. The group assigns responsibilities for implementation of changes in job design and monitoring of implementation to specified individuals.

2. A date is agreed for follow-up.

Step 6 (10 minutes)

The staff asks the participants to make comments on the exercise and the new behavior learnt from it.

Exercise 4
Transactional Analysis

Objectives

1. To diagnose the styles of handling interpersonal conflict with superior(s), subordinates, and peers.

2. To enhance the awareness of the positions of superior(s), subordinates, and peers.

3. To enhance authentic communication with a person's superior(s), subordinates, and peers.

Premeeting Preparation

1. Complete the ROCI–II (Forms A, B, and C), to be supplied by the staff, and construct the indices of your styles of handling interpersonal conflict with superior(s), subordinates, and peers, with the help of the staff.

2. Read Chapter 6 of this book. Additional readings may be assigned by the staff.

3. Write the parent, adult, and child responses to the five statements in Step 4 (1) on your writing tablet.

Requirements

1. Group size: Between 6 and 30.
2. Time required: 1 hour and 48 minutes.
3. Materials: Felt pens and writing tablets.
4. Physical arrangement: A large room where the trios can have private discussions. The room should have chairs that can be easily rearranged.

Procedures

Step 1 (5 minutes)
1. The group leader or staff discusses the objectives of the meeting.
2. The staff presents the schedule for the meeting.
3. The staff entertains questions from the participants.

Step 2 (30 minutes)
1. The staff presents the results of analysis of data collected on the ROCI–II. Additional data (especially on the effective use of the five styles of handling interpersonal conflict) that the staff may have collected through observation and interviews of group members may also be presented.
2. The staff and participants discuss the results and draw inferences.

Step 3 (2 minutes)
Break into subgroups of three members. You should choose members with whom you will be able to discuss your work-related problems openly.

Step 4 (25 minutes)
1. Write a Parent, Adult, and Child response to the following five statements: (The participants have done this before coming to the workshop.)
    a. Did you see the sales figures for this month?
    b. I have to finish this report today.
    c. What time is it?
    d. Jim, you are late.
    e. My supervisor is a competent person.

2. Discuss your responses to the preceding statements with your group members.

3. Write a group response (Parent, Adult, and Child) for each of the five statements.

Step 5 (6 minutes)

Think of a work incident that occurred between you and your supervisor. Quickly relate the story to the other members. Agree upon which of the three stories would make the best role-playing exercise.[2]

The individual to whom the incident occurred is designated as member A who becomes the observer. The other two are designated B and C.

Step 6 (5 minutes)

The designated members are assigned the following instructions:

Member B: Assume you are the supervisor in the situation described by member A. Start at the beginning and role-play it through to conclusion. Play the role according to how you would feel and behave if you were in the situation. Make up what is consistent with the story when you need to do so.

Member C: Assume you are the subordinate and follow the same role-playing instructions.

Member A: While observing, do not interrupt the role playing. Watch for the following:

1. Primary ego states from which each is communicating.
2. Changes in ego states as the exercise progresses.
3. Complementary, crossed, and ulterior transactions.

Step 7 (15 minutes)

1. Member A describes his observations on role-playing to Members B and C.

2. The triad members discuss the following:
   a. What did each of the role players try to accomplish?
   b. How would you characterize the final solution(s) arrived at by members B and C? Starting with the ego state of the supervisor, would you say the transaction was (a) arent to Child, (b) Child to Parent, (c) Adult to Adult, or (d) Child to Child?
   c. How did the subordinate feel about the transactions?
   d. What would appear to be possible consequences of the transactions?
   e. How could the situation have best been handled in terms of the following?
       (a) Type of communication.
       (b) Specific approaches to overcome conflict.
       (c) Solutions.

Step 8 (10 minutes)

Member A's are to report some of their observations to the total group. Open discussion of results follows.

Step 9 (10 minutes)

The staff asks the participants to make comments on the exercise and the new behavior learned from it.

Exercise 5
Managing Interpersonal Conflict

Objectives

1. To diagnose what styles of handling interpersonal conflict the participants use to deal with what situations.

2. To help the participants learn the effective use of each style to deal with different situations.

Premeeting Preparation

1. Complete the ROCI–II (Forms A, B, and C), to be supplied by the staff, and construct the indices of your styles of handling interpersonal conflict with superior(s), subordinates, and peers, with the help of the staff.

2. Read Chapter 6 of this book. Additional readings may be assigned by the staff.

Requirements

1. Group size: Between 5 and 30.

2. Time required: 2 hour, 15 minutes.

3. Materials: Felt pens, masking tape, writing tablets, magic markers, and newsprints.

4. Physical arrangements: A large room with chairs that can be easily rearranged.

Procedure

Step 1 (5 minutes)

1. The staff discusses the objectives of the exercise.

2. The staff presents the schedule of the exercise.

3. The staff entertains questions from the participants.

Step 2 (15 minutes)

1. The staff presents the results of analysis of data collected on the ROCI–II from the participants' organization. Additional data that the staff may have collected (especially on what styles are used to handle what types of situations) through observation and interviews of group members should also be presented.

2. The staff and participants discuss the results and draw inferences.

Step 3 (45 minutes)

1. Break into subgroups of five or six members.

2. Elect a leader for your subgroup.

3. List on the newsprint at least three situations where each of the five styles are appropriate.

Step 4 (45 minutes)

A fishbowl exercise may be arranged for this purpose.

1. Post on the walls the newsprint listings of the situations where each style is appropriate.

2. The subgroup leaders present the situations identified by their subgroups.

3. The subgroup leaders prepare the final list of situations where each style is appropriate.

Step 5 (15 minutes)

1. The group members with the help of the staff compare their lists of situations with the one resented in this book (Table 3–1).

Step 6 (10 minutes)

1. The staff asks the participants to make comments on the exercise and the new behavior learnt from it.

2. A schedule for follow-up is agreed upon.

Exercise 6
Team Building

Objectives

1. To assess the amount of intragroup conflict and the styles of handling such conflict.

2. To reach consensus on the goals of the group. This may involve adding new goals and dropping or redefining existing goals.

3. To analyze the tasks that are performed to attain the group's goals. This may involve adding new tasks and dropping or redefining existing tasks to attain the revised goals.

4. To assign or reassign the tasks to the group members.

5. To examine the group processes and the interpersonal relationships among the group members.

Requirements

1. Group size: 6 to 40.

2. Time: 7 hours, 45 minutes.

3. Materials: Felt pens, magic markers, writing tablets, masking tape, and newsprint pads.

4. Physical arrangements: A large room with chairs that can be easily rearranged.

Premeeting Preparation

1. Complete the ROCI–I and ROCI–II (Form C), to be supplied by the staff, and construct indices of the amount of conflict in your group and your styles of handling conflict with your group members. The items of the ROCI–I can be altered to measure conflict within a specific group (e.g., item no. 4 can be altered as, "In the marketing department, we do lots of bickering over who should do what job"). The items in the ROCI–II may be altered to make the information useful to the group members (e.g., Item No. 1 may be altered as, "I try to investigate an issue with my group members to find a solution acceptable to us").

2. Read chapter 7 of this book. Additional readings may be assigned by the staff.

Procedures

Step 1 (5 minutes)

1. The group leader or staff explains the objectives of the meeting.

2. The staff presents the schedule for the meeting.

3. The group leader and/or the staff entertains questions from the participants.

Step 2 (20 minutes)

1. The staff presents the findings of conflict diagnosis performed on the group members through the ROCI–I and ROCI–II. The staff also discusses the summary of data collected through observations and interviews from group members.

2. The staff and participants discuss the results of data analysis and draw inferences.

Step 3 (45 minutes)

1. Break into subgroups of 5 and 6 members to evaluate the existing goals of the group to prepare a revised list of goals.

2. Elect a leader for your subgroup.

3. List the revised goals of your group on the newsprint pads.

Step 4 (45 minutes)

A fishbowl exercise may be arranged for this step.

1. Post the newsprint listing of the revised group goals on the walls.

2. The subgroup leaders present the goals identified by their subgroups to the group.

3. The group prepares the final list of goals.

Step 5 (10 minutes)

The subgroup leaders rank the final list of goals in importance with the help of group members.

Step 6 (60 minutes)

1. Break into subgroups of five or six members to prepare a list of tasks that must be performed to attain the goals agreed upon in Step 4.

2. Assign each subgroup to work on the tasks for one or two group goals prepared in Step 4.

3. Elect your subgroup leader.

4. List the tasks needed to attain the group goals assigned to you on newsprint.

Step 7 (60 minutes)

A fishbowl exercise may be arranged for this purpose.

1. Post the newsprint listing of the tasks on the walls.

2. The subgroup leaders present the tasks identified by their subgroups to the group.

3. The group discusses and integrates the tasks identified by the subgroups.

4. The group prepares the final list of tasks that are needed to attain the revised goals.

Step 8 (30 minutes)

1. The group leader, with the help of subgroup leaders, assigns responsibilities for different tasks to group members.

2. The interdependent activities among group members are discussed and clarified. Some individuals may be made specifically responsible for the management of interface activities between units within the group.

Step 9 (45 minutes)

 1. Break into subgroups of five or six.

 2. Elect your subgroup leader.

 3. Discuss the problems that are hindering the attainment of group goals. The subgroup members may like to discuss the group processes, such as leadership, decision making, communication, motivation processes, and interpersonal issues, such as styles of handling conflict, trust, support, and so on.

 4. Prepare separate listings of group processes and interpersonal issues on newsprint pads.

Step 10 (45 minutes)

A fishbowl exercise may be arranged for this purpose.

 1. Post the newsprint listings of group processes and interpersonal relations from the subgroups on the walls.

 2. The subgroup leaders present the problems relating to group processes and interpersonal issues.

 3. The group members discuss these problems and prepare a final list of problems that should be properly dealt with to improve group effectiveness.

 4. The participants rank the problems in order of importance.

 5. Each subgroup is made responsible for formulating solutions to one or more specific problems identified in Step 10 (3).

Step 11 (30 minutes)

 1. Join your subgroup to discuss the problem(s) assigned to your subgroup.

 2. Elect your subgroup leader.

 3. Prepare alternative solutions to the problem(s).

 4. List the solutions to problems on newsprint pads.

Step 12 (45 minutes)

 1. Post the newsprint listing of problem solutions on the walls.

 2. The subgroup leaders present the alternative solutions to their assigned problems.

 3. The group members discuss these solutions and reach agreement on the solutions.

Step 13 (10 minutes)

 1. The participants elect three or more members for developing strategies needed for the implementation of changes recommended by the group. The group members can indicate several broad strategies for the implementation of changes.

 2. The members are made responsible for securing approval for changes from the formal leader of the group. (On receiving the approval, they prepare

the strategies for implementation and follow these for making the planned changes.)

   3. Dates for follow-up are agreed upon.

Step 14 (15 minutes)

The staff asks the participants to make comments on the exercise and the new behavior they learned that can be used in their group.

Exercise 7
Intergroup Problem Solving

Objectives

   1. To diagnose the amount of conflict between two specific groups and how it is handled.
   2. To help the participants identify intergroup problems.
   3. To help the participants develop alternative solutions to these problems.
   4. To design plans for implementation of intergroup decisions.
   5. To help ingroup members learn the integrating style of handling conflict with outgroup members.

Requirements

   1. Group size: Between 15 and 35.
   2. Time required: 6 hours, 15 minutes for the first session and 2 hours 35 minutes for the second session.
   3. Materials: Felt pens, magic markers, writing tablets, masking tape, and newsprint pads.
   4. Physical arrangement: One large room and several smaller rooms with chairs that can be easily rearranged.

Premeeting Preparation

   1. Complete the ROCI–I and ROCI–II, to be supplied by the staff, and construct indices of the amount of conflict between the two groups and the styles of handling such conflict by the members of the two groups, with the help of the staff. The items of the instruments may be altered to make the information useful to the two conflicting groups. The items of the ROCI–I may be altered to measure conflict between two specific groups, such as maintenance and production departments (e.g., item no. 10 can be altered as, "There is cooperation between production and marketing departments"). The items of the ROCI–II may be altered to measure how a member of the R/D department handles conflict with marketing department (e.g., item no.

2 can be altered as, "I generally try to satisfy the needs of the members of marketing department").

3. Read Chapter 8 of this book. The staff may assign additional readings.

First Problem-Solving Session: Procedure

Step 1 (5 minutes)

1. The leaders of the two groups or staff present the objectives of the exercise.

2. The staff presents the schedule for the exercise.

3. The leaders of the participating groups and/or staff entertain questions from the participants.

Step 2 (10 minutes)

1. The staff presents the five major steps in problem solving.

2. The staff entertains questions from the participants.

Step 3 (30 minutes)

1. The staff presents the results of the analysis of data collected on the ROCI–I and II. The staff also presents the summary of additional data that may have been collected from the members of the participating groups through observation, interviews, and company records.

2. The staff and participants discuss the results and draw inferences.

Step 4 (45 minutes)

1. Break into homogeneous subgroups and meet separately to discuss and identify the intergroup problems.

2. Elect your subgroup leader.

3. List the intergroup problems on newsprint pads.

Step 5 (45 minutes)

A fishbowl exercise may be arranged for this step.

1. Post the newsprint listings of intergroup problems on the walls.

2. The subgroup leaders present the problems identified by their subgroups to the intergroup.

3. The intergroup discusses and integrates the problems identified by the subgroups. It prepares the final list of problems.

Step 6 (10 minutes)

1. The subgroup leaders rank the final list of problems.

2. Each subgroup is assigned to work on the solutions of one or more specific problems.

Step 7 (15 minutes)

The intergroup formulates criteria for solutions.

Step 8 (30 minutes)

1. Break into heterogeneous subgroups and meet separately to discuss and formulate alternative solutions to problems assigned to your subgroup with reference to Step 7.

2. Elect your subgroup leader.

3. List the alternative solutions to problems on the newsprint pads.

Step 9 (45 minutes)

A fishbowl exercise may be arranged for this purpose.

1. Post the newsprint listings of alternative solutions on the walls.

2. The subgroup leaders discuss the alternative solutions to their assigned problems.

3. The intergroup discusses and integrates the alternative solutions.

4. The subgroup leaders rank the alternative solutions to each problem.

Step 10 (30 minutes)

The subgroups created in Step 8 prepare a plan for implementation (including monitoring of implementation) of the problem solutions.

Step 11 (45 minutes)

A fishbowl exercise may be arranged for this step.

1. The subgroup leaders present the plans prepared by their respective subgroups.

2. The subgroup leaders prepare the final plan for implementation.

Step 12 (45 minutes)

1. The subgroup leaders, with the help of participants, identify the problem of implementation.

2. They prepare strategies for overcoming resistance to change. A force field analysis may be performed for this purpose.

Step 13 (5 minutes)

The intergroup assigns responsibilities for implementation and monitoring of implementation to specified individuals.

Step 14 (5 minutes)

The intergroup prepares a schedule for follow-up.

Step 15 (10 minutes)

The staff asks the participants to make comments on the exercise and the new behavior learned from it.

(The first problem solving session concludes here.)

Second Problem-Solving Session

Procedure

The objective of this session is to evaluate the impact of implementation of the plan as specified in Step 11 in the previous session and recommend corrective measures.

Step 1 (5 minutes)
1. The leaders of the participating groups or the staff present the objectives of the second session for problem solving.
2. The staff presents a schedule for the exercise.
3. They entertain questions from the participants.

Step 2 (30 minutes)
A fishbowl exercise may be arranged for this step.
The individuals who were responsible for the implementation and monitoring of implementation discuss the progress made in implementation and problems encountered.

Step 3 (45 minutes)
The intergroup discusses the impact of the plan and identifies the problems of implementation, if any.

Step 4 (15 minutes)
The intergroup may recommend corrective actions if the results of implementation deviate from the standards.

Step 5 (45 minutes)
1. The participants may respond to the ROCI–I and ROCI–II. They compute indices of the amount of conflict between the two groups and their styles of handling such conflict.
2. The conflict indices from the first session are compared with corresponding indices from the second session.
3. The staff and the participants discuss the changes in the amount of conflict and styles of handling intergroup conflict between the two sessions and draw inferences.

Step 6 (10 minutes)
The intergroup decides whether or not to recycle the problem-solving process.

Step 7 (5 minutes)

The staff asks the participants to make comments on the exercise and the new behavior learned from it.

Exercise 8
Organizational Mirroring

Objectives

1. To improve relationships among three or more groups.
2. To receive feedback from the work-related groups.

Premeeting Preparation

Read Chapter 7 of this book. The staff may assign additional readings.

Requirements

1. Group size: Between 30 and 80.
2. Time required: 5 hours, 20 minutes.
3. Materials: Felt pens, magic markers, writing tablets, masking tape, and newsprint pads.
4. Physical arrangements: A large room with chairs that can be easily rearranged.

Procedure

Step 1 (10 minutes)

1. The leaders of the participating groups and/or the staff explain the objectives of the exercise.
2. The staff presents the schedule for the exercise.
3. The leaders of the participating groups and the staff entertain questions from the participants.

Step 2 (30 minutes)

1. The staff presents the findings of the conflict diagnosis performed on the participating groups through interview and other methods.
2. The staff and the participants discuss the results of diagnosis and draw inferences.

Step 3 (60 minutes)

1. The members of work-related groups form a "fishbowl" to interpret and discuss the data presented by the consultant.

2. The host group members listen and take notes.

Step 4 (60 minutes)

The host group members form a "fishbowl" to discuss what they learned from work-related groups. They may ask for clarification from the leaders of work-related groups.

Step 5 (30 minutes)

1. Break into heterogeneous subgroups to identify the significant intergroup problems that must be solved to enhance the host group's effectiveness.

2. Elect a leader for your subgroup.

3. List the problems on newsprint pads.

Step 6 (45 minutes)

A fishbowl exercise may be performed for this step.

1. Post the newsprint listings of problems on the walls.

2. The subgroup leaders report the problems identified by their respective subgroups.

3. The subgroup leaders discuss these problems and prepare a final list for which actions are needed.

4. Each subgroup is made responsible to formulate the solutions of one or more problems.

Step 7 (45 minutes)

1. The subgroups formed before discuss their assigned problem(s) and formulate alternative solutions.

2. The subgroups prepare action plans and strategies for implementation of the solutions in the previous step.

Step 8 (30 minutes)

1. The leaders of the subgroups review and accept the action plans and strategies of implementation.

2. A schedule for follow-up is agreed upon.

Step 9 (10 minutes)

The staff asks the participants to make comments on the exercise and the new behavior learned from it.

Exercise 9
Analysis of Task Interdependence

Objectives

1. To analyze the interrelationships of tasks between the participating groups.

2. To prepare a list of interdependent task items and classify them into homogeneous clusters.

3. To assign the task clusters to groups and an integrative committee.

Requirements

1. Group size: 15 to 35.

2. Time required: 3 hours, and 55 minutes.

3. Materials: Felt pens, magic markers, writing tablets, masking tape, newsprint pads.

4. Physical arrangement: A large room with chairs which can be easily rearranged.

Premeeting Preparation

Read Chapter 8 of this book if you have not done so already. The staff may assign additional readings.

Procedure

Step 1 (10 minutes)

1. The leaders of the participating groups and/or staff discuss the objectives of the meeting.

2. The staff presents the schedule for the exercise.

3. The leaders of the participating groups and the staff entertain questions from the participants.

Step 2 (15 minutes)

1. The staff presents results of the analysis of diagnostic data that may have been collected from the participating groups.

2. The staff and participants discuss the results and draw inferences.

Step 3 (60 minutes)

1. Break into heterogeneous subgroups to identify the task items that create problems between the participating groups.

2. Elect a leader for your subgroup.

3. On newsprint, list the task items that create intergroup problems.

Step 4 (60 minutes)

A fishbowl exercise may be arranged for this step.

1. The subgroup leaders present the tasks identified by their subgroups to the intergroup.

2. The intergroup discusses and integrates the tasks identified by the subgroups. The intergroup prepares the final list of tasks.

Step 5 (45 minutes)

1. The subgroup leaders classify the tasks into several clusters on the basis of similarity of task items.

2. They assign a short title to each task cluster.

Step 6 (30 minutes)

1. The formal group leaders, with the help of subgroup leaders, assign the task clusters to participating groups. The task clusters must be assigned to the groups on the basis of congruence between the requirements of the tasks and skill, material, and other resources possessed by the groups for performing the tasks.

2. The task clusters that cannot be assigned to a particular group because no group has the expertise, resources, or authority to perform the tasks in these clusters should be assigned to a special committee formed for this purpose with three or more members from the participating groups.

Step 7 (5 minutes)

1. A special committee is made responsible for the supervision of implementation of changes agreed by the intergroup.

2. A date(s) for follow-up is agreed upon.

Step 8 (10 minutes)

The staff asks the participants to make comments on the exercise and the new behavior they learned from the exercise.

Notes

1. *The Rahim Organizational Conflict Inventory–I and II* (Forms A, B, & C) and the *Rahim Organizational Conflict Inventories: Professional Manual* are available from the Center for Advanced Studies in Management, 1574 Mallory Court, Bowling Green, KY 42103, USA (mgt2000@aol.com).

2. Steps 5 through 8 of this exercise are based on an exercise developed by M. D. Federer, Department of Psychology, California Polytechnic State University, San Louis, Obispo, California.

References

Abratt, R., Nel, D., & Higgs, N. S. (1992). An examination of the ethical beliefs of managers using selected scenarios in a cross-cultural environment. *Journal of Business Ethics, 11,* 29–35.

Ahose, D. K. (1995). *The effects of formal and informal relations on choice of interpersonal conflict resolution strategy.* Unpublished doctoral dissertation, Gonzaga University, Spokane, WA.

Amason, A. C. (1996). Distinguishing the effects of functional and dysfunctional conflict on strategic decision making: Resolving a paradox for top management teams. *Academy of Management Journal, 39,* 123–148.

Ambrož, M. (2005). The mediating role of the ombudsman in the protection of human rights. *International Journal of Social Welfare, 14,* 145–153.

Amason, A. C., & Shweiger, D. M. (1997). The effects of conflict on strategic decision making effectiveness and organizational performance. In C. K. W. DeDreu & E. Van de Vliert (Eds.), *Using conflict in organizations* (pp. 101–115). London: Sage.

Andersen, M. (1984, December 27). Voluminous arbitrator's decision returned on Hormel wage reductions. *Austin Daily Herald,* p. 3.

Andersen, M. (1985a, February 21). UFCW Int'l seeks meeting with P–9 R & F. *Austin Daily Herald,* p. 1.

Andersen, M. (1985b, March 1). P–9 levies charges against international union V-P. *Austin Daily Herald,* p. 1.

Andersen, M. (1985c, March 18). Arbiter sets Hormel wage at $8.75 per hour. *Austin Daily Herald,* p. 1.

Andersen, M. (1985d, March 25). P–9 strengthens attack on First Bank. *Austin Daily Herald,* p. 1.

Andersen, M. (1985e, May 3). Hormel offers defense on injury rates. *Austin Daily Herald,* p. 1.

Anderson, J. C., & Gerbing, D. W. (1988) Structural equation modeling in practice: A review and recommended two-step approach. *Psychological Bulletin, 103,* 411–423.

Anton, R. J. (1990). Drawing the line: An exploratory test of ethical behavior in negotiations. *International Journal of Conflict Management, 1,* 265–280.

Antonioni, D. (1998). Relationship between the big five personality factors and conflict management style. *International Journal of Conflict Management, 9,* 336–355.

Aram, J. D., Morgan, C. P., & Esbeck, E. S. (1971). Relation of collaborative interpersonal relationships to individual satisfaction and organizational performance. *Administrative Science Quarterly, 16,* 289–296.

Arbitrator will make call in Hormel–P–9 tiff. (1985, January 8). *Austin Daily Herald,* p. 1.

Argyris, C. (1964). *Integrating the individual and the organization.* New York: Wiley.

Argyris, C. (1974). Personality vs. organization. *Organizational Dynamics, 3* (2), 3–17.

Argyris, C. (1976). Single-loop and double-loop models in research and decision making. *Administrative Science Quarterly, 21,* 363–375.

Argyris, C. (1990). *Overcoming organizational defenses: Facilitating organizational learning.* Needham Heights, MA: Allyn & Bacon.

Argyris, C. (1994). Good communication that blocks learning. *Harvard Business Review, 72* (5), 77–85.

Argyris, C., & Schön, D. (1996). *Organizational learning–II.* Reading, MA: Addison-Wesley.

Aristotle (1). (1984). Nicomachean ethics (trans. W. D. Ross). In J. Barnes (Ed.), *The complete works of Aristotle: The revised Oxford translation.* Princeton, NJ: Princeton University Press. [The location of the reference is further specified in terms of book (Roman numeral) and chapter (Arabic numeral)].

Aristotle (2). (1984). Politics. (trans. B. Jowett). In J. Barnes (Ed.), *The complete works of Aristotle: The revised Oxford translation.* Princeton, NJ: Princeton University Press. [The location of the reference is further specified in terms of book (Roman numeral) and chapter (Arabic numeral)].

Asch, S. E. (1951). Effects of group pressure on the modification and distortion on judgements. In H. G. Guetzkow (Ed.), *Groups, leadership and men* (pp. 174–183). Pittsburgh: Carnegie Press.

Ashforth, B. E., & Mael, F. (1989). Social identity theory and the organization. *Academy of Management Review, 14,* 20–39.

Assael, H. (1969). Constructive role of interorganizational conflict. *Administrative Science Quarterly, 14,* 573–582.

Babin, B. J., & Boles J. S. (1996). The effects of co-worker involvement and supervisor support on service provider role. *Journal of Retailing, 72,* 57–76.

Baenen, J. (1986, August 31). Hormel's long strike ends, but some scars still linger. *Huntsville* [Alabama] *Times,* p. H–2.

Bagozzi, R. P., & Heatherton, T. F. (1994). A general approach to representing multifaceted personality constructs: Application to state self-esteem. *Structural Equations Modeling, 1,* 35–67.

Bagozzi, R. P., & Phillips, L. W. (1982). Representing and testing organizational theories: A holistic construal. *Administrative Science Quarterly, 27,* 459–489.

Bagozzi, R. P., Yi, Y., & Phillips, L. W. (1991). Assessing construct validity in organizational research. *Administrative Science Quarterly, 36,* 421–458.

Baker, J., Tjosvold, T., & Andrews, I. R. (1988). Conflict approaches of effective and ineffective project managers: A field study in a matrix organization. *Journal of Management Studies, 25,* 167–178.

Baritz, L. (1960). *The servants of power: A history of the use of social science in American industry.* Middletown, CT: Wesleyan University Press.

Baron, R. A. (1989). Personality and organization conflict: Effects of the Type A behavior pattern and self-monitoring. *Organizational Behavior and Human Decision Processes, 44,* 281–296.

Baron, R. A. (1990). Conflict in organizations. In K. R. Murphy & F. E. Saal (Ed.), *Psychology in organizations: Integrating science and practice* (pp. 197–216). Hillsdale, NJ: Erlbaum.

Baron, R. A. (1997). Positive effects of conflict: Insights from social cognition. In C. K. W. De Drew & E. Van de Vliert (Eds.), *Using conflict in organizations* (pp. 177–191). London: Sage.

Bass, B. M. (1960). *Leadership, psychology, and organizational behavior.* New York: Harper & Row.

Bass, B. M. (1965). *Organizational psychology.* Needham Heights, MA: Allyn and Bacon.

Bass, B. M. (1985). *Leadership and performance beyond expectations.* New York: Free Press.

Bass, B. M., & Yammarino, F. J. (1991). Congruence of self and others' leadership ratings of naval officers for understanding successful leadership. *Applied Psychology: An International Review, 40,* 437–454.

Bateson, G. (1972). *Steps to an ecology of mind.* San Francisco: Chadler.

Baucus, M. S., & Baucus, D. A. (1997). Paying the piper: An empirical examination of long-term financial consequences of illegal corporate behavior. *Academy of Management Journal, 40,* 129–151.

Bazerman, M. H., Tenbrunsel, A. E., & Wade-Benzoni, K. (1998). Negotiating with yourself and losing: Making decisions with competing internal preferences. *Academy of Management Journal, 23,* 225–241.

Beauchamp, T. L. (1988). Ethical theory and its application to business. In T. L. Beauchamp & N. E. Bowie (Eds.), *Ethical theory and business* (3rd ed., pp. 1–54). Englewood Cliffs, NJ: Prentice-Hall.

Beauchamp, T. L., & Bowie, N. E. (Ed.). (1997). *Ethical theory and business* (5th ed.). Upper Saddle River, NJ: Prentice-Hall.

Becker, H., & Geer, B. (1960). Latent culture: A note on the theory of latent social roles. *Administrative Science Quarterly, 5,* 304–313.

Beckhard, R. (1967). The confrontation meeting. *Harvard Business Review, 45* (2), 149–155.

Beckhard, R., & Harris, R. T. (1987). *Organizational transitions: Managing complex change.* Reading, MA: Addison-Wesley.

Beer, M., & Spector, B. (1993). Organizational diagnosis: Its role in organizational learning. *Journal of Counseling & Development, 71,* 641–650.

Beer, M., & Walton, A. E. (1987). Organization change and development. *Annual Review of Psychology, 38,* 339–367.

Behfar, K. J., & Thompson, L. L. (2007). Conflict within and between organizational groups: Functional, dysfunctional, and quasifunctional perspectives. In K. J. Behfar & L. L. Thompson (Eds.), *Conflict in organizational groups: New directions in theory and practice.* (pp. 3–35). Evanston, IL: Northwestern University Press.

Behfar, K. J., Peterson, R. S., Mannix, E. A., & Trochim, W. M. K. (2008). The critical role of conflict resolution in teams: A close look at the links between conflict type, conflict management strategies, and team outcomes. *Journal of Applied Psychology, 93,* 170–188.

Behrman, D., & Perreault, W. D., Jr. (1984). A role stress model of the performance and satisfaction of industrial salespersons. *Journal of Marketing, 48,* 9–21.

Belasco, J. A., & Alutto, J. A. (1969). Line and staff conflicts: Some empirical insights. *Academy of Management Journal, 12,* 469–477.

Bell, E. C., & Blakeney, R. N. (1977). Personality correlates of conflict resolution modes. *Human Relations, 30,* 849–857.

Bentler, P. M. (1990). Comparative fit indexes in structural models. *Psychological Bulletin, 107,* 238–246.

Bentler, P. M., & Bonett, D. G. (1980). Significance tests and goodness-of-fit in the analysis of covariance structures. *Psychological Bulletin, 88,* 588–606.

Ben-Yoav, O., & Banai, M. (1992). Measuring conflict management styles: A comparison between the MODE and ROCI–II instruments using self and peer ratings. *International Journal of Conflict Management, 3,* 237–247.

Berlyne, D. E. (1960). *Conflict, arousal, and curiosity.* New York: McGraw-Hill.

Bernard, J. (1957). The sociological study of conflict. In International Sociological Association (Ed.), *The nature of conflict: Studies on the sociological aspects of international tensions.* UNESCO, Tensions and Technology Series (pp. 33–117). Paris: UNESCO.

Berne, E. (1961). *Transactional analysis in psychotherapy: A systematic individual and social psychiatry.* New York: Grove Press.

Berne, E. (1964). *Games people play: The psychology of human relationships.* New York: Grove Press.

Berne, E. (1972). *What do you say after you say hellow? The psychology of human destiny.* New York: Bantam.

Billingham, R. E., & Sack, A. R. (1987). Conflict tactics and the level of emotional commitment among unmarrieds. *Human Relations, 40,* 59–74

Bisno, H. (1988). *Managing conflict.* Newbury Park, CA: Sage.

Blake, R. R., & Mouton, J. S. (1961). Reactions to intergroup competition under win–lose conditions. *Management Science, 7,* 420–435.

Blake, R. R., & Mouton, J. S. (1964). *The managerial grid.* Houston, TX: Gulf.

Blake, R. R., & Mouton, J. S. (1984). *Solving costly organizational conflicts.* San Francisco: Jossey-Bass.

Blake, R. R., Mouton, J. S., & Sloma, R. L. (1965). The union-management intergroup laboratory: Strategy for resolving intergroup conflict. *Journal of Applied Behavioral Science, 1,* 25–57.

Blake, R. R., Shepard, H. A., & Mouton, J. S. (1964). *Managing intergroup conflict in industry.* Houston, TX: Gulf.

Blau, P. M. (1963). *The dynamics of bureaucracy: A study of interpersonal relations in two government agencies* (rev. ed.). Chicago: University of Chicago Press.

Boatright, J. R. (1997). *Ethics and the conduct of business* (2nd ed.). Upper Saddle River, NJ: Prentice Hall.

Bobbit, H. R., Jr., Breinholt, R. H., Doktor, R. H., & McNaul, J. P. (1978). *Organizational behavior: Understanding and prediction* (2nd ed.). Englewood Cliffs, NJ: Prentice-Hall.

Botkin, J. W., Elmandjra, M., & Malitza, M. (1979). *No limits to learning: Bridging the human gap: A report to the Rome.* Oxford: Pergamon Press.

Boulding, K. E. (1962). *Conflict and defense: A general theory.* New York: Harper & Row.

Boulding, K. E. (1968). Preface to a special issue. *Journal of Conflict Resolution, 12,* 409–411.

Bourgeois, L. J., III. (1985). Strategic goals, environmental uncertainty, and economic performance in volatile environments. *Academy of Management Journal, 28,* 548–573.

Brett, J. M. (1984). Managing organizational conflict. *Professional Psychology: Research and Practice, 15,* 664–678.

Brett, J. M., & Rognes, J. K. (1986). Intergroup relations in organizations. In P. S. Goodman and Associates (Eds.), Designing effective work groups (pp. 202–236). San Francisco: Jossey-Bass.

Brewer, M. B. (1979). In-group bias in the minimal intergroup situation: A cognitive-motivational analysis. *Psychological Bulletin, 86,* 307–324.

Brickman, P. (1974). Rule structure and conflict relationships: Readings in rule structure and conflict relationships. In P. Brickman (Ed.), *Social conflict* (pp. 1–36). Lexington, MA: D. C. Heath.

Brief, A. P., & Aldag, R. J. (1976). Correlates of role indices. *Journal of Applied Psychology, 61,* 468–472.

Brown, J. (1984, October 15). P–9 won't take wage cut without fight. *Austin Daily Herald*, p. 1.

Brown, K. M. (1994). Using role play to integrate ethics into the business curriculum: A financial management example. *Journal of Business Ethics, 13,* 105–110.

Brown, L. D. (1979). *Managing conflict among groups.* In D. A. Kolb, I. M. Rubin, & J. M. McIntyre (Eds.), *Organizational psychology: A book of readings* (3rd ed., pp. 377–389). Englewood Cliffs, NJ: Prentice Hall.

Brown, L. D. (1983). *Managing conflict at organizational interfaces.* Reading, MA: Addison-Wesley.

Browne, P. J., & Cotton, C. (1975). The topdog/underdog syndrome in liner–staff relationships. *Personnel Journal, 54* (8), 443–444.

Burke, R. J. (1969). Methods of resolving superior–subordinate conflict: The constructive use of subordinate differences and disagreements. *Organizational Behavior and Human Performance, 5,* 393–411.

Burke, W. W. (1987). *Organization development: A normative view.* Reading, MA: Addison-Wesley.

Burke, W. W. (1994). *Organization development: A process of learning and changing* (2nd ed.). Reading, MA: Addison-Wesley.

Byrne, J. A. (1993, December 20). The horizontal corporation: It's about managing across, not up and down. *Business Week,* pp. 76–81.

Callanan., G., Benzing, C. D., & Perri, D. F. (2006). Choice of conflict-handling strategy: A matter of context. *Journal of Psychology, 140,* 269–288.

Cameron, K. (1980, Autumn). Critical questions in assessing organizational effectiveness. *Organizational Dynamics,* pp. 66–80.

Cameron, K. S. (1981). Domains of organizational effectiveness in colleges and universities. *Academy of Management Journal, 24,* 25–47.

Cameron, K. S. (1984). The effectiveness of ineffectiveness. In B. M. Cummings & L. L. Cummings (Eds.), *Research in organizational behavior* (Vol. 6, pp. 235–285). Greenwich, CT: JAI.

Cameron, K. S. (1986). Effectiveness as paradox: Consensus and conflict in conceptions of organizational effectiveness. *Management Science, 32,* 539–553.

Campbell, D. T. (1967). Stereotypes and the perception of group differences. *American Psychologist, 22,* 817–829.

Campbell, J. P. (1977). On the nature of organizational effectiveness. In P. S. Goodman & J. M. Pennings (Eds.), *New perspectives of organizational effectiveness* (pp. 13–55). San Francisco: Jossey-Bass.

Campbell, D. T., & Fiske, D. W. (1959). Convergent and discriminant validity by the multitrait–multimethod matrix. *Psychological Bulletin, 56,* 81–105.

Cartwright, D., & Zander, A. (Eds.). (1968). *Group dynamics: Research and theory* (3rd Ed.). New York: Harper & Row.

Chanin, M. N., & Schneer, J. A. (1984). A study of the relationship between Jungian personality dimensions and conflict-handling behavior. *Human Relations, 37,* 863–879.

Charlier, M. (1985, March 1). Ray Rogers's strategies are popular, but many union chiefs don't like him. *Wall Street Journal,* p. 38.

Charters, W. W. (1952). *A study of role conflict among foremen in a heavy industry.* Unpublished doctoral dissertation, University of Michigan.

Child, J. (1995). Follett: Constructive conflict. In P. Graham (Ed.), *Mary Parker Follett—Prophet of management: A celebration of writings from the 1920s.* Boston: Harvard Buisness School Press.

Chow, I. H., & Ding, D. Z. Q. (2002). Moral judgement and conflict handling styles among Chinese in Hong Kong and PRC. *Journal of Management Development, 21,* 666–679.

Cole, M. A. (1996). *Interpersonal conflict communication in Japanese cultural contexts.* Unpublished doctoral dissertation, Arizona State University, Tempe.

Corwin, R. G. (1969). Patterns of organizational conflict. *Administrative Science Quarterly, 14,* 507–520.

Coser, L. A. (1956). *The functions of social conflict.* Glencoe, IL: Free Press.

Coser, L. A. (1968). Conflict: III. Social aspects. In D. L. Sills (Ed.), *International encyclopedia of the social sciences* (Vol. 3, pp. 232–236). New York: Crowell Collier and Macmillan.

Cosier, R. A., & Dalton, D. R. (1990). Positive effects of conflict: A field assessment. *International Journal of Conflict Management, 1,* 81–92.

Cosier, R. A., & Rose, G. L. (1977). Cognitive conflict and goal conflict effects on task performance. *Organizational Behavior and Human Performance, 19,* 378–391.

Costa, P. T., Jr., & McCrae, R. R. (1985). *The NEO Personality Inventory.* Odessa, FL: Psychological Assessment Resources.

Crowne, D. P., & Marlowe, D. (1960). A new scale of social desirability independent of psychopathology. *Journal of Consulting Psychology, 14,* 349–354.

Crozier, M. (1964). *The bureaucratic phenomenon* (Author, Trans. from French). Chicago: University of Chicago Press.

Dahrendorf, R. (1959). *Class and class conflict in industrial society* (Author, Trans. from German, rev., and expanded). Stanford, CA: Stanford University Press.

Dalton, M. (1959). Conflicts between staff and line managerial officers. *American Sociological Review, 15,* 342–351.

Darwin, C. R. (1871). *The descent of man, and selection in relation to sex.* New York: Modern Library.

Davis, K. (1975). A law of diminishing returns in organizational behavior? *Personnel Journal, 54,* 616–619.

Dayal, I., & Thomas, J. M. (1968). Operation KPE: Developing a new organization. *Journal of Applied Behavioral Science, 4,* 473–506.

De Bono, E. (1986). *Conflicts: A better way to resolve them.* Middlesex, UK: Penguin Books.

Dechant, K., & Veiga, J. (1995). More on the folly. *Academy of Management Executive, 9,* 15–16.

DeChurch, L. A., & Marks, M. A. (2001). Maximizing the benefits of task conflict: The role of conflict management. *International Journal of Conflict Management, 12,* 4–22.

De Dreu, C., & Weingart, L. (2003). Task versus relationship conflict, team performance, and team member satisfaction. *Journal of Applied Psychology, 88,* 741–749.

Deutsch, M. (1949). A theory of cooperation and competition *Human Relations, 2,* 129–152.

Deutsch, M. (1969). Conflicts: Productive and destructive. *Journal of Social Issues, 25* (1), 7–41.

Deutsch, M. (1977). *The resolution of conflict.* New Haven, CT: Yale University Press.

Deutsch, M. (1990). Sixty years of conflict. *International Journal of conflict management, 1,* 237–263.

Dewar, R., & Werbel, J. (1979). Universalistic and contingency predictions of employee satisfaction and conflict. *Administrative Science Quarterly, 24,* 426–448.

Dewey, J. (1957). *Human nature and conduct.* New York: Modern Library. [originally published 1922]

Digest of earnings. (1984, November 23). *Wall Street Journal,* p. 14.

Dixit, A. K., & Nalebuff, B. J. (2008). *The art of strategy: A game theorist's guide to success in business and life.* W. W. Norton.

Downs, A. (1968). *Inside bureaucracy.* Boston: Little, Brown.

Dreu, C. De, & Vliert, E. Van de (Eds.). (1997). *Using conflict in organizations.* London: Sage.

Druckman, D., Broome, B. J., & Korper, S. H. (1988). Value differences and conflict resolution: Facilitation or delinking? *Journal of Conflict Resolution, 32,* 489–510.

Druckman, D., & Zechmeister, K. (1973). Conflict of interest and value dissensus: Propositions in the sociology of conflict. *Human Relations, 26,* 449–466.

DuBrin, A. J. (1972). *The practice of managerial psychology: Concepts and methods of manager and organization development* (pp. 211–227). New York: Pergamon Press.

Duncan, R., & Weiss, A. (1979). Organizational learning: Implications for organizational design. In B. Staw (Ed.), *Research in organizational behavior* (Vol. 1, pp. 75–123). Greenwich, CT: JAI Press.

Dune, M. J. (1989). Sex differences in styles of conflict management. *Psychological Reports, 65,* 1033–1034.

Dyr, W. G. (1987). *Team building: Issues and alternatives* (2nd ed.). Reading, MA: Addison-Wesley.

Eisenhardt, K. M., Kahwajy, J. L., & Bourgeois, L. J. (1997). Conflict and strategic choice: How top management teams disagree. *California Management Review, 39* (2), 42–62.

Eisenhardt, K. M., & Schoonhoven, C. (1990). Organizational growth: Linking founding team, strategy, environment, and growth among U.S. semiconductor ventures, 1878–1988. *Administrative Science Quarterly, 35,* 504–529.

Elliston, F. (1985). *Whistleblowing research: Methodological and moral issues.* New York: Praeger.

Etzioni, A. (1964). *Modern organizations.* Englewood Cliffs, NJ: Prentice-Hall.

Evan, W. M. (1962). Role strain and the norm of reciprocity in research organizations. *American Journal of Sociology, 68,* 346–354.

Eysenck, H. J., & Eysenck, S. B. G. (1968). *Manual for the Eysenck Personality Inventory.* San Diego, CA: Educational and Industrial Testing Service.

Fayol, H. (1949). *General and industrial management* (C. Storrs, Trans. from French). London: Pitman. [originally published 1916]

Fiedler, F. E. (1967). *A theory of leadership effectiveness.* New York: McGraw-Hill.

Fiedler, F., Mitchell, T., & Triandis, H. (1971). The cultural assimilator: An approach to cross-cultural training. *Journal of Applied Psychology, 55,* 95–102.

Fiol, C. M. (1994). Consensus, diversity and learning organizations. *Organization Science, 5,* 403–420.

Fisher, C. D., & Gitelson, R. (1983). A meta-analysis of the correlates of role conflict and ambiguity. *Journal of Applied Psychology, 68,* 320–333.

Fisher, R. J. (2006). *Intergroup conflict.* In M. Deutsch, P. T. Coleman, & E. C. Marcus (Eds.), *The handbook of conflict resolution: Theory and research* (2nd ed., pp. 176–222). San Francisco: Josssey-Bass.

Fisher, R., & Ury, W. (1981). *Getting to Yes: Negotiating agreement without giving in.* New York: Penguin Books.

Fisher, R., Ury, W., & Patton, B. (1991). *Getting to YES: Negotiating agreement without giving in* (2nd ed.). New York: Penguin Books.

Follett, M. P. (1940). Constructive conflict. In H. C. Metcalf & L. Urwick (Eds.), *Dynamic administration: The collected papers of Mary Parker Follett* (pp. 30–49). New York: Harper & Row. [originally published 1926].

Fordyce, J. K., & Weil, R. (1971). *Managing with people: A manager's handbook of organization development methods.* Reading, MA: Addison-Wesley.

Forsyth, D. L. (1983). *An introduction to group dynamics.* Monterey, CA: Brooks/Cole.

Forsyth, D. R. (1980). A taxonomy of ethical ideologies. *Journal of Personality and Social Psychology, 39,* 175–184.

Fox, H. L. (1998, August 13). Who needs corporate brands? *Marketing,* pp. 22–23.

Frankenhaeuser, M. (1977). Quality of life: Criteria of behavioral adjustment. *International Journal of Psychology, 12,* 99–100.

Frederickson, J. D. (1998). *Assessing the validity of the Rahim Organizational Conflict Inventory–II (ROCI–II).* Unpublished doctoral dissertation, University of Minnesota.

Freeman, R. E., & Gilbert, D. R. (1988). *Corporate strategy and the search for ethics.* Englewood Cliffs, NJ: Prentice Hall.

French, W., & Albright, D. (1998). Resolving a moral conflict through discourse. *Journal of Business Ethics, 17,* 177–194.

French, W. L., & Bell, C. H., Jr. (1999). *Organization development* (6th ed.). Englewood Cliffs, NJ: Prentice-Hall.

French, W. L., Bell, C. H., Jr., & Zawacki, R. A. (Eds.). (1989). *Organization development: Theory, practice, & research* (3rd ed.). Homewood, IL: BIP/Irwin.

French, J. R. P., & Caplan, R. D. (1972). Organizational stress and individual strain. In A. J. Marrow (Ed.), *The failure of success* (pp. 30–66). New York: AMACOM.

French, J. R. P., Jr., & Raven, B. (1959). The bases of social power. In D. Cartwright (Ed.), *Studies in social power* (pp. 150–167). Ann Arbor, MI: Institute for Social Research, University of Michigan.

Fried, Y., Ben-David, H. A., Tiegs, R. B., Avital, N., & Yeverchyahu, U. (1998). The interactive effect of role conflict and role ambiguity on job performance. *Journal of Occupational & Organizational Psychology, 71,* 19–28.

Friedkin, N. E., & Simpson, M. J. (1985). Effects of competition on members' identification with their subunits. *Administrative Science Quarterly, 30,* 377–394.

Garvin, D. A. (1993). Building a learning organization. *Harvard Business Review, 71* (4), 78–92.

Georgopoulos, B. S., & Tannenbaum, A. S. (1957). A study of organizational effectiveness. *American Sociological Review, 22,* 534–540.

Gerbing, D. W., & Anderson, J. C. (1993). Monte Carlo evaluations of goodness-of-fit indices for structural equation models. In K. A. Bollen & J. S. Long (Eds.), *Testing structural equation models* (pp. 40–65). Newbury Park, CA: Sage.

Gilboa, S., Shirom, A., Fried, Y., & Cooper, C. (2008). A meta-analysis of work demand stressors and job performance: Examining main and moderating effects. *Personnal Psychology, 61,* 227–271.

Gist, M. E., Locke, E. A., & Taylor, M. S. (1987). Organizational behavior: Group structure, process, and effectiveness. *Journal of Management, 13,* 237–257.

Goldman, A. L. (1991). *Settling for more: Mastering negotiating strategies and techniques.* Washington, DC: Bureau of National Affairs.

Goldman, R. M. (1966). A theory of conflict processes and organizational offices. *Journal of Conflict Resolution, 10,* 328–343.

Golembiewski, R. T. (1998). Dealing with doubt and cynicism about organization change, the old-fashioned way: Empirical data about success rates in OD and QWL. In M. A. Rahim, R. T. Golembiewski, & C. C. Lundberg (Eds.), *Current topics in management* (Vol. 3, pp. 17–35). Stamford, CT: JAI Press.

Golembiewski, R. T., & Blumberg, A. (1968). The laboratory approach to organization change: "Confrontation design." *Academy of Management Journal, 11,* 199–210.

Goodman, P. S., & Pennings, J. M. (Eds.). (1977). *New perspectives on organizational effectiveness.* San Francisco: Jossey-Bass.

Graham, P. (1998). Saying "no" to compromise; "yes" to integration. *Journal of Business Ethics, 17,* 1007–1013.

Gray, B. (1989). *Collaborating: Finding common ground for multiparty problems.* San Diego, CA: Jossey-Bass.

Greenberg, G., & Baron, R. A. (1997). *Behavior in organizations: Understanding and managing the human side of work* (6th ed.). Upper Saddle River, NJ: Prentice Hall.

Green, H. (1990). *On strike at Hormel: The struggle for a democratic labor movement.* Philadelphia: Temple University Press.

Guetzkow, H., & Gyr, J. (1954). An analysis of conflict in decision-making groups. *Human Relations, 7,* 367–381.

Guyette sees "problems" with arbitrator's ruling. (1984, December 28). *Austin Daily Herald,* p. 1.

Gulick, L. H., & Urwick, L. (Eds.). (1937). *Papers on the science of administration.* New York: Institute of Public Administration, Columbia University.

Hackman, J. R., & Oldham, G. R. (1975). Development of the job diagnostic survey. *Journal of Applied Psychology, 60,* 159–170.

Hackman, J. R., & Oldham, G. R. (1976). Motivation through the design of work: Test of a theory. *Organizational Behavior and Human Performance, 16,* 250–279.

Hackman, J. R., & Oldham, G. R. (1980). *Work redesign.* Reading, MA: Addison-Wesley.

Hackman, J. R., & Vidmar, N. (1970). Effects of size and task type in group performance and member reactions. *Sociometry, 33,* 37–54.

Hage, D., & Klauda, P. (1989). *No retreat, no surrender: Labor's war at Hormel.* New York: William Morrow.

Haiman, F. S. (1951). *Group leadership and democratic action.* Boston: Houghton Mifflin.

Hall, J. (1969). *Conflict management survey: A survey of one's characteristic reaction to and handling conflict between himself and others.* Canoe, TX: Teleometrics International.

Hall, J., & Williams, M. S. (1966). A comparison of decision making performances in established and ad-hoc groups. *Journal of Personality and Social Psychology, 3,* 214–222.

Hall, R. H. (2002). *Organizations: Structure, processes, and outcomes.* (8th ed.).Upper Saddle River, NJ: Prentice-Hall.

Hammer, W. C., & Organ, D. W. (1978). *Organizational behavior: An applied psychology approach.* Dallas, TX: Business Publications.

Hammock, G. S., & Richardson, D. R. (1991). Aggression as one response to conflict. *Journal of Applied Social Psychology, 22,* 298–311.

Hampton, D. R., Summer, C. E., & Webber, R. A. (1982). *Organizational behavior and human performance.* Glenview, IL: Scott, Foresman.

Harman, H. H. (1967). *Modern factor analysis* (2nd ed.). Chicago: University of Chicago Press.

Harris, T. A. (1969). *I'm OK You're OK: A practical guide to transactional analysis.* New York: Harper & Row.

Harris, T. A., & Harris, A. (1985). *Staying OK.* New York: Harper & Row.

Hart, L. B. (1991). *Learning from conflict: A handbook for trainers and group leaders* (2nd Ed.). Amherst, MA: Human Resource Development.

Hater, J. J., & Bass, B. M. (1988). Superiors' evaluations and subordinates' perceptions of transformational and transactional leadership. *Journal of Applied Psychology, 73*, 695–702.

Hernez-Broome, G., Steed, J., Lundberg, S. (2004). The right thing? Leaders speak out on corporate ethics. *Leadership in Action, 24* (4), 3–6.

Herzberg, F., Mausner, B., & Snyderman, B. (1959). *The motivation to work.* New York: Wiley.

Hoffman, L. R., & Maier, N. R. F. (1961). Quality and acceptance of problem solutions by members of homogeneous and heterogeneous groups. *Journal of Abnormal and Social Psychology, 62*, 401–407.

Holzworth, J. (1983). Intervention in a cognitive conflict. *Organizational Behavior and Human Decision Process, 32*, 216–231.

Hormel moves annual meeting. (1984, December 27). *Austin Daily Herald,* p. 1.

Hormel profitability report. (1990, July 20). La Crosse, WI: A. G. Edwards.

Hormel shows 10% earnings reduction. (1984, August 17). *Austin Daily Herald,* p. 1.

Hormel union can't strike until August. (1985, March 28). *Austin Daily Herald,* p. 1.

Hormel willing to go to bargaining table. (1985, August 19). *Austin Daily Herald,* p. 1.

House, R. J. (1971). A path-goal theory of leadership effectiveness. *Administrative Science Quarterly, 16*, 321–338.

House, R. J., & Rizzo, J. R. (1972). Role conflict and ambiguity as critical variables in a model of organizational behavior. *Organizational Behavior and Human Performance, 7*, 467–505.

Hunger, J. D., & Stern, L. W. (1976). An assessment of the functionality of the superordinate goals in reducing conflict. *Academy of Management Journal, 19*, 591–605.

Husted, B. W., Dozier, J. B., McMahon, J. T., & Kattan, M. W. (1996). The impact of cross-national carriers of business ethics on attitudes about questionable practices and form of moral reasoning. *Journal of International Business Studies, 27*, 391–411.

Jackson, S. E., & Schuler, R. S. (1985). A meta-analysis and conceptual critique of research on role ambiguity and role conflict in work settings. *Organizational Behavior and Human Decision Processes, 36*, 16–78.

James, M., & Jongeward, D. (1971). *Born to win: Transactional analysis with gestalt experiments.* Reading, MA: Addison-Wesley.

Jamieson, D. W., & Thomas, K. W. (1974). Power and conflict in the student–teacher relationship. *Journal of Applied Behavioral Science, 10*, 321–336.

Janis, I. J. (1971, November). Groupthink. *Psychology Today,* pp. 43–44, 46, 74–76.

Janis, I. L. (1982). *Groupthink* (2nd Ed.). Boston, MA: Houghton Mifflin.

Jarboe, S. C., & Witteman, H. R. (1996). Intragroup conflict management in task-oriented groups. *Small Group Research, 27*, 316–333.

Jehn, K. A. (1994). Enhancing effectiveness: An investigation of advantages and disadvantages of value-based intragroup conflict. *International Journal of Conflict Management, 5*, 223–238.

Jehn, K. A. (1995). A multimethod examination of the benefits and determinants of intragroup conflict. *Administrative Science Quarterly, 40*, 256–282.

Jehn, K. A. (1997a). A qualitative analysis of conflict types and dimensions in organizational groups. *Administrative Science Quarterly, 42*, 530–557.

Jehn, K. A. (1997b). To agree or not to agree: The effects of value congruence, individual demographic dissimilarity, and conflict of workgroup outcomes. *International Journal of Conflict Management, 8*, 287–305.

Jehn, K. A., Greer, L., Levine, S., & Szulanski, G. (2008). The effects of conflict types, dimensions, and emergent states on group outcomes. *Group Decision and Negotiation, 17*, 465–495.

Jehn, K. A., & Mannix, E. A. (2001). The dynamic nature of conflict: A longitudinal study of intragroup conflict and group performance. *Academy of Management Journa, 44,* 238–251.

Jehn, K. A., Northcraft, G. B., & Neale, M. A. (1999). Why differences make a difference: A field study of diversity, conflict, and performance in workgroup. *Administrative Science Quarterly, 44,* 741–763.

Jehn, K. A., Rispens, S., & Thatcher, S. M. B. (2010). The effects of conflict asymmetry on workgroup and individual outcomes. *Academy of Management Journal, 53,* 596–616.

Johnson, P. E. (1989). *Conflict in school organizations and its relationship in school climate.* Unpublished doctoral dissertation, Auburn University, AL.

Jones, G. R., George, J. M., & Hill, C. W. L. (1998). *Contemporary management.* Boston, MA: McGraw-Hill.

Jones, R. E., & Melcher, B. H. (1982). Personality and the preference for modes of conflict resolution. *Human Relations, 35,* 649–658.

Jones, R. E., & White, C. S. (1985). Relationships among personality, conflict resolution styles, and task effectiveness. *Group & Organization Studies, 10,* 152–167.

Jöreskog, K. G. (1971). Simultaneous factor analysis in several populations. *Psychometrika, 36,* 409–426.

Jöreskog, K. G., & Sörbom, D. (1988). *LISREL 7.* Chicago: SPSS.

Julian, J. W., & Perry, F. A. (1967). Cooperation contrasted with intra-group and intergroup competition. *Sociometry, 30,* 79–90.

Jung, C. G. (1923). *Psychological types.* London: Routledge and Kegan Paul.

Kahn, R. L., & Byosiere, P. (1992). Stress in organizations. In M. D. Dunnette & L. M. Hough (Eds.), *Handbook of industrial and organizational psychology* (Vol. 3, pp. 571–650). Palo Alto, CA: Consulting Psychologists Press.

Kahn, R. L., Wolfe, D. M., Quinn, P. R., Snoak, J. D., & Rosenthal, R. A. (1964). *Organization stress: Studies in role conflict and ambiguity.* New York: Wiley.

Kaplan, N. (1959). The role of the research administrator. *Administrative Science Quarterly, 4,* 20–42.

Katz, R. (1977). The influence of group conflict on leadership effectiveness. *Organizational Behavior and Human Performance, 20,* 265–286.

Keeley, M. (1978). A social-justice approach to organizational evaluation. *Administrative Science Quarterly, 23,* 272–292.

Keenan, D. (1984). *A study to determine the relationship between organizational climates and management styles of conflict as perceived by teachers and principals in selected school districts.* Unpublished doctoral dissertation, West Virginia University.

Keller, R. T. (1989). A test of the path-goal theory of leadership with need for clarity as a moderator in research and development organizations. *Journal of Applied Psychology, 74,* 208–212.

Keller, R. T. (1992). Transformational leadership and the performance of research and development project groups. *Journal of Management, 18,* 489–501.

Keller, R. T., Szilagyi, A. D. Jr., & Holland, W. E. (1976). Boundary-spanning activity and employee reactions: An empirical study. *Human Relations, 29,* 699–710.

Kelly, J. (1974). *Organizational behavior* (rev. ed.). Homewood, IL: Irwin.

Kelly, J., & Kelly, L. (1998). *An existential-systems approach to managing organizations.* Westport, CT: Quorum.

Kennedy, E. J., & Lawton, L. (1993). Ethics and services marketing. *Journal of Business Ethics, 121,* 785.

Kerlinger, F. N. (1986). *Foundations of behavioral research* (3rd ed.). New York: Holt, Rinehart and Winston.

Kerr, S. (1995). On the folly of rewarding A, while hoping for B. *Academy of Management Executive, 9*, 7–14. [originally published 1975]

Kilmann, R. H., & Mitroff, I. I. (1979). Problem defining and the consulting/intervention process. *California Management Review, 21* (3), 26–33.

Kilmann, R. H., & Thomas, K. W. (1975). Interpersonal conflict-handling behavior as reflections of Jungian personality dimensions. *Psychological Reports, 37*, 971–980.

King, L. A., & King, D. W. (1990). Role conflict and role ambiguity: A critical assessment of construct validity. *Psychological Bulletin, 107*, 48–64.

Kochan, T. A., Huber, G. P., & Cummings, L. L. (1975). Determinants of intraorganizational conflict in collective bargaining in public sector. *Administrative Science Quarterly, 20*, 10–23.

Kohlberg, L. (1969). Stage and sequence: The cognitive-developmental approach to socialization. In D. A. Goslin (Ed.), *Handbook of socialization: Theory and research* (pp. 347–480). Chicago: Rand-McNally.

Kohlberg, L. (1971). *From is to ought: How to commit the naturalistic fallacy and get away with it in the study of moral development.* New York: Academic Press.

Kolb, D. M. (1988). Corporate ombudsman and organizational conflict resolution. *Journal of Conflict Resolution, 31*, 673–691.

Korbanik, K., Baril, G. L., & Watson, C. (1993). Managers' conflict management style and leadership effectiveness: The moderating effects of gender. *Sex Roles, 29*, 405–420.

Kotey, B., & Meredith, G. G. (1997). Relationships among owner/manager personal values, business strategies, and enterprise performance. *Journal of Small Business Management, 35* (2), 37–62.

Kozan, M. K. (1989). Cultural influences on styles of handling interpersonal conflicts: Comparisons among Jordanian, Turkish, and U.S. managers. *Human Relations, 9*, 787–799.

Krejci, V. A. (1986). *Chronology of industry and company events, 1975–1986.* Unpublished manuscript, George A. Hormel & Co., Austin, MN.

Kroon, M. B. R., Hart, P. 'T., & Kreveld, D. V. (1991). Managing group decision making processes: Individual versus collective accountability and groupthink. *International Journal of Conflict Management, 2*, 91–115.

Knudson, R. M., Sommers, A. A., & Golding, S. L. (1980). Interpersonal perception and mode of resolution in marital conflict. *Journal of Personality and Social Psychology, 38*, 751–763.

Kurdek, L. A. (1994). Conflict resolution styles in gay, lesbian, heterosexual nonparent, and heterosexual parent couples. *Journal of Marriage and the Family, 56*, 705–722.

LaPorte, R. T. (1965). Conditions of strain and accommodation in industrial research organizations. *Administrative Science Quarterly, 10*, 21–38.

Lawrence, P. R. (2001). The contingency approach to organization design. In R. T. Golembiewski (Eds.), *Handbook of organizational behavior* (2nd ed., pp. 7–17). New York: Marcel Dekker.

Lawrence, P. R., & Lorsch, J. W. (1967a). Differentiation and integration in complex organizations. *Administrative Science Quarterly, 12*, 1–47.

Lawrence, P. R., & Lorsch, J. W. (1967b). *Organization and environment.* Homewood, IL: Irwin-Dorsey.

Lax, D. A., & Sebenius, J. K. (1986). *The manager as negotiator: Bargaining for cooperation and competitive gain.* New York: Free Press.

Lee, C.-W. (1990). Relative status of employees and styles of handling interpersonal conflict: An experimental study with Korean managers. *International Journal of Conflict Management, 1*, 327–340.

Lee, C.-W. (1996). Referent role and conflict management styles: An empirical study with Korean central government employees. *Korean Review of Public Administration, 1* (1), 237–252.

Lens, V. (2004). Principled negotiation: A new tool for case advocacy. *Social Work, 49,* 506–513.

Levy, M. B. (1989). *Integration of lovestyles and attachment styles: Cross-partner influences and a clarification of concepts, measurement, and conceptualixzation.* Unpublished doctoral dissertation, University of South Carolina.

Lewin, K. (1948). *Resolving social conflicts: Selected papers on group dynamics.* Ed. by G. W. Lewin. New York: Harper & Row.

Likert, R. (1967). *The human organization: Its management and value.* New York: McGraw-Hill.

Likert, R., & Likert, J. G. (1976). *New ways of managing conflict.* New York: McGraw-Hill.

Litterer, J. A. (1966). Conflict in organization: A re-examination. *Academy of Management Journal, 9,* 178–186.

Local P–9 will strike. (1985, August 15). *Austin Daily Herald,* p. 1.

Lourenco, S. V., & Glidewell, J. C. (1975). A dialectical analysis of organizational conflict. *Administrative Science Quarterly, 20,* 489–508.

Lusch, R. F. (1976a). Channel conflict: Its impact on retailer operating performance. *Journal of Retailing, 52* (2), 3–12, 89–90.

Lusch, R. F. (1976b). Sources of power: Their impact on intrachannel conflict. *Journal of Marketing Research, 13,* 382–390.

Luthans, F., Rubach, M. J., & Marsnik, P. (1995). Going beyond total quality: The characteristics, techniques, and measures of learning organizations. *International Journal of Organizational Analysis, 3,* 24–44.

Mack, R. W. (1965). The components of social conflict. *Social problems, 12,* 388–397.

Mack, R. W., & Snyder, R. C. (1957). Analysis of social conflict: Toward an overview and synthesis. *Journal of Conflict Resolution, 1,* 212–248.

Maier, N. R. F., & Verser, G. C. (1982). *Psychology in industrial organizations* (5th ed.). Boston: Houghton Mifflin.

Manheim, H. L. (1960). Intergroup interaction as related to status and leadership differences between groups. *Sociometry, 23,* 415–427.

March, J. G., & Simon, H. A. (1958). *Organizations.* New York: Wiley.

Mayo, E. (1933). *The human problems of an industrial civilization.* New York: Macmillan.

McDonald, A. (1972). Conflict at the summit: A deadly game. *Harvard Business Review, 50* (2), 59–68.

McGrath, J. E. (1976). Stress and behavior in organizations. In M. D. Dunnette (Ed.), *Handbook of industrial and organizational psychology* (Vol. 1, pp. 1351–1395). Chicago: Rand-McNally.

McKeon, R. (1951). Philosophy and method. *Journal of Philosophy, 48,* 653–682.

Miles, R. H. (1975). An empirical test of causal inference between role perceptions of conflict and ambiguity and various personal outcomes. *Journal of Applied Psychology, 60,* 334–339.

Miles, R. H. (1980). *Macro organizational behavior.* Santa Monica, CA: Goodyear.

Miles, R. H., & Perreault, W. D., Jr. (1976). Organizational role conflict: Its antecedents and consequences. *Organizational Behavior and Human Performance, 17,* 19–44.

Mills, C. W. (1959). *The sociological imagination.* New York: Oxford University Press.

Mills, N. (1986, April 26). Why Local P–9 is going it alone. *Nation,* pp. 578–581.

Misquita, V. C. (1998). *Exploration of factors leading to organizational commitment of the subordinate in unionized environment.* Unpublished doctoral dissertation, Illinois Institute of Technology, Chicago.

Mitroff, I. I. (1998). *Smart thinking for crazy times: The art of solving the right problems.* San Francisco: Berrett-Koehler.

Mitroff, I. I., & Emshoff, J. R. (1979). On strategic assumption-making: A dialectical approach to policy and planning. *Academy of Management Review, 4,* 1–12.

Mitroff, I. I., & Featheringham, T. R. (1974). On systemic problem solving and the error of the third kind. *Behavioral Science, 19,* 383–393.

Moberg, P. J. (1998). Predicting conflict strategy with personality traits: Incremental validity and the five factor model. *International Journal of Conflict Management, 9,* 258–285.

Mooney, J. D., & Reiley, A. C. (1939). *The principals of organization.* New York: Harper & Row.

Morano, R. A. (1976). Managing conflict for problem solving. *Personnel Journal, 55* (8), 393–394.

Morris, J. H., Steers, R. M., & Koch, J. L. (1979). Influence of organization structure on role conflict and ambiguity for three occupational groupings. *Academy of Management Journal, 22,* 58–71.

Morris, M. W., Williams, K. Y., Leung, K., Larrick, R., Mendoza, M. T., Bhatnagar, D., Li, J., Kondo, M., Luo, J-L, & Hu, J-C. (1998). Conflict Management Style: Accounting for Cross-national differences. *Journal of International Business Studies, 29,* 749–747.

Morse, J. J., & Lorsch, J. W. (1970). Beyond theory Y. *Harvard Business Review, 48* (3), 61–68.

Mosak, H. H., & LeFevre, C. (2003). The resolution of "intrapersonal conflict." *Journal of Individual Psychology, 32* (1), 19–26.

Mulki, J. P., Jaramillo, J. F., & Locander, W. B. (2009). Critical role of leadership on ethical climate and salesperson behaviors. *Journal of Business ethics, 86,* 125–141.

Munduate, L., Ganaza, J., & Alcaide, M. (1993). Estilos de gestion del conflicto interpersonal en las organizaciones [Conflict management styles in organizations]. *Rivista de Psicologia Social, 8* (1), 47–68.

Murray, E. J. (1968). Conflict: I. Psychological aspects. In D. L. Sills (Ed.), *International encyclopedia of the social sciences* (Vol. 3, pp. 220–226). New York: Crowell and Macmillan.

Musser, S. J. (1982). A model for predicting the choice of conflict management strategies by subordinates in high-stakes conflicts. *Organizational Behavior and Human Performance, 29,* 257–269.

Myers, I. B. (1962). *Manual: The Myers-Briggs type indicator.* Princeton, NJ: Educational Testing Service.

Neale, M. A., & Northcraft, G. B. (1991). Behavioral negotiation theory: A framework for conceptualizing dyadic bargaining. In L. L. Cummings & B. M. Staw (Eds.), *Research in organizational behavior* (Vol. 14, pp. 147–190). Greenwich, CT: JAI Press.

Neff, E. K. (1986). *Conflict management styles of woman administrators in the twelve state universities in Ohio.* Unpublished doctoral dissertation, Bowling Green State University, Ohio.

Nemeth, C., Connell, J., Rogers, J., & Brown, K. (2001). Improving decision making by means of dissent. *Journal of Applied Psychology, 31,* 48–58.

Netemeyer, R. G., Johnston, M. W., & Burton, S. (1990). Analysis of role conflict and role ambiguity in a structural equations framework. *Journal of Applied Psychology, 75,* 148–157.

Neuhauser, P. (1988). *Tribal warfare in organizations.* Cambridge, MA: Ballinger.

Newton, T. J., & Keenan, A. (1987). Role stress reexamined: An investigation of role stress predictors. *Organizational Behavior and Human Decision Processes, 40,* 346–368.

Nicotera, A. M., & Dorsey, L. K. (2006). Individual and interactive processes in organizational conflict. In J. G. Oetzel & Ting-Toomey, S. (Eds.), *The SAGE handbook of conflict communication: Integrating theory, research, and practice* (pp. 293–325). Thousand Oaks, CA: Sage.

Nightingale, D. (1974). Conflict and conflict resolution. In G. Strouss, R. E. Miles, C. C. Snow, & A. S. Tannenbaum (Eds.), *Organizational behavior: Research and issues* (pp. 141–163). Madison, WI: Industrial Relations Research Association.

Nunnally, J. C. (1978). *Psychometric theory* (2nd ed.). New York: McGraw-Hill.

Oaklander, H., & Fleishman, E. A. (1964). Patterns of leadership related to organizational stress in hospital settings. *Administrative Science Quarterly, 8,* 520–532.

Oh, E-S. (1997). *A comparison of NCAA division I athletics directors' and coaches' conflict management styles and influential factors that affect the conflict management styles.* Unpublished doctoral dissertation, University of Kansas, Lawrence.

Olson, M. E. (1968). *The process of social organization.* New York: Holt, Rinehart, & Winston.

Organ, D. W., & Greene, C. N. (1974). Role ambiguity, locus of control, and work satisfaction. *Journal of Applied Psychology, 59,* 101–102.

Orpen, C. (1979). The effects of job enrichment on employee satisfaction, motivation, involvement, and performance: A field experiment. *Human Relations, 32,* 189–217.

Pandey, S., & Kumar, E. S. (1997). Development of a measure of role conflict. *International Journal of Conflict Management, 8,* 187–215.

Park, R. E., & Burgess, E. W. (1929). *Introduction to the science of sociology* (3rd ed.). Chicago: University of Chicago Press. [originally published 1921]

Parsons, T. (1949). *Essays in sociological theory: Pure and applied.* Glencoe, IL: Free Press.

Pascale, R. T. (1990). *Managing on the edge: How the smartest companies use conflict to stay ahead.* New York: Simon and Schuler.

Paulhaus, D. L. (1984). Two-component models of socially desirable responding. *Journal Personality and Social Psychology, 46,* 598–609.

Pearson, M, & Monoky, J. F. (1976). The role of conflict and cooperation in channel performance. In K. L. Bernhardt (Ed.), *Marketing: 1776–1976 and beyond* (pp. 240–244). Chicago: American Marketing Association.

Pelled, L. H. (1996). Demographic diversity, conflict, and work group outcomes: An intervening process theory. *Organization Science, 7,* 615–631.

Pelled, L. H., Eisenhardt, K. M., & Xin, K. R. (1999). Exploring the black box: An analysis of work group diversity, conflict, and performance. *Administrative Science Quarterly, 44,* 1–28.

Pelz, D. C., & Andrews, F. M. (1976). *Scientists in organizations: Productive climates for research and development.* New York: Wiley.

Penn, W. Y., & Collier, B. D. (1985). Current research in moral development as a decision support system. *Journal of Business Ethics, 4,* 131–137.

Pennings, J. M. (1992). Structural contingency theory: A reappraisal. In B. M. Staw & L. L. Cummings (Eds.), *Research in organizational behavior* (Vol. 14, pp. 269–310). Greenwich, CT: JAI Press.

Persico, J., Jr. (1986). *Levels of conflict, worker performance, individual conflict styles, type of work, organizational characteristics and the external environment of the organization.* Unpublished doctoral dissertation, University of Minnesota.

Peterson, M. F., Smith, P. B., Akande, A., Ayestaran, S., Bochner, S., Callan, V., Cho, N. G., Jesuino, J. C., D'Amorin, M., Francois, P-H., Hofmann, K., Koopman, P., Leung, K., Lim, T. K., Mortazavi, S., Munene, J., Radford, M., Ropo, A., Savage, G., Setiadi, B., Sinha, T. N., Sorenson, R., & Viedge, C. (1995). Role conflict, ambiguity, and overload: A 21–nation study. *Academy of Management Journal, 38,* 429–452.

Pettijohn, C., Pettijohn, L., & Taylor, A. (2008). Salesperson perceptions of ethical behaviors: Their influence on job satisfaction and turnover intentions. *Journal of Business ethics, 78,* 547–557.

Phillips, E., & Cheston, R. (1979). Conflict resolution: What works? *California Management Review, 21*(4), 76–83.

Pilkington, C. J., Richardson, D. R., & Utley, M. E. (1988). Is conflict stimulating? Sensation seekers' responses to interpersonal conflict. *Personality and Social Psychology Bulletin, 14,* 596–603.

Pondy, L. R. (1967). Organizational conflict: Concepts and models. *Administrative Science Quarterly, 12,* 296–320.

Porcello, J. V., & Long, B. C. (1994). Gender role orientation, ethical and interpersonal conflicts, and conflict handling styles of female managers. *Sex Roles, 31,* 683–701.

Posner, B. Z. (1986). What's all the fighting about? Conflicts in project management. *IEEE Transactions on Engineering Management, EM–33,* 207–211.

Poundstone, W. (1992). *Prisoner's dilemma.* New York: Doubleday.

Premeaux, S. (2009). The link between management behavior and ethical philosophy in the wake of the Enron convictions. *Journal of Business Ethics, 85,* 13–25.

Prein, H. C. M. (1976). Stijlen van conflicthantering [Styles of handling conflict]. *Nederlands Tijdschrift voor de Psychologie, 31,* 321–346.

Pruitt, D. G. (1983). Strategic choice in negotiation. *American Behavioral Scientist, 27,* 167–194.

Pruitt, D. G., & Carnevale, P. J. (1993). *Negotiation and social conflict.* Buckingham: Open University Press.

Pruitt, D. G., & Kim, S. H. (2004). *Social conflict: Escalation, stalemate, and settlement.* New York: McGraw-Hill Higher Education.

Pruitt, D. G., & Rubin, J. Z. (1986). *Social conflict: Escalation, stalemate, and settlement.* New York: Random House.

Psenicka, C., & Rahim, M. A. (1989). Integrative and distributive dimensions of styles of handling interpersonal conflict and bargaining outcome. In M. A. Rahim (Ed.), *Managing conflict: An interdisciplinary approach* (pp. 33–40). New York: Praeger Publishers.

Putnam, L. L., & Wilson, C. E. (1982). Communicative strategies in organizational conflicts: Reliability and validity of a measurement scale. In M. Burgoon (Ed.), *Communication yearbook 6* (pp. 629–652). Beverly Hills, CA: Sage.

Rahim, M. A. (1977). The management of organizational intergroup conflict: A contingency model. *Proceedings of the 8th annual meeting of the Midwest American Institute for Decision Sciences* (pp. 247–249). Cleveland, OH.

Rahim, M. A. (1979). The management of intraorganizational conflicts: A laboratory study with organization design. *Management International Review, 19* (1), 97–106.

Rahim, M. A. (1980). Some contingencies affecting interpersonal conflict in academia: A multivariate study. *Management International Review, 20* (2), 117–121.

Rahim, M. A. (1981). Organizational behavior courses for graduate students in business administration: Views from the tower and battlefield. *Psychological Reports, 49,* 583–592.

Rahim, M. A. (1983a). A measure of styles of handling interpersonal conflict. *Academy of Management Journal, 26,* 368–376.

Rahim, M. A. (1983b). Measurement of organizational conflict. *Journal of General Psychology, 109,* 189–199.

Rahim, M. A. (1983c). *Rahim Organizational Conflict Inventory–I.* Palo Alto, CA: Consulting Psychologists Press.

Rahim, M. A. (1983d). *Rahim Organizational Conflict Inventory–II, Forms A, B, & C.* Palo Alto, CA: Consulting Psychologists Press.

Rahim, M. A. (1983e). *Rahim organizational conflict inventories: Professional manual.* Palo Alto, CA: Consulting Psychologists Press.

Rahim, M. A. (1985). Referent role and styles of handling interpersonal conflict. *Journal of Social Psychology, 126,* 79–86.

Rahim, M. A. (1990). Moderating effects of hardiness and social support on the relationships of conflict and stress to job burnout and performance. In M. A. Rahim (Ed.), *Theory and research in conflict management* (pp. 4–14). New York: Praeger.

Rahim, M. A. (1997). Styles of managing organizational conflict: A critical review and synthesis of theory and research. In M. A. Rahim, R. T. Golembiewski, & L. E. Pate (Eds.), *Current topics in management* (Vol. 2, pp. 61–77). Greenwich, CT: JAI Press.

Rahim, M. A. (2002). Toward a theory of managing organizational conflict. *International Journal of Conflict Management, 13,* 206–235.

Rahim, M. A. (2004). *Rahim organizational conflict inventories: Professional manual* (2nd ed.). Bowling Green, KY: Center for Advanced Studies in Management.

Rahim, M. A., Antonioni, D., Psenicka, C. (2001). A structural equations model of leader power, subordinates' styles of handling conflict and job performance. *International Journal of Conflict Management, 12,* 191–211.

Rahim, M. A., & Bonoma, T. V. (1979). Managing organizational conflict: A model for diagnosis and intervention. *Psychological Reports, 44,* 1323–1344.

Rahim, M. A., & Pelled, L. H. (1998, June). *Rethinking the structure of conflict: Toward a four-dimensional conceptualization.* Paper presented at the annual conference of the International Association for Conflict Management, College Park, Maryland.

Rahim, M. A., Buntzman, G. F., & White, D. (1999). An empirical study of the stages of moral development and conflict management styles. *International Journal of Conflict Management, 10,* 154–171.

Rahim, M. A., Garrett, J. E., & Buntzman, G. F. (1992). Ethics of managing interpersonal conflict in organizations. *Journal of Business Ethics, 11,* 423–432.

Rahim, M. A., & Magner, N. R. (1994). Convergent and discriminant validity of the Rahim Organizational Conflict Inventory–II. *Psychological Reports, 74,* 35–38.

Rahim, M. A., & Magner, N. R. (1995). Confirmatory factor analysis of the styles of handling interpersonal conflict: First-order factor model and its invariance across groups. *Journal of Applied Psychology, 80,* 122–132.

Rahim, M. A., & Psenicka, C. (1995). Convergent and discriminant validity of the Rahim Organizational Conflict Inventory. *Perceptual and Motor Skills, 81,* 1075–1078.

Rahim, M. A., Magner, N. R., & Shapiro, D. L. (2000). Do fairness perceptions influence styles of handling conflict with supervisors: What fairness perceptions, precisely? *International Journal of Conflict Management, 11,* 9–31.

Rands, M., Levinger, G., & Mellinger, G. D. (1981). Patterns of conflict resolution and marital satisfaction. *Journal of Family Issues, 2,* 297–321.

Rapoport, A. (1960). *Fights, games, and debates.* Ann Arbor, MI: University of Michigan Press.

Raven, B. H., & Kruglanski, A. W. (1970). Conflict and power. In P. Swingle (Ed.), *The structure of conflict* (pp. 69–109). New York: Academic Press.

Renwick, P. A. (1975). Perception and management of superior–subordinate conflict. *Organizational Behavior and Human Performance, 13,* 444–456.

Renwick, P. A. (1977). The effects of sex differences on the perception and management of superior–subordinate conflict: An exploratory study. *Organizational Behavior and Human Performance, 19,* 403–415.

Rest, J. (Ed.). (1986). *Moral development: Advances in research and theory.* New York: Praeger.

Rest, J. R., & Thomas, S. J. (1986). Relation of moral judgment development to formal education. *Developmental Psychology, 21,* 709–714.

Rettig, J. L., & Amano, M. M. (1976). A survey of ASPA experience with management by objectives, sensitivity training and transactional analysis. *Personnel Journal, 55,* 26–29.

Reve, T., & Stern, L. W. (1979). Interorganizational relations in marketing channels. *Academy of Management Review, 4,* 405–416.

Rizzo, J. R., House, R. J., & Lirtzman, S. I. (1970). Role conflict and ambiguity in complex organizations. *Administrative Science Quarterly, 15,* 150–163.

Robbins, S. P. (1974). *Managing organizational conflict: A nontraditional approach.* Englewood Cliffs, NJ: Prentice-Hall.

Roberts, W. L. (1997). *An investigation of the relationship between principal's self-efficacy beliefs and their methods of managing conflict with teachers.* Unpublished doctoral dissertation, Auburn University, AL.

Robey, D., Farrow, D. L., & Franz, C. R. (1989). Group process and conflict in system development. *Management Science, 35,* 1172–1191.

Roethlisberger, F. J. (1965). The foreman: Master and victim of double talk. *Harvard Business Review, 43* (5), 22–26ff.

Rogers, D. L., & Molnar, J. (1976). Organizational antecedents of role conflict and ambiguity in top level administrators. *Administrative Science Quarterly, 21,* 598–610.

Roloff, M. E. (1987). Communication and conflict. In C. R. Berger & S. H. Chaffee (Eds.), *Handbook of communication science* (pp. 484–534). Newbury Park, CA: Sage.

Rosen, R. A. H. (1970). Foreman role conflict: An expression of contradictions in organizational goals. *Industrial and Labor Relations Review, 23,* 541–552.

Ross, R. S., & Ross, J. R. (1989). *Small groups in organizational settings.* Englewood Cliffs, NJ: Prentice-Hall.

Rotter, J. B. (1966). Generalized expectancies for internal versus external control of reinforcement. *Psychological Monographs, 80* (whole No. 609).

Rubenstein, B. (1990, March 14). Divided and conquered: A trust violated. *Minneapolis City Pages,* pp. 6–10.

Rubin, J. Z. (1994). Models of conflict management. *Journal of Social Issues, 50* (1), 33–45.

Ruble, T. L., & Thomas, K. W. (1976). Support for a two-dimensional model for conflict behavior. *Organizational Behavior and Human Performance, 16,* 143–155.

Rutland, J. M. (1983). *Performance and intra-group conflict: A study of mountain climbers.* Unpublished doctoral dissertation, University of Washington.

Saaty, T. L. (1990). The Analytic Hierarchy Process in conflict management. *International Journal of Conflict Management, 1,* 47–68.

Sales, S. M. (1969). Organizational role as a risk factor in coronary disease. *Administrative Science Quarterly, 14,* 325–336.

Sampson, R. C. (1955). *The staff role and management: Its creative uses.* New York: Harper & Row.

Schein, E. H. (1980). *Organizational psychology.* Englewood, Cliffs, NJ: Prentice-Hall.

Schein, E. H. (1990). Organizational culture. *American Psychologist, 45,* 109–119.

Schein, E. H. (1993). How can organizations learn faster? The challenge of entering the green room. *Sloan Management Review, 35* (2), 85–92.

Schellenberg, J. A. (1996). *Conflict resolution: Theory, research, and practice.* Albany, NY: State University of New York Press.

Schelling, T. C. (1980). *The strategy of conflict.* Cambridge, MA: Harvard University Press.

Schmidt, S. M., & Kochan T. A. (1972). Conflict: Toward conceptual clarity. *Administrative Science Quarterly, 17,* 359–370.

Schmitt, N., & Stults, D. N. (1986). Methodology review: Analysis of multitrait–multimethod matrices. *Applied Psychological Measurement, 10,* 1–22.

Schmidt, W. H., & Tannenbaum, R. (1960). Management of differences. *Harvard Business Review, 38* (6), 107–115.

Schnake, M. E., & Cochran, D. S. (1985). Effect of two goal-setting dimensions of perceived intraorganizational conflict. *Group & Organization Studies, 10,* 168–183.

Schneer, J. A., & Chanin, M. N. (1987). Manifest needs as personality predispositions to conflict-handling behavior. *Human Relations, 40,* 575–590.

Schriesheim, C. A., & Denishi, A. S. (1981). Task dimensions as moderators of the effects of instrumental leadership: A two-sample replicated test of path-goal leadership theory. *Journal of Applied Psychology, 66,* 589–597.

Schriesheim, C. A., & Murphy, C. J. (1976). Relationships between leader behavior and subordinate performance: A test of some situational moderators. *Journal of Applied Psychology, 61,* 634–641.

Schweiger, D., Sandberg, W., & Ragan, J. W. (1986). Group approaches for improving strategic decision making: A comparative analysis of dialectical inquiry, devil's advocacy, and consensus approaches to strategic decision making. *Academy of Management Journal, 29,* 51–71.

Schwenk, C. R., & Thomas, H. (1983). Effects of conflicting analyses on managerial decision making: A laboratory experiment. *Decision Sciences, 14,* 467–482.

Seiler, J. A. (1963). Diagnosing interdepartmental conflict. *Harvard Business Review, 41* (5), 121–132.

Senge, P. M. (1990). *The fifth discipline: The art and practice of the learning organization.* New York: Doubleday.

Senge, P. M., Kleiner, A., Roberts, C. Ross, R. B., & Smith, B. J. (1994). *The fifth discipline fieldbook.* New York: Doubleday.

Serrin, W. (1984, December 10). Meat workers battle Hormel on wage cuts. *New York Times,* p. A–18.

Shaw, M. E. (1981). *Group dynamics: The dynamics of small group behavior* (3rd Ed.). New York: McGraw-Hill.

Sherif, M. (1958). Superordinate goals in the reduction of intergroup conflict. *American Journal of Sociology, 63,* 349–356.

Sherif, M., Harvey, O. J., White, B. J., Hood, W. R., & Sherif, C. W. (1961). *Intergroup conflict and cooperation: The robbers cave experiment.* Norman: Institute of Group Relations, University of Oklahoma.

Shockley-Zalabak, P. (1981). The effects of sex differences on the preference for utilization of conflict styles of managers in a work setting: An exploratory study. *Public Personnel Management, 10,* 289–295.

Simmel, G. (1955). *Conflict* (K. H. Wolff, trans.) and *The web of group-affiliations* (R. Bendix, Trans.). Glencoe, IL: Free Press. [originally published in German, 1908]

Simon, H. A. (1976). The birth of an organization. In H. A. Simon (Ed.), *Administrative behavior* (pp. 315–334). New York: Free Press. [Original work published 1953]

Simmons, T. L., & Peterson, R. S. (2000). Task conflict and relationship conflict in top management teams: The pivotal role of intragroup trust. *Journal of Applied Psychology, 85,* 102–111.

Sipka, T. A. (1969). *Social conflict and re-construction.* Unpublished doctoral dissertation, Boston College.

Slater, S. F. (1995, November–December). Learning to change. *Business Horizons,* pp. 13–20.

Smith, B. D., & Principato, F. (1983). Effects of conflict and field structure on arousal and motor responses. *British Journal of Psychology, 74,* 213–222.

Smith, C. G. (1966). A comparative analysis of some conditions and consequences of interorganizational conflict. *Administrative Science Quarterly, 10,* 504–529.

Sohi, R. S. (1996). The effects of environmental dynamism and heterogeneity on salespeople's role perceptions, performance and job satisfaction. *European Journal of Marketing, 30,* 49–68.

Sorenson, P. S., & Hawkins, K. (1995). Gender, psychological type and conflict style preference. *Management Communication Quarterly, 9,* 115–127.

Soutar, G., McNeil, M. M., & Molster, C. (1994). The impact of the work environment on ethical decision making: Some Australian evidence. *Journal of Business Ethics, 31,* 327.

Stanley, J. D. (1981). Dissent in organizations. *Academy of Management Review, 6,* 13–19.

Stark, R. (2007). *Sociology* (10th ed.). Beverly, MA: Wadsworth.

Steers, R. M. (1975). Problems in the measurement of organizational effectiveness. *Administrative Science Quarterly, 20,* 546–558.

Steers, R. M. (1977). *Organizational effectiveness: A behavioral view.* Santa Monica, CA: Goodyear.

Stein, A. A. (1976). Conflict and cohesion: A review of the literature. *Journal of Conflict Resolution, 20,* 143–172.

Stern, L., & Gorman, R. H. (1969). Conflict in distribution channels: An exploration. In L. W. Stern (Ed.), *Distribution channels: Behavioral dimensions* (pp. 156–175). Boston: Houghton Mifflin.

Stern, L. W., Sternthal, B., & Craig, C. S. (1973). Managing conflict in distribution channels: A laboratory study in distribution channels. *Journal of Marketing Research, 10,* 169–179.

Stewart, I. (2007). *Transactional analysis counseling in action* (3rd ed.). Thousand Oaks, CA: Sage.

Stewart, K. L. (1978). What a university ombudsman does: A sociological study of everyday conduct. *Journal of Higher Education, 49,* 1–22.

Struch, N., & Schwartz, S. H. (1989). Intergroup aggression: Its predictors and distinctness from in-group bias. *Journal of Personality and Social Psychology, 56,* 364–373.

Szilagyi, A. D., Jr., Sims, H. P., Jr., & Keller, R. T. (1976). Role dynamics, locus of control, and employee attitudes and behavior. *Academy of Management Journal, 19,* 259–276.

Tajfel, H. (1970). Experiments in intergroup discrimination. *Scientific American, 223* (5), 96–102.

Tajfel, H. (1981). *Human groups and social categories: Studies in social psychology.* Cambridge, England: Cambridge University Press.

Tajfel, H., & Turner, J. C. (1986). The social identity theory of intergroup behavior. In S. Worchel & W. G. Austin (Eds.), *Psychology of intergroup relations* (pp. 7–24). Chicago: Nelson-Hall.

Taylor, F. W. (1911). *The principles of scientific management.* New York: Harper & Row.

Tedeschi, J. T., Schlenker, B. R., & Bonoma, T. V. (1973). *Conflict, power and games: The experimental study of interpersonal relations.* Chicago: Aldine.

Terhune, K. W. (1970). The effects of personality in cooperation and conflict. In P. Swingle (Ed.), *The structure of conflict* (pp. 193–234). New York: Academic Press.

Thibaut, J. W., & Kelley, H. H. (1959). *The social psychology of groups.* New York: Wiley.

Thomas, K. W. (1976). Conflict and conflict management. In M. D. Dunnette (Ed.), *Handbook of industrial and organizational psychology* (pp. 889–935). Chicago: Rand-McNally.

Thomas, K. W. (1977). Toward multi-dimensional values in teaching: The example of conflict behaviors. *Academy of Management Review, 2,* 484–490.

Thomas, K. W., & Kilmann, R. H. (1974). *Thomas-Kilmann conflict MODE instrument.* New York: XICOM.

Thomas, K. W., & Kilmann, R. H. (1978). Comparison of four instruments measuring conflict behavior. *Psychological Reports, 42,* 1139–1145.

Thomas, K. W., & Schmidt, W. H. (1976). A survey of managerial interests with respect to conflict. *Academy of Management Journal, 19,* 315–318.

Thompson, H. B., & Werner, J. M. (1997). The impact of role conflict/facilitation on core and discretionary behaviors: Testing a mediated model. *Journal of Management, 23,* 583–601.

Thompson, J. D. (1967). *Organizations in action.* New York: McGraw-Hill.

Thompson, L., & Leonardelli, G. J. (2004). The big bang: The evolution of negotiation research. *Academy of Management Executive, 18,* 113–117.

Ting-Toomey, S., Gao, G., Trubisky, P., Yang, Z., Kim, H. S., Lin, S.-L., & Nishida, T. (1991). Culture, face maintenance, and conflict styles of handling interpersonal conflict: A study in five cultures. *International Journal of Conflict Management, 2,* 275–296.

Tjosvold, D. (1984). Effects of crisis orientation on managers' approach to controversy in decision making. *Academy of Management Journal, 27,* 130–138.

Tjosvold, D. (1990). The goal interdependence approach to communication in conflict: An organizational study. In M. A. Rahim (Ed.), *Theory and research in organizations* (pp. 15–27). New York: Praeger.

Tjosvold. D., & Johnson, D. W. (Eds.). (1983). *Productive conflict management: Perspectives for organizations.* New York: Irvington.

Tocalli-Beller, A. (2003). Cognitive conflict, disagreement and repetition in collaborative groups: Affective and social dimensions from an insider's perspective. *Canadian Modern Language, 62,* 143–171.

Tompkins, T. C. (1995). Role of diffusion in collective learning. *International Journal of Organizational Analysis, 3,* 69–85.

Torrance, E. P. (1954). The behavior of small groups under the stress of conditions of survival. *American Sociological Review, 19,* 751–755.

Tracy, L., & Johnson, T. W. (1981). What do the role conflict and role ambiguity scales measure? *Journal of Applied Psychology, 66,* 464–469.

Trevino, L. K., & Victor, B. (1992). Peer reporting of unethical behaviors: A social context perspective. *Academy of Management Journal, 35,* 38–64.

Trubisky, P., Ting-Toomey, S., & Lin, S-L. (1991). The influence of individualism–collectivism and self-monitoring on conflict styles. *International Journal of Intercultural Relations, 15,* 65–84.

Tsui, A. S. (1990). A multiple-constituency model of effectiveness: An empirical examination at the human resource subunit level. *Administrative Science Quarterly, 35,* 458–483.

Turner, A. N., & Lawrence, P. R. (1965). *Industrial jobs and the worker: An investigation of response to task attitudes.* Boston: Harvard University Press.

Tutzauer, F., & Roloff, M. E. (1988). Communication processes leading to integrative agreements: Three paths to joint benefits. *Communication Research, 15,* 360–380.

Uline, C. L., Tschanen-Moran, M., & Perez, L. (2003). Constructive conflict: How controversy can contribute to school improvement. *Teachers College Record, 105,* 782–816.

VandenBos, G. R. (Ed.). (2007). *APA dictionary of psychology.* Washington, DC: American Psychological Association.

Van de Vliert, E. (1990). Small group conflicts. In J. B. Gittler (Ed.), *Annual review of conflict knowledge and conflict resolution* (Vol. 2, pp. 83–118). Hamden, CT: Garland.

Van de Vliert, E., & Kabanoff, B. (1990). Toward theory-based measures of conflict management. *Academy of Management Journal, 33,* 199–209.

Velasquez, M. G. (1988). *Business ethics: Concepts and cases.* Englewood, NJ: Prentice-Hall.

Vigil-King, D. C. (2000). Team conflict, integrative conflict-management strategies and team effectiveness: A field study. *Dissertation abstracts international* (Section B: The Science and Engineering), *61* (1–B), p. 573.

Visser, M. (2007). Deutero-learning in organizations: A review and a reformulation. *Academy of Management Review, 32,* 659–667.

Vroom, V. H., & Yetton, P. W. (1973). *Leadership and decision-making.* Pittsburgh, PA: University of Pittsburgh Press.

Wall, J. A., Jr., & Blum, M. W. (1991). Negotiations. *Journal of Management, 17,* 273–303.

Wall, J. A., Jr., & Callister, R. R. (1995). Conflict and its management. *Journal of Management, 21,* 515–558.

Wall, V. D., Jr., & Galanes, G. (1986). The SYMLOG dimensions and small group conflict. *Central States Speech Journal, 37,* 61–78.

Wall, V. D., Jr., & Nolan, L. L. (1986). Perceptions of inequity, satisfaction, and conflict in task-oriented groups. *Human Relations, 39,* 1033–1052.

Walton, R. E., & Dutton, J. M. (1969). The management of interdepartmental conflict: A model and review. *Administrative Science Quarterly, 14,* 73–84.

Walton, R. E., Dutton, J. M., & Cafferty, T. P. (1969). Organizational context and interdepartmental context. *Administrative Science Quarterly, 14,* 522–542.

Walton, R. E., & McKersie, R. B. (1965). *A behavioral theory of labor negotiations: An analysis of a social interaction system.* New York: McGraw-Hill.

Wardlaw, S. P. (1988). *Conflict handling styles and project manager effectiveness.* Unpublished master's thesis, Air University, Wright Patterson Air Force Base, OH.

Watkins, K. E., & Golembiewski, R. T. (1995). Rethinking organization development for the learning organization. *International Journal of Organizational Analysis, 3,* 86–101.

Watson, W. (1985). *The architectonics of meaning.* Albany: State University of New York Press.

Weber, M. (1947). *The theory of social and economic organization* (A. M. Henderson & T. Persons, trans. from German). New York: Oxford University Press. [originally published 1929]

Weider-Hatfield, D., & Hatfield, J. D. (1995). Relationships among conflict management styles, levels of conflict, and reactions to work. *Journal of Social Psychology, 135,* 687–698.

White, H. (1961). Management conflict and sociometric structure. *American Journal of Sociology, 67,* 185–199.

Whyte, G. (1989). Groupthink reconsidered. *Academy of Management Review, 14,* 40–56.

Whyte, W. H. (1967). Models for building and changing organizations. *Human Organizations, 26,* 22–31.

Wilder, D. A. (1986). Social categorization: Implications for creation and reduction of intergroup bias. In L. Berkowitz (Ed.), *Advances in experimental social psychology* (Vol. 19, pp. 293–355). New York: Academic Press.

Wilmot, W. W., & Hocker, J. L. (2007). *Interpersonal conflict* (7th ed.). New York: McGraw-Hill.

Wilson, J. A., & Jerrell, S. L. (1981). Conflict: Malignant, beneficial, or benign. In J. A. Wilson (Ed.), *New directions for higher education: Management science applications to academic administration* (pp. 105–123). San Francisco, CA: Jossey-Bass.

Wong, P. S. P., Cheung, S. O., & Leung, K. Y. (2008). Moderating effect of organizational learning type on performance improvement. *Journal of Management Engineering, 24* (3), 162–173.

Yerkes, R. M., & Dodson, J. D. (1908). The relation of strength of stimulus to rapidity of habit-formation. *Journal of Comparative Neurological Psychology, 18,* 459–482.

Yetton, P. W., & Bottger, P. C. (1983). The relationships among group size, member ability, social decision schemes, and performance. *Organizational Behavior and Human Performance, 32,* 145–159.

Yeung. A. C. L., Lai, K-H., Yee, R. W. Y. (2007). Organizational learning, innovativeness, and organizational performance: A qualitative investigation. *Intedrnational Journal of Production Research, 45,* 2459–2477.

Young, C. M. (1984). *The relationship between rhetorical sensitivity and conflict management styles.* Unpublished master's thesis, University of Georgia, Athens.

Yuchtman, E., & Seashore, S. E. (1967). A system resource approach to organizational effectiveness. *American Sociological Review, 32,* 891–903.

Author Index

Subject Index

Breinigsville, PA USA
13 April 2011
259745BV00001B/3/P